Dine with Thomas Jefferson and Fascinating Guests

Other Books by James Gabler

Passions: The Wines and Travels of Thomas Jefferson

How To Be A Wine Expert

Wine into Words: A History and Bibliography of Wine Books in the English Language

An Evening with Benjamin Franklin and Thomas Jefferson: Dinner, Wine, and Conversation

God's Devil, a Novel

The Secret Formula, a Novel

Dine with Thomas Jefferson and Fascinating Guests

James M. Gabler

Bacchus Press Ltd
Palm Beach, FL

Dine with Thomas Jefferson and Fascinating Guests

International Standard Book Number 978-0-692-03152-0

Cover Design by Ranilo Cabo

Book design by Maureen Cutajar
www.gopublished.com

Published and distributed by:
Bacchus Press Ltd
146 Sunset Avenue
Palm Beach, Florida 33480
410-960-1002
bacchuspr@aol.com

To Anita, Morgan, Tricia

Contents

Introduction

Thomas Jefferson was America's first wine and food connoisseur. His great learning experiences took place during his five years in France (1784-1789) where he acquired a knowledge and appreciation of wine and food that no American of his time would rival.

Dine with Thomas Jefferson and Fascinating Guests is a fact-based account of twenty-five dinners at Monticello, White House, Paris, London, Philadelphia, and the Burgundy wine country. The dinners center on three of Jefferson's passions: wine, food and travel and present a panoramic view of Thomas Jefferson's social life.

Throughout his life we know what wines Jefferson purchased and possessed, what foods he served at Monticello, the White House and his Paris residence, and generally who his dinner guests were. We know that Jefferson's dinners were open to a wide range of subjects that usually centered on his passions: gardening, architecture, books, music, travel, wine, food, and reminiscing about his five years in France and the men and women who had effected historical events. What we do not know, with some exceptions, is what was discussed at a particular dinner and by whom, and precisely what wines and foods were served because this information has not been recorded-- historical gaps.

For example, we know that Jefferson and Franklin dined together at Franklin's residence in Passy, France on August 12, 1784. We know they were both wine enthusiasts. We also know the general contents of Franklin's wine cellar and what foods he had contracted with his maitre d'hôtel to furnish for each of his dinners. What we do not know, because history does not tell us, is what they talked about, who else was present, and precisely what they ate and drank at this dinner.

This historical gap problem is present throughout all the dinners. The only way around this dilemma was to use historical license to create dialogue and events based on historical facts. Therefore, the dinners though fact-based should be viewed as historical fiction. To verify the factual basis for anything said or done simply turn to the Dinner Source Notes at the end of the book. There are more than 400 such notes, many of which are annotated. They provide authority for the factual sources drawn upon, authority for support of what is said and done, and add significant follow-through information.

Jefferson was not an epicure when he left for France on July 5, 1784, because, at the time, it was impossible in America to become an epicure. There was not a single commercial winery in operation in America. Although Madeira was available to wealthy Americans, wine was not a staple and generally not available or, when available, of very poor quality. Most Americans drank rum, brandies made in home stills from fruits, rye and corn whiskey, gin, malt liquors, and hard cider. Heavy drinking, a serious problem in 18th century America, caused Jefferson to take up his pen in retirement in passionate advocacy of wine as the beverage of temperance and health. Pleading for a reduction of the heavy taxes on wine, he said, "I think it is a great error to consider a heavy tax on wines, as a tax on luxury. On the contrary it is a tax on the health of our citizens. It is a legislative declaration that none but the richest of them shall be permitted to drink wine, and in effect a condemnation of all the middling and lower conditions of society to the poison of whiskey, which is destroying them by wholesale, and ruining their families."[1]

Eighteenth century colonial and post-colonial American meals were heavily influenced by English traditions and followed a sort of meat and potatoes routine. Although all kinds of fish abounded in America's rivers, fish was not a common dietary staple. Open-hearth roasting was the principle way of cooking, and meats, game, and vegetables were usually boiled, fried and stewed. Sour food was not unusual and accepted as normal. Dinner often featured boiled pastes under the name of puddings, and the sauces, even for roast beef, were melted butter with potatoes and other vegetables swimming in hog's lard, butter, or fat.[2]

Travel in 18th century America was at best difficult. One traveled by walking, on horseback, or public stage or private carriage, and there was no such thing as hiring a carriage or horses from post to post as in England and France. The roads were dirt and in most cases not much more than Indian trails plagued with deep ruts, tree stumps, and other travel impediments. Because of a lack of bridges, travel included many river crossings which often meant fording a river on horseback or by canoe.

American taverns lacked the basic amenities of comfort and convenience and were far behind those in England and France. One traveler described them as being "indifferent for bed or table but good for horses." Sleeping quarters often consisted of one large room where lodgers slept on straw bedding with blankets but no sheets. Tavern food varied from good to bad, or as an English traveler put it, "Instead of wishing it was better, I thanked God it was not worse."[3]

Before he left for France, Jefferson was aware that the culinary scene of Europe, especially France, was far more sophisticated than at home. As a student at William & Mary College he dined at the Governor's Palace where the meals were prepared by French cooks.[4]

At thirty he met Philip Mazzei, an Italian vintner, who arrived in Virginia to start America's first commercial vineyard. Jefferson supported Mazzei's vineyard efforts (which failed) and they became neighbors and friends. Mazzei was a frequent dinner guest at Monticello, and it was through Mazzei that Jefferson first became acquainted with Italian wines, olive oils, anchovies, Parmesan cheese, figs, and other Italian products that were impossible to buy in America.

Later in Annapolis when he served in Congress with James Monroe, they rented a house and Partout, a French chef, prepared their meals including beef, turkey, duck, veal, and oysters with cider and wine purchased at Mann's, one of America's better taverns.

Jefferson went to France with a palate familiar with French cooking, and to insure that he took advantage of its culinary opportunities, he brought along his slave-servant James Hemings "for the particular purpose of learning French cookery."[5]

Jefferson loved to have friends and guests to dinner and no expense was too much. By combining good food and wine, and interesting conversation with the three rules of his table, "no toasts, no politics, and no restraints," his dinner parties were sought-after social events wherever he resided: Monticello, the White House, Paris, and Philadelphia. He was such a considerate host that on his death bed he absolutely insisted that the last visitor to see him alive, Henry Lee, dine that evening at Monticello saying, "You must dine here--my sickness makes no difference."[6]

During the ten months Franklin and Jefferson were in Paris together, Franklin and John and Abigail Adams gave frequent dinner parties attended by Jefferson and other members of the American contingent and their French friends. When Franklin left to return home and Adams became minister to England, Jefferson succeeded Franklin as minister to France and remained in Paris for more than four years. His mansion on the Champs-Élysées became a gastronomic center where he entertained friends with choice wines and foods.

As president Jefferson accepted the social leadership expected of him turning the President's House (White House) into the most interesting social center in the raw new capital. His lavish dinners were prepared by a French chef on a large coal-burning stove in the basement. A typical White House dinner consisted of a first course of soups, meats, game, fish, poultry and vegetables all served simultaneously. The first course was followed by a second course, a profusion of sweet desserts. Dinner beverages were beer, cider, tea and coffee. Following the dessert course, the table cloth was removed and for the first time wine was served with an assortment of nuts, raisins, figs, dried fruits and crackers.

Jefferson, who seldom dined alone, discovered that fine wines and food were a great way to meet informally with his political friends and foes, never talking politics, but dropping a hint here and there of how he felt on a subject. He used these almost nightly dinners as a form of legislative lobbying. He usually did not mix Republicans and Federalists, and he thought out his guest lists so thoroughly that politicians from his own party came from different boardinghouses while Federalists were invited by boarding house bloc. The political effect of the dinners is perhaps best summed up by Vermont Federalist Senator Stephen Bradley who snapped over an unpopular executive appointment and the lack of senatorial opposition, "The President's dinners have silenced them."

It would have been less expensive to lobby for votes. The presidential annual salary of $25,000 was generous and covered his expenses, but made no contribution toward his retirement. An egalitarian in public life, in private he spared no expenses for pleasure. Food totaled over $6,000 one year; wine $7,597 the first term; less the second term with his stock well in hand. Household and entertainment funds did not come out of the public coffers as they do today but from Jefferson's pocket. His expenditures for food and wine ran a footrace with his income. Income usually lost.[7]

During his eight years as President the executive mansion had two dining rooms. The formal dining room on the northwest corner was used sparingly for more elaborate functions and when ladies were in attendance. It had a dumbwaiter built into a doorway that rotated into a service area near the basement stairs where food was brought up. He had a similar arrangement for food service at Monticello.[8]

His favorite place for dining was the smaller room. Chintz curtains hung at the windows, and the walls were decorated with "two elegant Girandoles and two looking Glasses."[9] Dinners here were usually men, and to eliminate any perception of rank he used an oval dining table. The dining room was equipped with four-tiered étagère dumbwaiters which were shaped like vertical Lazy Susans from which guests could serve themselves when not actually served by Mr. Jefferson. This arrangement insured privacy. "You see we are alone," he would say, "and our walls have no ears."

In retirement his wine tastes were changing with the world around him. Monticello's troubled economy was a factor in Jefferson's shift to lesser-known wines particularly from southern France. His obvious favorites were from Languedoc in southern France: Claret de Bergasse, Limoux, Ledenon, Bellet, and Muscat de Rivesaltes. Jefferson cut back on the quality of his wines--but not on quantity--and his dinner guests continued to eat heartily--duck, oysters, cheese, lamb, beef, turkey, chicken and herring were standard dinner foods.[10]

He continued to import the red wines of Tuscany. Occasionally he ordered white Hermitage which he referred to as a *bonne bouche* [good taste]. White Hermitage from the vineyards of M. Jourdan, which he considered one of the best wines of France, had on his palate a *un peu de la liqueur*, "silky, soft, smooth in contradistinction to the dry, hard or rough ... barely a little sweetish, so as to be sensible and no more, and this is exactly the quality I esteem."[11]

Jefferson's love for travel speaks for itself with trips to London, the English countryside, Paris, Amsterdam, Frankfurt, Heidelberg, Strasbourg, New York, Philadelphia, Washington, upstate New York, and parts of New England. His three-and-a-half month trip through southern France took him through Provence, over the Alps into northern Italy, along the French and Italian rivieras with visits to the great Roman antiquities of Gaul, the vineyards of Burgundy, Côte Rôtie, Hermitage, Bordeaux and the Loire Valley. One year later he traveled to Holland, down the Rhine with wine tastings at famous vineyards, and Champagne. He loved to reminisce about his travels and they form an important part of many dinner conversations.

Eighteenth century wine glasses were smaller than present wine glasses. Details of Jefferson's wine glasses that span the time periods 1760-1770, 1770-1780, late 18th century, and 1810-1840 will be found in Appendix G.

My principal source of wine information was *Passions: The Wine and Travels of Thomas Jefferson*, and authorities cited therein, a book I wrote twenty years ago, which is still in print.

The diaries, journals and letters of Senators William Plumer, Manasseh Cutler, Samuel L. Mitchill, John Quincy Adams, and the President's personal secretary, Isaac A. Coles, were rich sources of information about what foods and wines were served, what was discussed, what happened, and who attended presidential dinners. Regarding Jefferson's meals I have also relied on two excellent books: *Dining at Monticello*, Damon Lee Fowler, editor, and Marie Kimball's *Thomas Jefferson's Cook Book*.

I acknowledge and thank Lucia "Cinder" Stanton, former Director of Research at Monticello, for suggestions and information about several of the dinners, Dr. William Franklin for reading the manuscript and his helpful suggestions, Maureen Cutajar for formatting the print and EBook editions, Ranilo Cabo for the cover design, Eileen Huston and Carrie Cort for suggestions, and my wife, Anita, for reading the manuscript, her thoughtful ideas, and her unstinting encouragement.

For those who might want to quickly find the answer to a Jefferson question, I suggest checking the Thomas Jefferson Foundation Inc. website at www.monticello.org. It is a rich source of information, which I consulted freely.

Citizen Jefferson, Monticello

As a student at William and Mary College, Thomas Jefferson studied fifteen hours daily, including vacations.[1] Thirty-five year-old George Wythe, a scholarly lawyer, took the tall and bony six-foot-two, 19-year-old Jefferson into his Williamsburg law office for a five year apprenticeship. After his admission to the bar his law practice prospered. On the social side Jefferson traveled in Virginia Governor Francis Fauquier's circle of educated men who enjoyed music, literature and knowledge.

The young, red-haired Jefferson also found entertainment is less intellectual pursuits such as drinking punch at Raleigh's, Campbell's, Charlton's, Vaughan's and other taverns, winning and losing at backgammon, buying a horse, seeing a tiger in a traveling show, and day-dreaming of spending two or three years traveling through Europe.[2]

Why a bachelor who practiced law in Williamsburg wanted to build a house on top of a mountain, a long and arduous horse ride away from the valley, is not known. But at age twenty-four Monticello became his ambition, soon to be translated into a life-long passion.

A home, a profession, the only thing missing was a wife. Martha Wayles Skelton, a 23-year-old widow would join the 28-year-old Jefferson at Monticello following their marriage on New Year's 1772.[3]

Setting: Monticello, November 1773

Present are Thomas Jefferson, 30, Philip Mazzei, 43, Thomas Adams, a Virginia merchant returning from London, Maria Martin, Mazzei's wife-to-be, her 12-year-old daughter, and several Italian vineyard workers.

It is nearly five o'clock when Thomas Adams, Philip Mazzei and his entourage approach the entrance to Thomas Jefferson's Monticello, a 35 room house astride a mountaintop near Charlottesville, Virginia. Mr. Jefferson is standing by the dining room fireplace reading a book. He is tall, about six foot two and a half, with thick coppery hair, a sharp chin, straight-edged nose, and friendly hazel eyes. The room is essentially square with a high ceiling. The walls are painted chrome yellow and lined with copies of master paintings, prints with an American focus, and an assortment of engravings and architectural drawings.

Jefferson learned about an hour ago that Thomas Adams, an Augusta County neighbor, and a number of companions are traveling from Williamsburg and expected to stop at Monticello. Since there are no public lodging facilities close to Monticello, the visitors will need dinner and sleeping accommodations. Jefferson looks around the dining room, a rectangular mahogany table and three small tables are set with silver flatware and wine glasses.

Suddenly noises and loud voices emanate from the entrance area. He places the book on the fireplace mantel and moves in the direction of the parlor to investigate. It turns out to be what he thought, the arrival of his Augusta County neighbor, Thomas Adams and companions.

On seeing Thomas Adams, Jefferson strides across the room and greets his friend. Adams, who has been working in London the past several years, shakes Jefferson's hand and says, "Thomas, it is kind of you to have us as unexpected guests. Please meet my friend Philip Mazzei. I've told Philip much about you, and he insisted that we stop here so he could meet you."

Mazzei and Jefferson shake hands. Mazzei is slight of build, at least a half foot shorter than Jefferson, sharp facial features, and dark hair coifed in tight rolls. Clearly pleased to meet Jefferson, Mazzei introduces his fiancée Maria Martin, and her twelve year old daughter, and identifies the men traveling with him as vineyard workers.

Mazzei speaks with an accent but his English is clear, and Jefferson's first impression is favorable. Waving his hand in the direction of the dining room Jefferson says, "I knew you would arrive tired and hungry so dinner was prepared in advance and it is ready."

Adams, Mazzei, Mrs. Martin, her daughter, and Jefferson sit at the large dinner table and the workers at the smaller tables.

Jefferson stands and addressing Mazzei says, "Normally we don't serve wine until the meal is finished and the table cloth removed, but in deference to the Italian tradition of serving wine before and with dinner, an exception will be made."

Jefferson walks to the fireplace, opens a door on the right side of the fireplace mantel and removes a bottle of wine. Returning to the table he removes the cork, pours the wine and says, "It's Madeira and I think you will like it."

"I've never seen wine stored in the side of a fireplace." Mazzei says.

"It is not a storage area. It is a dumbwaiter built into the sides of the fireplace mantel. The wine cellar is located directly below the dining room and on instructions from me a servant places a bottle of wine in the box and pulls it up to the dining room. The same method in reverse is used to return empty bottles."[1]

"Where is the food prepared?" Mazzei asks.

"The kitchen is in the basement located under the south terrace and connected to the house by an all-weather passageway. The food is carried through the passageway, up a staircase and placed on tiered shelves on the other side of that door," Jefferson says, pointing toward a door. "The door rotates from the center. After food is placed on the shelves, servants turn the door and it rotates into the dining room."

"Another type of dumbwaiter?"

Jefferson nods. "Yes. I think of it as a revolving service door."[2]

"How does the food come to the table from the dumbwaiter?" Mrs. Martin asks.

"The food is brought to the table by servants." And with those words the door swings round and shelves loaded with food appear.

"I hope you will forgive us if the food is not warm and up to our usual standards, but it was prepared on short notice."

"Please, no apologies," Thomas Adams says. "We are delighted to be here."

As the conversation moves around the table, servants place before the guests two glazed hams, chicken pie with a thick brown crust, and a boiled leg of mutton on a bed of mashed turnips, sliced carrots, and white beans.

Jefferson sips his wine and looks at Mazzei. "Do you like the wine, Mr. Mazzei?"

"Please, call me Philip. Yes, it is excellent. I grew up in a mountain village in Tuscany and Madeira was not a common beverage."

"How did you end up living in London?"

"As a young man I studied medicine at the Santa Maria Nuova Hospital in Florence, but I was dismissed for drinking wine before taking communion on Holy Thursday."

"What a bad turn," Jefferson says sympathetically.

"Well, yes and no. I went to Leghorn and established a medical practice. But being restless I left for Smyrna, Turkey, where I continued to practice medicine. But life in Smyrna was boring, so after two and a half years I bought a supply of Turkish opium and a few other items and sailed for England in December, 1755. In London I sold the Turkish opium for a good profit, rejected offers to resume my medical practice, and made a living teaching Italian to the British gentry. The profits from the sale of the Turkish goods gave me the idea of opening a shop specializing in wines, silks, olive oil, anchovies, parmesan cheese and other Italian products that were almost impossible to buy in London."

Mazzei sips his wine thoughtfully. "My first exposure to good Madeira was through my American friends living in London."

Jefferson's eyebrows arch, "How did you meet them?"

"The Grand Duke of Tuscany sent an order for two Franklin stoves. I knew Benjamin Franklin was living in London. I found his address, knocked on his door, and persuaded him to help me find the stoves. It was through Dr. Franklin that I met Thomas Adams, and Thomas introduced to me to his circle of Virginia friends. My political persuasions were and remain in tune with the growing American rebellious spirit, and I succumbed to the urgings of Franklin and Adams to come to America to live."[3]

"What are your plans?"

"Philip has come to America for the purpose of growing European grapes and making wine, planting olive trees and producing olive oil, and growing silk worms and making silk," Thomas Adams says.[4]

"Where will Philip plant his vineyard?"

"I acquired from the Virginia Assembly 1,000 acres for Philip. However, he found the land offer unacceptable because it was divided into many parcels and separated by great distances.[5] I'm building a house in Augusta County and have offered to sell him land adjoining my estate. That is where we will set out for tomorrow," Adams says.

"Do you have plans for the grape varietals you will plant?" Jefferson's enthusiasm for the Mazzei project is obvious in the pitch of his voice and the look in his eyes.

"Yes," Mazzei says. "My plans call for planting 10,000 vines from France, Italy, Sicily, Spain and Portugal, planting about 4,000 olive trees from places where the best oil is made, and a sufficient quantity of silk worm eggs from Italy and Sicily to make silk."

"Do you have the funds to complete the project?"

"No, but Mr. Adams thinks there will be sufficient interest in the production of quality wine in Virginia which will allow me to form a partnership and raise the necessary money."

"How much will a share cost?"

"We are thinking of pricing a share at fifty pounds sterling," Adams says.

"What got you interested in wine?"

"I grew up in a mountain village in Tuscany surrounded by vineyards. My father and grandfather were winemakers. When I first opened my shop in London the English told me that Tuscan wine was a pleasant summer drink but it didn't keep. I remembered as a child that my grandfather would never drink a wine less than a year old. It was my belief that Tuscan wines spoiled because they were mishandled by the English merchants, so I ordered Tuscan wines from some Italian cousins, but over the summer this wine also spoiled. Later on a trip through Burgundy I observed the vinification methods and noted that the Burgundians did not adulterate their wines.

"When I explained this difference to an Italian wine dealer, he admitted that our forefathers never adulterated wines. He pointed out, too, that the inhabitants of Chianti treated wine much less than others did and that some did not treat it at all.[6] I purchased a large quantity of unadulterated wines from this wine dealer and less than a third of it spoiled.

"On another trip to Florence, I discovered an excellent red wine from Carmignano produced on a small vineyard owned by a tailor by the name of Cartei. I offered to buy his entire vintage and to pay him eleven percent more than his asking price on condition that he not strengthen his wine with alcohol. But Cartei would not agree, explaining that if he did not strengthen his wine it would not be good and he would lose prestige.

"I finally succeeded in buying Cartei's vintage and, after bottling it in London, it improved with age. One evening at a friend's house for dinner he had his servant 'bring in a bottle of Burgundy, one of Bordeaux, and one of Cartei's wine, which had been bottled for six or seven years.' We drank the wines without knowing which wine was which. The guests expressed a preference for Cartei's wine. They were amazed to learn that it was nothing more than the wine of Carmignano.[7] I like to think that I single-handedly improved the quality of Italian wines drunk in England."

Jefferson has been studying the little Italian and he likes what he sees and hears. There is energy and confidence in his manner and voice. "I'm interested in making quality wines in Virginia, and your project sounds exciting. I will become a partner. For now, however, I'm sure everyone is tired. Let's meet in the morning and we can talk further about it."

Early the next morning, Mazzei and Jefferson go for a walk through Monticello's surrounding hillsides, and Mazzei finds the vineyard land he is looking for, a 400-acre tract adjoining Monticello to the east. He names it Colle. Jefferson later describes the land Mazzei selected as "having a southeast aspect and an abundance of lean and meager spots of stony and red soil, without sand, resembling extremely the Côte of Burgundy from Chambertin to Montrachet where the famous wines of Burgundy are made."[8]

When Mazzei and Jefferson return home, everyone is up. Looking at Jefferson, Adams says, "I see by your expression that you have taken him away from me. I knew you would do that." Jefferson smiles, and without looking at him, but staring at the table, says, "Let's have breakfast first and then we'll see what we can do."[9]

What Mazzei and Jefferson talked about on this early-morning walk is not recorded, but it sparked a lifetime friendship. Jefferson became a partner in Mazzei's vineyard project, the first commercial vineyard venture in America.

Mazzei's viticulture experiment also captured the imagination of the Virginia gentry and George Washington, George Mason, Governor Earl Dunmore, Thomas Randolph, Thomas Adams, and Washington's stepson John Park Custis became partners at fifty pounds sterling per share. Jefferson later acquired a second share by buying the interest of Thomas Randolph. Mazzei was given four shares and the right to use for his household such necessaries as he produced.[10]

Fifteen years later on a muggy June afternoon Thomas Jefferson is seated at Café Le Procope, a venerable Paris restaurant frequented by Rousseau, Voltaire, Benjamin Franklin, John Adams, Lafayette, John Paul Jones and other famous men and women.[11] To Jefferson's surprise Philip Mazzei enters, sees his Virginia friend and hurries over.

"I arrived in Paris late this morning and immediately went to your place on the Champs Elysées. No one knew where you were, but when I was leaving through the courtyard a young girl suggested I look for you here," an excited Mazzei says.

Jefferson stands, welcomes his old friend, and invites Mazzei to join him for a glass of wine.

Over his wine Mazzei says, "I know that time moves on but I often think about my failed vineyard venture, and it makes me sad." His lips tighten. "After settling at Colle, my enthusiasm for the winemaking adventure was infused by what I saw and was told. I learned from my men that the surrounding woods yielded over 200 varieties of wild grapes. I personally identified thirty-six varieties on the property—good, fair and bad in quality. I chose six of the best varieties to make two barrels of wine, one of which I kept for myself and the other I gave to my men.

"The murderous frost that struck the Charlottesville area in May 1774 killing the European vines my men had planted didn't defeat my enthusiasm. You may recall that two months later I told you, 'In my opinion, when this country is populated in proportion to its size, the best wine in the world will be made here.' It must be remembered that the grapes from which I made the two barrels of wine were picked from the top of trees in a very dense woods, and the vine had a tremendous number of branches. When I pulled the cork three months later, it was like the sparkling wine of Champagne. I do not believe that nature is as favorable to growing vines in any country as this. I measured two vines which were more than a foot and a half in circumference. The shoots of the lugliola grape produced branches of such a length that my good Vicenzo Rossi told me, 'Master, don't write of this to our village, because they won't believe it, and you'll pass for a liar.'"[12]

"It was bad circumstances," Jefferson says. "The war intervened and when you went to Europe as a financial agent for the State of Virginia there was no one to keep it going. Who would have thought when you rented Colle to the interned Hessian General Riedesel that his horses in one week would destroy 'the whole labor of three or four years and thus end an experiment, which, from every appearance, would in a year or two more have established the practicability of that branch of culture in America.'"[13]

Mazzei shakes his head in disgust. "Who knows," Jefferson says with a shrug. "If Riedesel's horses hadn't destroyed your venture perhaps something else would have."

Mazzei looks nonplus. "What are you talking about?"

"An Englishman by the name of Isaac Weld visited Colle after it was disbanded and concluded that the experiment failed because 'the vines which the Italians found growing there were different, as well as the soil, from what they had been in the habit of cultivating, and they were not much more successful in the business than the people of the country.' Weld went on to presage that 'We must not, however, conclude that good wine can never be manufactured upon these mountains. It is well known that the vines, and the mode of cultivating them, vary as much in different parts of Europe as the soil in one country differs from that in another. It will require some time, therefore, and different experiments to ascertain the particular kind of vine, and the mode of cultivating it, best adapted to the soil of these mountains.'"[14]

Mazzei smiles and shakes his head, "I never thought I would hear Thomas Jefferson agree with an Englishman."

"I didn't say I agree with him," Jefferson says with an impish grin. "Let's not dine here. Let's call on Condorcet and then pay our respects to Lavoisier and the Duke of Rochefoucauld before returning home to dine with Short."[15]

Minister Jefferson, France
1784 – 1789

In May 1784 Congress appoints Thomas Jefferson a commissioner to join Benjamin Franklin and John Adams in Paris to negotiate treaties of commerce with European countries. Jefferson will live in Paris five years, one year as a commissioner and four years as minister plenipotentiary.

On July 5, 1784, the 41-year old Jefferson, his 11-year old daughter Martha, and an 18-year old slave-servant, James Hemings, sail from Boston for France aboard the *Ceres*. This is the beginning of a five year adventure during which Jefferson acquires a depth of knowledge and an appreciation of wine and food that no American of his time will rival.

There are only six other passengers aboard and one of those is the owner of the ship, Nathaniel Tracy. Martha recalls that the food was excellent. Four days before sailing Martha's father has the foresight to buy forty-eight bottles of Hock (a white German wine) for the voyage, which he shares with his fellow passengers. They have perfect weather, and with tailwinds their twenty-day passage is unusually fast. Jefferson amuses himself on a daily basis by recording in his account book weather data, whale and shark sightings, and teaching himself Spanish with the use of a dictionary and the study of *Don Quixote*.[1]

After landing in Le Harve, France and traveling through the French countryside, Jefferson and his daughter approach Paris on August 8 by way of Saint-Germain-en-Laye, Marly, and Nanterre, having seen along the way a spectrum of palaces, bridges, towns, woods, and hillsides in vines and wheat. They cross the Seine at Pont de Neuilly and ride down the Champs-Elysées stopping at the Grille de Chaillot, one of twenty-four barriers or tollhouse gates that ring Paris for the purpose of collecting taxes on all goods coming into the city. About a year later Jefferson will live in a mansion directly across from the Grille de Chaillot.

On entering Paris Jefferson's carriage continues down the Champs-Elysées to Place Louis XV, past the Tuileries Gardens, and along rue Saint Honoré to rue Richelieu where he takes rooms at a hotel.

Four days after his arrival, Jefferson visits Benjamin Franklin who, at the time, is serving as America's first minister (ambassador) to France. Franklin came to France in December 1776 to obtain money and arms for the American Revolution and to forge, if possible, an alliance with France. Franklin was successful in achieving these goals and, in doing so, he became the most popular and respected man in France.[2]

Setting: August 12, 1784, Hôtel de Valentinois, Benjamin Franklin's residence in Passy, a village three miles from Paris

Present are Benjamin Franklin, 78, Benjamin Franklin Bache, two days shy of his 15th birthday, Thomas Jefferson, 41.

Jefferson has been in Paris just four days but this is his third visit to the Palais Royal, the center of the city's social life and the most interesting place for entertainment and shopping in all Europe. Enclosed on three sides by elegant apartment houses, the Palais Royal's lower levels house cafes, restaurants, coffee houses, art galleries, theaters, shops of all kinds, gambling-houses, and a variety of facilities for vice. According to a local habitué "there is no spot in the world comparable to the Palais Royal. Visit London, Amsterdam, Madrid, Vienna, you will see nothing like it; a prisoner could live here free from care for years with no thought of escape."

Walking in the gardens during daylight hours is a fashionable Parisian pastime. It is the place to hear the latest gossip, observe women's fashions, and to see and be seen. At night it is a different scene with courtesans and other evening pleasures available. Jefferson has taken up power walking as an exercise, and has promised himself that until he establishes permanent quarters, he will walk daily in the Palais Royal gardens.

Walking at a rapid pace through the beautiful gardens, Jefferson's thoughts shift between dinner at Benjamin Franklin's place in Passy, and the positive impression the Palais Royal has made on him. He keeps thinking about how a similar project replicated in the Shockoe Hill neighborhood in Richmond would benefit the city and its promoters.[3]

Promptly at 3 o'clock Jefferson leaves his temporary quarters at the Hôtel d'Orleans for a 3:30 dinner appointment at Benjamin Franklin's residence in Passy. Although the distance to Passy is just three miles, the travel time is nearly a half hour because the average carriage speed is only seven miles-an-hour.[4]

Dr. Franklin's note said that he occupies a portion of an estate, Hôtel de Valentinois, owned by a wealthy French merchant, Jacques-

Donatien LeRay de Chaumont. The Leray de Chaumont mansion is, however, more imposing than Jefferson had imagined. It is perched on top of a hill and surrounded by elevated terraces, stately gardens, a lake, and avenues of linden trees leading down to the Seine with views of Paris and the Bois de Boulogne.

Benjamin Franklin's welcome is warm and friendly. Their hugs and exclamations are genuine and it is obvious they are delighted to see one another after an absence of eight years. Franklin seems taller than Jefferson remembers, at least five feet nine or ten, but otherwise his smooth round face, high domed forehead, and thinning grey hair are little changed. He is still overweight, but the twinkle in his eyes and strong voice belie his age.

"How is Temple?" Jefferson asks.

"I'm sorry to say Temple is not home, and he will be disappointed to have not been here to greet you." The thought of Temple brings a smile to the old man's face.

"He is like every young man his age, interested in women and hunting, but all in all he is doing well."

A young man enters and wraps his arms around Franklin's waist. "This is my youngest grandson, Benny Bache," Franklin says with pride, placing his arm around the young man. "Benny lives with me. In two days he will turn fifteen and he is full of energy. I have set up a printing press and Benny is extraordinarily gifted in operating it. I think printing and publishing will be his professions."[5]

"Happy birthday, Benny," Jefferson says shaking Benny's hand and making a mental note of how much he looks like his grandfather.

"Thomas, did you bring your children to France?"

"Just my oldest daughter Martha. She is eleven. I have arranged for her admission to the Convent of Panthemont located on the Left Bank. It was recommended by the Marquis de Chastellux as the best private school for young women in Paris. My two younger daughters, Mary and Lucy Elizabeth, are in Virginia in the care of my sister-in-law and her husband, Elizabeth and Francis Eppes."[6]

"I have never met your children, and I can't wait to meet Martha."

20

"And she is excited to meet you." Looking around the spacious drawing room, Jefferson says, "I'm impressed with your living quarters."

Franklin smiles, "Thank you, Thomas. It offers a 'fine house, a large garden to walk in, an abundance of acquaintances,' and beautiful sunrises and sunsets. In addition I am on very friendly terms with Monsieur LeRay de Chaumont, his wife, Marie-Thérèse, and their four charming daughters and son, who is a carousing friend of Temple's. Monsieur de Chaumont has been a great friend and benefactor of our country."

"In what way?"

"His enterprises have supplied America with more arms, ammunition and clothing than any other single source. It was through his auspices that John Paul Jones obtained the *Bonhomme Richard*, and over the past eight years he has allowed John Adams, John Jay, Silas Deane, and my private secretary, Edward Bancroft, to live here. He has also served as a warm personal friend and valuable adviser on intimate and complex dealings with French government officials.[7]

"Let's go on a short tour and we'll make an important stop at the wine cellar and select the dinner wines." Walking with a noticeable limp and his right arm draped around his grandson's waist, Benjamin Franklin heads for outside.

"I see you walk with difficulty. What is that about?"

Franklin stops, turns, and fixes his guest with an unhappy stare, "Gout. Why? I have eaten and drank too freely and indulged my legs in indolence. I have had a long dialogue with Madam Gout. She has castigated me for playing chess when I should take walks in the pure air of the finest gardens with beautiful women, and engage in agreeable and constructive conversation. She has reminded me how many times I have promised myself to exercise and violated my promises because it was too cold, or too warm, too windy, too moist, or whatever else I pleased, when in truth it was too nothing but my insuperable love of ease!" Franklin nods in the direction of a desk, "Benny, please get Mr. Jefferson a copy of my dialogue with Madam Gout."

Benny walks to the desk, opens a drawer, removes a paper and hands it to Jefferson. Jefferson glances at it and reads: Dialogue Between

Franklin and the Gout. Midnight, 22 October, 1780. "Written nearly four years ago."

"Yes, and because I have not taken her advice I merit these cruel sufferings."

Franklin and Jefferson walk through the elevated terraces and marvel at the beauty of the gardens and avenues of linden trees. From a terrace that looks back to Paris, but pointing in the direction of the Bois de Boulogne, Franklin says, "It was on this spot this past November that I watched the balloon ascension from the Chateau de la Muette of the Montgolfier brothers, Charles and Robert. It was the first time humans were lifted into the air."

"That must have been a thrilling experience."

"It was. The balloon rose rapidly until it entered the clouds, when it seemed to me scarce bigger than an orange and soon after became invisible." He pauses. "Aside from the excitement of seeing humans travel through the air, I'm almost embarrassed to say what thoughts entered my mind."

Jefferson studies his friend, "What were your thoughts?"

"That the balloon might become an effective instrument of war and possibly give a new turn to human affairs. Convincing sovereigns of the follies of wars may perhaps be one effect of it; since it will be impracticable for the most potent of them to guard his dominions. Five thousand balloons, capable of raising two men each, would not cost more than five ships of the line; and where is the prince who can afford to cover his country with troops in defense as ten thousand men descend from the clouds in many places and do an infinite deal of mischief before a force can be brought together to repel them?"

Walking along a dark corridor Franklin abruptly stops. He walks to a large wooden door and with the help of his grandson slides it open. Benny lights a lantern and, voila, there in full view is Benjamin Franklin's wine cellar filled with more than a thousand bottles, including red Bordeaux, Burgundies, Champagnes, Madeiras, Sherries and casks of wine.[9]

"Impressive," Jefferson says nodding his head in approval. "From our time together in Philadelphia I knew you enjoyed Madeira, but this," he says with a wave of the hand, "is far more than just a cask or two of Madeira."

"I have impressed you twice in the past half hour. That is two times more than I accomplished in our two years together in Congress," Franklin says with a chuckle.

"Not so. You constantly impressed me back then and you continue to impress me."

"When I lived in Philadelphia my drinking was pretty much confined to rum punch and Madeira. During my years in England the range was wider. At club gatherings wine, often claret, but also punch, porter and beer were served. Some of the best claret I drank was during my visits to Scotland at friends' dinner parties."[10]

"Scotland? I didn't know Scotland was a wine drinking country."

"It is and it's interesting how it evolved. Although Scotland and England were a united kingdom after 1603, by the turn of the eighteenth century all the political power was in the English Parliament in London. This was a period of strained relations between England and France, and French wine was prohibited in the United Kingdom from 1679 to 1685 and again from 1690 to 1696. When the French wine prohibition was lifted, the Methuen Treaty of 1703 between England and Portugal raised the duties on French wine by fifty percent more than Iberian wine duties. What had once been a flow of French claret to England became a trickle."[11]

"Which, I suppose, increased the price of claret, and made it so expensive that it was available only to the wealthy," Jefferson says.

"That was the situation in England, but not in Scotland. Scotland had a tradition of importing and drinking French claret that went back to the thirteenth century, when Scots' merchants sailed directly to Bordeaux, then the capital of the English province of Gascony.[12] The Scots jealously guarded their wine-trading rights with France, and paid little attention to Parliament's restrictive wine laws. Throughout the eighteenth century vast amounts of claret were smuggled into Scotland. The common method of announcing its arrival was for the ship's captain to send a hogshead of claret through the town on a cart, and anyone who wanted to buy it had only to go to the cart with a jug. All sections of society bought and drank the smuggled wine."[13]

"How did the smugglers avoid getting caught by English custom ships?"

"That, of course, was the smuggler's risk, but the coastline of Scotland is daunting, so catching the smuggler was near impossible. Also, contraband wine was usually not shipped direct from Bordeaux but rerouted via Dutch ports. So you see, while England suffered through the eighteenth century with strong port and little claret, Scotland was knee-deep in claret."[14]

"Other than your club activities where else did you buy wine in London?"

"I bought wine from a local wine merchant and from a Burgundian winemaker with the unlikely name of Thomas O'Gorman. O'Gorman sent me a hogshead (57 gallons) of wine of what he called 'the right sort for you.' I even received wine from home. A Pennsylvania vintner by the name of Thomas Livezey sent me wine he made from 'some small wild grapes.' I told Livezey that his wine was excellent and that I was applying the wine 'towards winning the hearts of the friends of our country.' My London wine merchant was very desirous of knowing what quantity of it might be had and at what price.[15] Yes, there is so much to love about France, and its wines are a big part of my love affair."

"How many bottles do you have?"

"I don't know, but I would estimate about a thousand."[16]

"All French?"

"There are some Madeiras and Spanish sherry but most of the wines are white Burgundies and Bordeaux reds."

"From whom do you buy your French wines?"

"I buy most of my Bordeaux wines through John Bondfield, the American Consul in Bordeaux, and from V. & P. French & Nephew. Most of my Burgundies come from Saussett and Masson, and Thomas O'Gorman. O'Gorman once sent me seven *feuillettes* (foy-yets) of wine, six red and one white, of the 1775 vintage. I recall Bondfield shipping me two hogsheads of Médoc wines for inspection with the promise of two more if the wine met my approval. From V. & P. French & Nephew in Bordeaux, Temple ordered for my account 480 bottles of the best claret fit for immediate consumption. The wine was represented to be better than any claret they had previously sent me."[17]

"What is a *feuillette?*"

"A wooden cask containing 114 liters. We will have wine with dinner so while we're here, Thomas, please select the dinner wines."

"I will defer to your experienced palate, but I prefer white Burgundy and red Bordeaux."

Franklin walks to a corner of the cellar and pulls down a bottle. "This is a Burgundy I have enjoyed." He hands it to Benny. He moves to another part of the cellar, lifts a bottle from a bin and hands it to Jefferson. "This wine was sent to me by John Bondfield with the comment, 'The best Bordeaux available.'"

"The best Bordeaux available," Jefferson mumbles with obvious satisfaction.

Later the two American diplomats relax over dinner in elegant but simple surroundings. The table is set with a white table cloth, ivory-colored plates, silverware, wine glasses, and flowers.

"My dinner arrangements allow for a joint of beef, veal or mutton, fowl or game, and fish, when fresh and available as it is this evening, two vegetables with hors d'oeuvres of butter, pickles and relishes, and desserts of fruits, fruit preserves, cheeses, biscuits, bonbons, and ice cream.[18] This evening my cook has prepared salmon, fresh from the Loire River, and a delicious veal roast with peas and asparagus. Thomas, I know peas are your favorite vegetable so I ordered them special."

"Thank you. It sounds like a delicious meal. I am very much looking forward to enjoying and learning more about French cooking."

"Ah, French wines, foods and women, have been a revelation. And now it is your turn," the savvy old host says with a smile and twinkle in his eyes.

"I've often wondered," Jefferson says, "what was the essential turning point in the war? Was it Burgoyne's surrender at Saratoga?"

Franklin stops. "It was the turning point in my efforts to form a Treaty of Alliance with France and bring France into the war. France wanted the alliance, but so long as the war went badly for us, the king's minister of foreign affairs, Comte de Vergennes, would do nothing more than surreptitiously furnish us help in the form of arms and money. Vergennes was fearful we would lose the will to persevere with the war. The summer and fall of 1777 were full of bad news: Washington's evacuation of New York, General William Howe's advance on Philadelphia, and the march of General Burgoyne's army south from Canada. In November, we learned that Philadelphia had fallen to Howe's army. Despite the bleak news, I was convinced that we could successfully maintain the war. Just before noon on December 4, I received the news of a staggering American military victory; Burgoyne's entire army had surrendered at Saratoga!"

The salmon comes to the table and the conversation is suspended as the two revolutionaries savor it. The sauce is light and delicate and gives the salmon an exquisite taste that Jefferson has never experienced before. Franklin can tell from his friend's countenance that he is enjoying the fish. "Do you like it?"

Jefferson nods, "Yes, very much, and the green beans that accompany it are perhaps the best I've ever eaten."

"I don't know why it is but French green beans are indeed special." Franklin takes a sip of his white wine. "But, of course, it could also be the company that makes it special," he says, winking at his grandson Benny.

"Did Burgoyne's surrender change the diplomatic picture?"

"Completely," a smiling Franklin says. "Two days after receiving the news of the American victory at Saratoga, Vergennes's emissary, Conrad-Alexandre Gérard, called to congratulate us and to invite us to renew our proposal for an alliance. I drafted the proposal, and we submitted it. The British also realized that Burgoyne's defeat had changed the complexion of the war and that it had the potential of sparking a

French alliance. I had a positive feeling about the French when I left Count Vergennes's office. A few days later the king's council, with Louis XVI's consent, voted in favor of a treaty of amity and commerce and a treaty of alliance was signed on February 6," Franklin says.[19]

The veal roast is served on a large silver platter. A servant slices it with a knife that looks like a saber. It is covered in a rich, hot sauce that gives off a marvelous aroma. A large slice of rare veal is placed on each plate. Franklin watches as Jefferson and Benny cut into their meat. Sipping the red wine Franklin says to his friend, "Do you like the red wine?"

"It is my favorite of the evening. Whose is it?"

"Bondfield didn't mention the vineyard name. He said only that it was a first growth."

Jefferson swirls the wine and sips it thoughtfully. "It is a lovely wine with a full bouquet and rich flavor." Still thinking about the conversation he says, "Why wasn't General Burgoyne held captive like his officers? Why was he allowed to return to England?"

Franklin shrugs, "He was paroled and sent back to England on his promise not to engage in further hostilities. But that's not the end of the Burgoyne story. Congress revoked Burgoyne's parole, and because he was still technically a prisoner of war, he was required to return to America."[20]

"I don't recall Burgoyne returning," Jefferson says.

"No, here is what happened. Burgoyne engaged Edmund Burke to represent him. Burke had remained friendly to the American cause and wrote me and asked that I intercede on Burgoyne's behalf. He pointed out that in vigorously prosecuting the war, Burgoyne had been following the king's orders and the soldier's code. He then said, 'If I were not fully persuaded of your liberal and manly way of thinking, I should not presume, in the hostile situation in which I stand, to make an application to you. I apply, not to the Ambassador of America, but to Doctor Franklin the Philosopher; my friend; and the lover of his species.'"[21]

"Did you intercede?"

"It so happened that I had just received authority from Congress to offer Burgoyne's freedom in exchange for that of Henry Laurens who was being held a prisoner in the Tower of London after being captured at sea. I made that offer to Burke, and although the British ministry was not then ready to make the swap, Laurens was eventually set free, and Burgoyne was not required to return to America as a prisoner of war. A happy ending."[22]

"I ended up 'generals sitting' Burgoyne's two highest-ranking officers," Jefferson says with a chuckle.

"How did that happen?"

"After the surrender of Burgoyne at Saratoga more than 4,000 British and Hessian captured soldiers were marched from Boston into the Charlottesville area and interned as prisoners. The living conditions were bad when they arrived in my neighborhood. The barracks were unfinished, the weather was unbearable, and much of the food provisions spoiled.

"When I heard the rumors that the prisoners would be moved, I took the matter up with Governor Patrick Henry. 'Is an enemy so execrable,' I asked Henry, 'that, though in captivity, his wishes and comforts are to be disregarded and even crossed? I think not. It is for the benefit of mankind to mitigate the horrors of war as much as possible. The practice, therefore, of modern nations, of treating captive enemies with politeness and generosity, is not only delightful in contemplation, but really interesting to all the world, friends, foes, and neutrals.' Henry was understanding and agreed to keep them in the Charlottesville area and improve their living conditions. The barracks were completed, and they were giving gardens to tend and their own poultry.[23]

"Major General William Phillips, second in command to Burgoyne, rented Colonel Carter's place, Blenheim. Philip Mazzei went to Europe as a financial agent for the State of Virginia, but before leaving, he rented Colle to the ranking Hessian, Major General Baron Frederick Adolphus de Riedesel, who had been captured and interned along with his troops. His wife, the Baroness Friderike von Riedesel, and their three small daughters, joined the general.

"My wife, Martha, and I met the Riedesels at a dinner party given by General Phillips. The baroness was stout and handsome, wore riding boots, and charmed us with her operatic singing. The Riedesels became our friends, but our circle of friends among the prisoners was wider than our two families. War and politics were put aside as music furthered our friendship. I played the violin, with a young German captain, Baron de Geismar, also on the violin, and the baroness singing Italian arias."[24]

"Enough war stories. Thomas, I'm excited to introduce you to my French friends. The Marquis de Lafayette remains a great friend of all Americans, and every Monday he and his lovely wife, Adrienne, host a dinner for Americans in Paris. Some other friends to whom I will introduce you include Marquis de Condorcet, an enthusiast of human rights and a brilliant mathematician." Franklin reflects as he sips his wine. "Other men of distinction are Andre Morellet, an economist, the great chemist Antoine Lavoisier, Count Buffon, Intendant of the King's Garden and a world famous naturalist, the great sculptor Jean Antoine Houdon, the king's foreign minister Count Vergennes, and, of course, two of my favorite lady friends, Madame Brillon and Madame Helvétius. Thomas, you are going to find France an intellectual feast!"

"It sounds like a new and exciting experience for the 'savage of the mountains of America.'[25] But Benjamin, I've heard that your circle of women friends is quite extensive, and you're only going to introduce me to two of them?" Jefferson says with feigned disappointment.

"For you, Thomas, I'm going to make an exception and introduce you to all of my lady friends."

Franklin pours the last of the wine. "Temple told me that John Adams will arrive in Paris in a few days from London with Abigail, his 19-year old daughter, Nabby, and son, John Quincy. I am excited to have you and John in Paris with me to negotiate treaties of commerce with the nations of Europe and to renew our friendships."

On the carriage ride back to Paris the quality of the red wine that Franklin called a first growth remains on the new commissioner's mind. *When I place my first order for Bordeaux wines with John Bondfield, I will specify that he provide me with 'such wine' as I drank at Dr. Franklin's house.*[26]

Setting: December 31, 1784, Hôtel Antier, the residence of John and Abigail Adams in Auteuil, a suburb four miles from Paris

Present are John Adams, 49, Abigail Adams, 40, their daughter Nabby, 19, their son John Quincy, 17, Thomas Jefferson, 41, Jefferson's secretary William Short, 25, David Humphreys, 32, John Paul Jones, 37, Thomas Barclay, 56, Benjamin Franklin, 78, Marquis de Lafayette, 28, his wife Adrienne, 26.

The Adams residence in Auteuil is a white stone 25 room house located near the Bois de Boulogne where John Adams takes daily one and two hour walks.

Thomas Jefferson arrives promptly at 3:30 o'clock. The door is opened by a servant. Standing behind him is an attractive, diminutive woman, about five feet tall, brown hair, with cream-like smooth skin. It is one of Jefferson's favorite ladies, Abigail Adams. She extends her hand to the man she considers "one of the choice ones of the earth"[1] and in a soft voice says, "I know you have not been feeling well lately, and John and I thank you for coming to share New Year's Eve with our family and mutual friends."

"On the contrary, Abigail, I thank you and John for inviting me. I thought that after dinner John, Nabby, John Quincy and you might do me the pleasure of driving into Paris and welcoming-in the New Year at my place."

"What a splendid idea," Abigail says as she takes the handsome Virginian's arm.

To the left of the reception area is a large drawing room, or as the French say, salon, where a number of the guests are already gathered. To the right is the dining room with a long rectangular table set for dinner.

Abigail takes Jefferson's hand and moves into the drawing room. At each end of the room are large glass doors, one opens into a court and the other into a beautiful garden.[2] John Adams is by the fireplace stoking the fire.

"John seems preoccupied with the fire, so come, join me in greeting the guests." Abigail heads in the direction of Benjamin Franklin who is talking to a handsome young man at the far end of the room. He is John Paul Jones, a naval hero of mythic proportions throughout Europe.

Franklin exclaims, "Thomas, I see you are in good hands with the beautiful and charming Abigail Adams. And speaking of good hands this young man is Captain John Paul Jones. Thomas, I'm sure you have met Captain Jones."

"Yes, we have met on several occasions but my hope is to get to know Captain Jones far better in the months ahead."

"It will be my pleasure," Jones says extending his hand. Jones is small in stature but his handshake is firm and strong. He is in Paris in connection with collecting prize money and staying with Dr. Franklin "as I almost always do when in Paris."

"Abigail, along with your husband, Thomas and John Paul are two of my best friends, and I intend to see that their friendship grows," Franklin says.

Abigail knows that her husband is a bit jealous of Dr. Franklin, but she has admired him since she was a little girl.[3] "I have no doubt Dr. Franklin that your friendship will nourish theirs."

As Abigail maneuvers Jefferson across the room toward her nineteen year old daughter Nabby, she says, "In stature for a warrior Captain Jones is somewhat of a disappointment. From the intrepid character he justly supported in the American Navy, I expected to see a rough, stout, warlike Roman––instead of that I should sooner think of wrapping him up in cotton wool, and putting him into my pocket, than sending him to contend with cannon-balls. He is small in stature, well proportioned, soft in his speech, easy in his address, polite in his manners, vastly civil, understands all the etiquette of a lady's toilet as perfectly as he does the masts, sails and rigging of his ship. Under all this appearance of softness he is bold, enterprising, ambitious and active ... he is said to be a man of gallantry and a favorite amongst the French ladies ... he knows how often the ladies use the baths, what color best suits a lady's complexion, what cosmetics are most favorable to the skin."[4]

Young Abigail, who is affectionately called Nabby, in appearance looks like her mother, but in manner she is a bit stiff like her father. She too admires Mr. Jefferson and quickly confesses to him that she has been sizing up the young men. "I find that as a group, American men, especially young men, are too stiff and reserved and that they would be better off adopting some of the French ease of manner."

"I agree that the French exhibit a politeness and conviviality that we lack." With a small chuckle he adds, "Anyone in particular in mind?"

She nods her head in the direction of David Humphreys. "I find Col. Humphreys too soldier like. I suppose that comes from serving as an aide de camp to General Washington. On our second meeting I thought him a sensible man, but his address is not agreeable. Later when he presented me with a copy of his poem, Armies of the America, I was surprised to learn that he is a poet. That impressed me and I noted in my diary that Col. Humphreys has taken the most effectual means of gaining my good opinion; no more reflections upon the stiffness of his manner must proceed from me."[5]

"What about that young man?" Jefferson says, looking in the direction of his secretary, William Short.

"William?" Jefferson nods. "William has 'some of that ease of French manner that I admire.' He is sociable and pleasant 'without the least formality or affectation of any kind. He converses with ease and says many good things.' But I understand he has a French lady friend."[6]

"Excuse me, Nabby," her mother says, "but I see the Marquis de Lafayette and his lovey wife, Adrienne, have arrived. Thomas, let's welcome them."

As they move across the room in the direction of the Lafayettes, Abigail says, "Of all the French women I have met, there are none that I hold in higher esteem than Adrienne. She is an anomaly . . ."

"In what way is she an anomaly?" Jefferson asks.

"She is a good and amiable lady, exceedingly fond of her children and attentive to their education, passionately attached to her husband!!! Think about it Thomas, a French lady and fond of her husband!!!"

Abigail and Adrienne fall into a tête-à-tête. Jefferson and Lafayette discuss their mutual interest in Madeira and decide to share a pipe (110 gallons) of Madeira with Jefferson assigned the task of buying it.[8]

"I see that we are being called to dinner. Thomas, you will sit between John and me." Abigail takes his arm and they move into the dining room.

"Are you aware that dinner tonight is going to be served 'French style," Abigail says.

"What is French style?"

"It's a curious custom. When company are invited to dine, gentlemen meet, they seldom or never sit down, but are standing or walking from one part of the room to the other, with their swords on, and their *chapeau de Bras*, which is a very small silk hat, always worn under the arm. These they lay aside while they dine, but resume them immediately after dinner. At dinner the ladies and gentlemen are mixed, and you converse with him who sits next you, rarely speaking to persons across the table, unless to ask if they will be served with anything from your side. Conversation is never general as with us or when company quit the table, they fall into a tête-à-tête of two, when the conversation is in a low voice, and a stranger, unacquainted with the customs of the country, would think that everybody had private business to transact. And on with the conversation very pleasantly, with scarcely a word from any other person, til we have finished our ice cream. When the wine begins to pass round the table a little more freely, all their tongues begin to be in motion."[9]

"French style or not," Jefferson says, "I cannot imagine sitting next to you at dinner and not falling into a tête-à-tête."

"I have my complaints with the French but certainly their cookery is not one on them," Abigail says, as the first course of oyster soup and breast of guinea hen with mushrooms in a clear gravy are served with a dry white wine.

A servant pours the wine. John Adams turns and says, "Dinner at our house is always accompanied by wine. 'I acquired an early taste of French hospitality and French wines when I landed at Bordeaux six years ago and was invited aboard a French vessel to have dinner with the captain. The first dish was a fine French soup, which I confess I liked very much. Then a dish of boiled meat. Then the lights of a calf, dressed one way and the liver another. Then roasted mutton. Then fricasseed mutton. A fine salad and something very like asparagus, but not it. The bread was very fine, and it was baked on board. We had then prunes, almonds, and the most delicate raisins I ever saw. Dutch cheese–then a dish of coffee–then a French cordial and wine and water, excellent Claret with our dinner. None of us understood French—none of them English.'[10]

"The next day I received my first lesson on the Bordeaux wine hierarchy from J. C. Champagne, a négociant from Blaye, who rated Chateaux Margaux, Haut-Brion, Lafite and Latour the best wines of Bordeaux and referred to them as 'First Growths.' That afternoon, I dined in the fashion of the country. We had fish and beans and salad, and Claret and Champagne and Mountain Wine."[11]

As the next course is served and conversation drifts around the table, John waits while a servant fills his glass with red wine. "As good as my introduction to French cooking and wine was back then, dinner tonight is as good," he says as glazed rump of beef with sauce hachée and roast hindquarter of lamb are passed around the table. "When I lived in Holland hachée was a favorite meal of mine. It is a Dutch tradition."

Jefferson watches as Adams savors the beef and onion stew. "I too like it. How does this hachée measure up to Dutch hachée?"

Adams smiles. "Maybe it is because it's New Year's Eve and I'm with my family and friends, but regardless, this hachée is as good as any I've had. And I like this wine. I sampled it and ordered a 60 gallon cask of it."[12]

"Where is it from?" Jefferson asks.

"Gaillac in southeastern France. It is a good wine and extremely cheap."

Jefferson agrees that the meal is outstanding and says that the quality of French cooking continues to impress him. "I have apprenticed my servant James Hemings to several caterers to learn the art of French cooking."

Adams gives Jefferson a quizzical look. "Do you think he can learn it?"

"I do. James is quite bright." Jefferson mentions Abigail's ambivalent comments about John Paul Jones and a moment of thoughtful silence follows. "Captain Jones should not be judged on the basis of his size. I met him for the first time about five years ago while staying at the Hôtel de l'Epée Royale in L'Orient and hosted Jones and the officers of the *Poor Richard* at an elegant dinner where we 'practiced the old American custom of drinking to each other' which I confess 'is always agreeable to me.' Our conversation covered 'some hints about language and glances about women, and produced this observation, that there are two ways of learning French commonly recommended–take a mistress and go to the comedy.'

"I came away from this meeting with the impression that Jones is the most ambitious and intriguing officer in the American Navy. Jones has art, and secrecy, and aspires very high. You see the character of the man in his uniform and that of his officers and Marines, variant from the uniforms established by Congress. Golden Button holes, for himself–two Epaulettes–Marines in red and white instead of green.

"Eccentricities and irregularities are to be expected from him–they are in his character, they are visible in his eyes. His voice is soft and still and small, his eye has keenness and wildness and softness in it."[13]

Abigail leans in toward her husband, "Thomas has suggested that we ride into Paris after dinner and welcome in the New Year at his place. I would like to do that."

"Fine," her husband says and takes a sip of wine. "Thomas, what do you think of this dessert wine?

Jefferson swirls the wine in his glass and takes a sip. "It's a good sweet wine. What is it?"

"It is from a place in southern France called Frontignan, bordering the Mediterranean. I just received it from The Hague where I have my wines stored. I think it has improved since I last tasted it."

"I will try to serve as good a wine to help us welcome in the New Year."

Setting: March 1785, Franklin's villa in Passy, a suburb of Paris

Present are Benjamin Franklin, 79, Franklin's lady friends Madame Helvétius, 64, and Madame Brillon, about 45, Marquis de Lafayette, 28, Adrienne Lafayette, 26, John Paul Jones, 37, Franklin's landlord LeRay de Chaumont, 59, his wife Marie-Thérèse, about 55, John Adams, 49, Abigail Adams, 40, 'Nabby' Adams, 19, Franklin's personal secretary and friend, Edward Bancroft, 40, and Thomas Jefferson, 41.

Although the Congressional commission papers appointing Thomas Jefferson minister plenipotentiary to succeed Benjamin Franklin have not arrived, the guests know the transition is just months away. Accordingly, there is a feeling that this is Benjamin Franklin's farewell dinner party.

Suddenly the door bursts open and Franklin's lady friend, the famous Madame Helvétius, whom Franklin calls 'our lady of Auteuil', enters with a careless and jaunty air. Upon seeing ladies who are strange to her she bawls out, "Ah, Mon Dieux! Where is Franklin? Why did you not tell me there were ladies here! How I look!" Her hair is frizzled, and over it she has a small straw hat with a dirty gauze half-handkerchief tied over it.

It is clear that Abigail is shocked by Madame Helvétius's appearance and behavior. Abigail whispers to her daughter, "I should have been greatly astonished if the Doctor had not told me that in this lady I would see a genuine French woman and one of the best women in the world. For this I must take the Doctor's word, but I should have set her down as a very bad one, although 60 years of age and a widow."[1]

The ever alert Franklin notices Abigail's annoyance with Helvétius's behavior and comes over to her.

"Ask the doctor what you asked me," Abigail says to Nabby.

Nabby is clearly embarrassed and mumbles, "Is the woman who just entered the room, and the attractive younger woman she is now talking to, the two French women who have been the recipients of your fervor and attention during your time in France?" Franklin smiles and nods. "Who are they?"

"Anne-Louise de Harancourt, Brillon de Jouy, known as Madame Brillon, and Anne-Catherine Helvétius. They have been the two main women in my life during my eight and a half years in France."

"How did you meet them?"

"Through my circle of Passy friends."

"I suppose," Abigail says, "it is as my husband said, 'This is a time in your life when at the age of seventy-odd you have neither lost your love of beauty nor your taste for it.'"[2]

An impish smile forms on Franklin's face. "Someone mentioned the kindness of the French ladies to me, and here is how I explained it: 'This is the most civilized nation upon earth. Your first acquaintances endeavor to find out what you like, and they tell others. If it is understood that you like mutton, dine where you will, you find mutton. Somebody, it seems, gave it out that I loved ladies, and then everybody presented me their ladies (or the ladies presented themselves) to be embraced, that is have their necks kissed. For as to the kissing of lips or cheeks, it is not the mode here: the first is considered rude, and the other may rub off the paint.'"[3]

"Tell us about Madame Brillon and Madame Helvétius," Abigail says.

Franklin's eyes take on a nostalgic look. "I first met Madame Brillon soon after I arrived in Paris. We took an immediate fancy to one another. She was in her thirties, and according to you, Abigail, she is 'one of the handsomest women in France,'[4] and married to a philandering husband twenty-four years her senior. Of course, our age difference is even greater, nearly forty years. Nevertheless, Madame Brillon and I became close friends, and she became particularly dependent on me when in the spring of 1779 she discovered her husband's affair with Mademoiselle Jupin, the governess of their children.

"She once told me that people had the audacity to criticize her pleasant habit of sitting on my knee, and mine of always asking her for what she always refused.[5]

"There is a dichotomy to our relationship, the paternal and the sensual. Every time I see Madame Brillon, I am guilty of breaking the Commandment that forbids coveting one's neighbor's wife. I told her that the best way to get rid of a certain temptation is to comply with and satisfy it.[6]

"Unfortunately, all my amorous advances were repulsed by her commitment to virtue, saying 'You are a man, and I am a woman, and while we might think along the same lines, we must speak and act differently. Perhaps there is no great harm in a man having desires and yielding to them; a woman may have desires, but she must not yield.' It was not that she did not have desires, for she told me that 'in the matter of desire, I am as great a sinner as yourself.'"[7]

Franklin's eyes flash in the direction of Madame Helvetius and he continues, "My other serious amour is with Madame Helvétius. She is the lady who just entered the room screaming, 'Mon Dieux! Where is Franklin?' She is a wealthy widow whose estate in Auteuil is within walking distance of my place. Although approaching sixty when I met her, she is still attractive and vivacious, and fifteen years my junior. She maintains the intellectual salon her late husband established and that is where I met her. Statesmen, philosophers, historians, poets, and men of learning of all sorts are drawn around her.[8]

"We have a routine where I visit her in Auteuil once a week and she visits me once a week. On one occasion when I failed to show up and she complained, I told her, 'Madame, I am waiting till the nights are longer.'"[9]

"Is it true, Dr. Franklin, that you proposed marriage to Madame Helvétius and she rejected your proposal?" Abigail says.

A slight smile creases the doctor's lips. "Her response was a bit more subtle than a blatant 'no,' but the effect was the same. She said that she had resolved to be faithful to the memory of her late husband, a former farmer-general and philosopher. Mortified I went home that night and dreamed that I was in the Elysian Fields where I met Monsieur Helvétius. He received me with much courtesy, having known me by reputation, he said, for some time. He asked me many things about the war and about the present state of religion, liberty, and government in France. 'You ask nothing then,' I said to him, 'about your dear friend Madame Helvétius; and yet she still loves you to excess. I was with her less than an hour ago.'

'Ah!' he said, 'you remind me of my former happiness. But we must forget if we are to be happy here. For several years at first, I thought of nothing but her. At last, I am consoled. I have taken another wife; the most likely I could find. She is not, it is true, altogether so beautiful, but she has so much good sense and plenty of wit, and she loves me infinitely. She studies continually to please me, and she has just now gone out to search for the best nectar and ambrosia 'to regale me with this evening. Stay with me and you will see her.'

'I perceive,' I said, 'that your former wife is more faithful than you; she has had several good offers and refused them all. I confess to you that I love her, to madness; but she was cruel to me and absolutely rejected me for love of you.'

'I pity you,' he said, 'in your misfortune, for she is indeed a good and beautiful woman, and very amiable.' "Then the new Madame Helvétius came in with the nectar. Immediately I recognized her as Madame Franklin, my former wife. I claimed her again, but she said coldly: 'I was a good wife to you for forty-nine years and four months, almost half a century. Be content with that, I have formed a new connection here, which will last for an eternity.'

"Indignant at this refusal from my Eurydice, I at once resolved to quit these ungrateful shades, return to this good world, and see again the sun and Madame Helvétius. And when I saw her, I told her of my dream and said, 'Here I am. Let us avenge ourselves.'"[10]

"Did her rejection affect your friendship?"

"No, we remain close friends."

Nabby notices a man that she has not seen before. Nodding in the direction of a tall, trim, rather handsome man who moves about with an air of confidence, she says to her father, "I have not seen that handsome gentleman before. Who is he?"

John Adam looks across the room at Edward Bancroft who is engaged in animated conversation with Thomas Jefferson. "First, Nabby, he is married. Second, he has a French mistress. And third, he is too old for you."

"Don't talk silly, papa. I'm not looking at him as a romantic prospect. I've never seen him before, and so I want to know who he is."

"His name is Edward Bancroft. He is an expatriate American who resides in London when he is not in Paris. He is a physician, scientist and writer. He is a close friend of Dr. Franklin's and has served as Dr. Franklin's personal secretary for the past eight years."

"What is it that you don't like about him?"

"What makes you think I don't like him?"

"Your tone of voice and attitude."

"Well, Nabby, you are right. I don't like some of his personal habits."

"Such as?"

"He is married but maintains a mistress, conduct of which I highly disapprove. He has written a novel which no doubt appeals to many readers, and procured a considerable better sale by the plentiful abuse and vilification of Christianity which he took care to insert in it. He is a meddler in stocks and is not to be trusted in his stock speculation activities. He will descend into the deepest and darkest retirements and recesses of the brokers and jobbers, Jews as well as Christians to gain an advantage with his stock speculations." Adams pauses and takes in a deep breath. "Some of his dining habits also offend me."[11]

"Such as?"

"He seasons his food with enormous amounts of cayenne pepper, assisted by generous amounts of Burgundy. This 'sets his tongue a running at a most licentious rate both at the table and after dinner' and his conversation gives me a 'great pain.'[12] Do you wish to hear more?"

Nabby is smiling to herself, "Yes, papa."

"The Bible and the Christian religion are his most frequent subjects of invective and ridicule, but the royal court is also included, especially the queen. The queen's intrigues with the Duchess de Polinac, her constant dissipation, her habits of expense and profusion, her giddy thoughtless conduct are almost constant topics of his tittle tattle."[13]

"Those are concerns I have heard others express about the queen."

Adams looks at his daughter sternly. "While I am expelling my annoyances of Dr. Bancroft, there is something else. Among his many activities and pursuits he reviews books. His review of the first volume of my work *Defense of the Constitution of Government of the United States of America* was very ungracious."

"What did he say, papa?"

"The opening sentence of his review says it all, 'We have not met with a greater disappointment, in our literary labors, than we have experienced with respect to the work now before us.' I'm sure Dr. Franklin would give you a different opinion of Dr. Bancroft."[14]

At dinner Madame Helvétius takes a seat between Franklin and Adams. Abigail sits next to Jefferson. As dinner is being served, Abigail says, "Look, she carries on most of the conversation at dinner, frequently locking her hand into the Doctor's and sometimes spreading her arms upon the backs of both the Doctor and my husband. Now look at her, she is throwing her arm carelessly about the Doctor's neck." Mrs. Adams shakes her head in disgust.

For the first course Franklin's guests have a choice of fricasseed chicken, mutton chops, and a veal roast, and desserts of sponge cake with fruit preserves, cheeses, bonbons and ice cream. White and red wine freely circulate round the table.

To the chagrin of Abigail and daughter Nabby, Helvétius is not through with her exhibitions. After dinner she throws herself on a settee where Abigail points out she is showing "more than her feet," to which Nabby adds, "Odious indeed do our sex appear when divested of those ornaments with which modesty and delicacy adorn them."[15]

Franklin stands and the dinner table falls silent. "I want to propose a toast to two of the bravest and exemplary men I have ever known. He raises his wine glass, "To the Marquis de Lafayette and Captain John Paul Jones, both of whom have risked their lives, fortunes and sacred honor in the pursuit of freedom."

Everyone stands and lifts their glasses, *To Marquis de Lafayette and Captain John Paul Jones.*

Franklin remains standing. "I've never told this story in public but I have the permission of my friend Captain Jones to tell it now. It's a humorous story but it could have ended tragically. When John Paul is in Paris he usually stays with me. One day after Captain Jones left Passy in March 1779, a local clergyman advised Madame de Chaumont and me of what he called a scandal. Captain Jones, he told us, had tried to rape the wife of the gardener of our estate at about seven o'clock on the evening before he left. I wrote to Jones that the wife had related to us all the circumstances, some of which were not fit for me to write.

"The serious part of it was that three of her sons were determined to kill Captain Jones if he had not left when he did. The rest occasioned some laughing, for the 'old woman was one of the grossest, coarsest, dirtiest, and ugliest that we may find in a thousand. Madame de Chaumont said it gave her a high idea of the strength of appetite and courage of the Americans.'[16]

"Madame de Chaumont and I had another chuckle when my investigation revealed that the old woman's assailant was a chambermaid who had stolen one of Captain Jones's uniforms. It was the last night of the carnival before Lent. As a practical joke, the chambermaid, dressed as Captain Jones, and on meeting the old woman in the darkened garden, took it into her head to test the old woman's chastity, which the old woman passed by pushing her attacker away and running to her husband." Everyone laughs.

"I seem to recall hearing somewhere that Marquis de Lafayette and Captain Jones made plans to raid English coastal cities during the war. Whatever came of those plans?" someone calls out.

"Since we have the author of the daring plan here at the dinner table, I think the Marquis de Lafayette should tell you how it came about."

The Marquis stands. "After my country signed the Treaty of Alliance with the United States in February 1778, I returned to France with the intention of returning to America with a French army. My expedition in this regard, however, was delayed. Impatient, I came up with the idea to launch surprise attacks on English coastal cities, in particular Bath, because 'the best of London society comes together in Bath this time of year.' I thought that the terror that we could spread would be felt much more intensely, and that Bath would furnish some well-qualified hostages.[17]

"The king's tentative approval of the plan sent my blood boiling. I wrote Admiral d'Estaing, 'If you undertake an attack on England and land troops and I am not there with you, I shall hang myself!'"[18]

"I was told of the plans," Franklin says, "and I endorsed the expedition with enthusiasm. I admired the activity of Layette's genius, and the strong desire he had for being continually employed against the common enemy. I too was certain that the coasts of England and Scotland were open and defenseless. And I told Lafayette, 'There are also many rich towns near the sea, which 4000 or 5000 men, landing unexpectedly, might easily surprise and destroy, or exact from them a heavy contribution, taking a part in ready money and hostages for the rest. It would spread terror to greater distances and the whole would occasion movements and marches of troops that would put the enemy to prodigious expense and harass them exceedingly.'

"In war, attempts thought to be impossible do often for that very reason become possible and practicable, because nobody expects them and no precautions are taken to guard against them. Those are the kind of undertakings of which the success affords the most glory. In that same conversation I mentioned that 'much will depend on a prudent and brave sea commander who knows the coasts.' I had, of course, John Paul Jones in mind.[19]

"Captain Jones was sent for and arrived at Passy in early April. He and Lafayette spent long hours planning the operation. Because I knew nothing about naval maneuvers, I relied on Antoine de Sartine, the French naval minister, who prepared the plans for the incursions into England after conferring with Lafayette and Jones.

"Since I was the ranking American representative in France, Captain Jones was my charge. I knew Jones was brave and daring, but also impetuous and touchy on matters of rank, and I was very concerned that a conflict might develop between him and General Lafayette, who would ultimately be in command. Therefore, I cautioned Jones. 'It has been observed that joint expeditions of land and sea forces often miscarry, through jealousies and misunderstanding between the officers of the different corps. This must happen when there are little minds actuated more by personal views of profit or honor to themselves than by the warm and sincere desire of good to their country. Knowing you both as I do, and your just manner of thinking on these occasions, I am confident nothing of the kind can happen between you, and that it is unnecessary for me to recommend to either of you that condescension, mutual goodwill and harmony, which contribute so much to success in such undertakings.' Jones and Lafayette got my message, and they exchanged letters."[20]

Jones speaks out, "I told Lafayette, 'Where men of fine feeling are concerned there is very seldom any misunderstanding. Without any apology I shall expect you to point out my errors, when we are together alone, with perfect freedom.' And always the gentleman, Lafayette responded, 'I'll be happy to divide with you whatever share of glory may expect us.'"[21]

"I reminded Captain Jones that General Lafayette outranked him and would command the ground forces, but the command of the ships will be entirely in you, in which I am persuaded that whatever authority his rank might in strictness give him, he will not have the least desire to interfere with you. Because the operation joined not simply land and sea forces but also Americans and French, 'a cool prudent conduct in the chiefs is therefore the more necessary.' But I told Jones, he need not fear. 'There is honor enough to be got for both of you if the expedition is conducted with a prudent unanimity.'

"I followed this exhortation with formal instructions to Jones. Captain Jones was to accept the French forces Lafayette brought him and conduct them wherever the Marquis requested. Once the troops were landed, Jones was to assist them by all means in his power. He must stay close. I specifically told him, 'You are during the expedition never to depart from the troops so as not to be able to protect them or to secure their retreat in case of a repulse.' Jones said that I could count on him."[22]

"So, what happened?" Abigail asks.

"The king changed his mind. He decided against a series of incursions and chose a full-scale invasion of Great Britain involving more than 40,000 troops, but that too was abandoned."[23]

"What did you do, Captain Jones?" Madame Helvétius says.

"I took the ship the French provided me through the patronage of our friend LeRay de Chaumont, the *Duc de Duras*, refitted it, and christened it the *Bonhomme Richard*. With the invasion of England called off, I put out to sea. In September 1779, I met off the coast of England the *Serapis*, a larger, more heavily armed vessel. The two ships sailed toward one another with cannons blasting away. Two of my 18-pound cannons exploded in the faces of the gunners, ripping away a chunk of the starboard side. 'The battle thus begun continued with unremitting fury.'[24] The destruction and carnage aboard the *Bonhomme Richard* was incredible, and I realized that we could not win a cannon duel with the better-equipped *Serapis*. I maneuvered the *Bonhomme Richard* so that it collided with the *Serapis*, and the sailing master and I bound the two ships together by lashing a rope around the *Serapis's* jib boom and the *Bonhomme Richard's* mizzenmast.

"The battle now raged above deck with my sharpshooters in control, but below deck the heavy cannons of the Serapis were taking their toll on us. Both ships were on fire and their decks covered with blood and dead bodies.[25] As the *Bonhomme Richard* began to sink, the captain of the *Serapis*, convinced that he had won, called out, 'Have you struck? Do you call for quarter?' And though my ship is sinking beneath me, I could think of only one reply, 'I have not yet begun to fight.'[26]

"With the raging battle entering its fourth hour and my marines in control of the upper decks, a sailor named William Hamilton climbed the rigging that extended over the deck of the *Serapis*. He carried a bucket of grenades and a lighted slow match. Hamilton lit several grenades and lobbed them toward an open hatch below. One of the bombs rolled into the hatch and exploded, setting off a chain reaction of explosions among the loose powder cartridges in the gun deck. Fire spread like lightning, and the men and cannons of the *Serapis* were decimated."[27]

Franklin interjects, "Jones told me himself, 'A person must have been an eyewitness to form a just idea of the scenes of carnage, wreck and ruin which everywhere appeared. Humanity cannot but recoil and lament that war should be capable of producing such fatal consequences.'"[28]

"Captain Jones," Madame Brillon calls out, "what happened next?"

"The *Serapis's* captain, his name was Pearson, climbed to the quarter-deck and struck his colors. I issued the order to 'cease firing,' and I accepted Pearson's sword at the surrender ritual aboard the *Bonhomme Richard*. Attempts to save my ship were futile, so I and my crew went aboard the *Serapis* and watched from there as the *Bonhomme Richard* sank to a watery grave."[29]

Someone at the table starts clapping and applause spreads around the table. Franklin lifts his glass and says, "To freedom loving brave men everywhere."

Setting: Paris, September 20, 1785, Hôtel de Landron,
Thomas Jefferson's residence in the Cul-de Sac Taitbout

Present are Jefferson, 42, John Ledyard, 34, David Humphreys, 32, David Franks, 46, Thomas Barclay, 57, and William Short, 26.

After two months in temporary quarters Jefferson moves to a handsome three story house on the Right Bank with a courtyard and two gardens. The house is unfurnished and Jefferson purchases furniture, dishes, flatware, wine glasses, carpets, etc. His friend Thomas Barclay helps stock his wine cellar with "2 casks of very good brandy two years old, each cask containing 42 gallons."[1]

Jefferson assembles a household staff consisting of Marc, the *maître d' hôtel*, Le-grand, *valet de chambre*, and Saget, the *frotteur*, whose sole job is to keep the red tile and parquet floors clean by whirling around the rooms with brushes strapped to his feet "dancing here and there like a Merry Andrew."[2] During the year Jefferson resides at the Hôtel de Landron all of his meals are catered. His slave-servant James Hemings is apprenticed to several caterers to learn the art of French cooking so that, when trained, he will become Jefferson's chief cook.[3]

The American circle of Jefferson's friends includes two who live with him, David Humphrey, Secretary of the American Legation, and William Short, a native Virginian and Jefferson's private secretary.

Another member of the group assembled in the drawing room is John Ledyard, an American navigator and explorer of "fearless courage and enterprise." Ledyard is wearing a dark shirt with an open neck collar and Turkish breeches. In comparison to the other men he is not tall, about five-seven, but he has a thick neck, broad shoulders, blond hair, sharp nose, and blue eyes. Ledyard's appearance and manner exude energy and strength.[4]

A tall and erect Thomas Jefferson enters. "Gentlemen, I see that we are being summoned to dinner." He is at least six feet two with a trim, powerful looking physique that comes from daily exercise that includes five and six mile power walks through the Bois de Boulogne and around Paris. His thick coppery hair is powered, and he is dressed in a front cutaway tailcoat fashioned from red silk damask, patterned with alternating large and small rosettes, an ivory satin collar and lapels, a ruffled ivory silk cravat, with matching silk breeches, stockings, and buckled shoes.

A fifteen-foot table is the center piece of the dining room and the guests take their places in no assigned order. A waiter in livery enters carrying two decanters of white wine and places them on a side table next to Mr. Jefferson. As Jefferson pours the wine he says, "Gentleman, I have a theater engagement so I might have to leave a little early but there is no reason for you to rush."

As the wine passes around Thomas Barclay says, "What is the wine?"

"It's from Burgundy. I first tasted this wine at Dr. Franklin's house."

As the conversation moves around the table, William Short says, "What brought you to France, Mr. Ledyard?"

"To make my fortune."

"How?"

"By getting financial backing for a trading idea I had for buying animal furs in the Pacific Northwest and selling them for three times as much in China. And with the money from the fur sales, buying Chinese tea, silk, and porcelain and selling it here in France and throughout Europe."

"What gave you the idea?"

"Years earlier I had explored the Pacific Northwest with Captain Cook and witnessed the Russian fur trade. I knew of the abundance and richness of the furs available and how cheaply they could be purchased."

"Were you successful?"

"I formed a partnership with John Paul Jones with plans to take two ships to the Northwest coast and establish a fur trading factory. But for reasons I don't entirely understand, we were not able to secure the approval of the French government. So, here I am, happy to be at Mr. Jefferson's table among his circle of distinguished American friends."

Ledyard looks around the table.[5] "Colonel David Humphreys, former aide-de-camp to General Washington during our glorious war, and now Secretary to the American Legation, whose stout warlike stature hides a man devoutly fond of women, wine and religion, provided they are each of good quality."[6]

That's not George Washington's perception of Humphreys, Jefferson thinks. *He told me, 'In him you will find a good scholar, natural and acquired abilities, great integrity, and more than a share of prudence.'*[7]

"There sits my good friend Thomas Barclay who sacrificed his career as a successful Philadelphia merchant to serve his country as Consul General with the task of settling all United States public accounts in Europe.

"David Franks, revolutionary veteran, diplomatic courier, drinking companion and member of my 'set of such moneyless rascals that have never appeared since the epoch of Falstaff,' a patriot who left his position as president (parnas) of his Spanish and Portuguese synagogue to serve as a volunteer soldier in General Montgomery's army in the battle for Quebec.[8]

"And you, sir, graduate of William and Mary College, co-founder of Phi Beta Kappa, lawyer, and private secretary to our distinguished host."

"How did you get to know Mr. Jefferson?" Humphreys asks.

"I was in L'Orient when notified that my plan to start the fur trade business had been rejected by the French government. Thomas Barclay was the consul there. He suggested I seek assistance through the U.S. legation, and I came to Paris. When I got here I immediately went to see Minister Jefferson. At our first meeting we discussed the science of the compass, Indian dialects, our passion for books and walking, and within an hour we were like brothers. Our minister kindly lets me dine with him and has taken me into his circle of friends which included dining with the venerable Dr. Franklin. He has become like a brother to me."

Servants enter pushing three wooden étagères or dumbwaiters consisting of four-tiered open shelves on casters on which food has been placed. The servants maneuver the dumbwaiters around the room and position them between the guests so that each guest can serve himself.

"I had not seen the use of these serving devices before I dined here with Minister Jefferson," Ledyard says.

"Actually," Short says, "they are a method of serving food that has become fashionable in wealthy French and English homes."[9]

In deference to their host, Jefferson's guests wait until he begins serving. Jefferson ladles on to his plate chicken with rice, onions and carrots. From the bottom shelf he selects a croquette of roasted veal, and from another shelf a slice of French beefsteak with potatoes and peas, and says, "Please, don't wait. Serve yourselves before the food gets cold."

A waiter enters carrying a silver tray containing a decanter of red wine. He places the tray on a side table. Jefferson pours the wine and says, "John walked here from his place in Saint-Germain-en-Laye, and I suppose he has worked up a considerable appetite."

"Saint-Germain-en-Laye is twelve miles out," Short says. "You walked from there?"

"Yes. I make these trips to Paris often."

Smiling, Jefferson hands Ledyard a glass of wine. "Since the end of the war it has been my desire to have the western part of the North American continent explored. John is a prodigious walker. At my suggestion he has agreed to walk from Paris across Russia and then take a vessel to Nootka Sound and make his way to the continent of the United States. From there he will cross on foot from the Pacific Ocean to Virginia."[10]

All heads turn in the direction of Ledyard.

"I heartily approve the project and will apply to Monsieur de Simoulin, the Russian minister, and to Baron de Grimm, private agent for the Empress, to make application in my name to the Empress to grant Ledyard permission as an American citizen to travel through her dominions."[11]

Ledyard says, "I am the same age at which my father died but I am healthy, active, vigorous and strong." *It will make me famous and bring me honor*, he thinks.

David Franks shakes his head in astonishment. "You are saying that you plan to walk around the world?"

Jefferson interjects, "Yes, and to ensure that John will be able to record significant geological data such as the height of mountains, I have suggested that he tattoo two marks on his arm exactly a foot apart. In this way he can break off a stick of that length and estimate heights by measuring shadows." He takes a sip of wine. "What do you think of the wine, John?"

Ledyard nods, "I like it very much. I will have to inculcate in my memory its bouquet and taste because I'm sure I won't drink wines like this on my travels across Russia."

"Speaking of your travels, have you decided on an itinerary?" Thomas Barclay says.

"Yes. I plan to travel to Copenhagen and on to Stockholm arriving when the Gulf of Bothnia is frozen. I will cross the gulf in a sledge and travel to Petersburg and Moscow before crossing Siberia to Okotsk. From there I will take a fishing vessel to Kamchatka and cross to the North American continent by boat."[12]

"What will you do if the Gulf of Bothnia is not frozen solid? You know that happens when there are warm winters," Barclay says.

"I will have no choice but to head in the direction of the Arctic Circle and circumambulate the gulf, a distance of 1200 miles rather than the 120 miles directly across the gulf," he says with a shrug.

"As I mentioned I will solicit Empress Catherine's permission through Baron Grimm and Monsieur de Simoulin to allow John to pass through Russia to the western coast of America." Jefferson tips his glass in the air and says, "John, you are a welcome addition to my table."

The waiters begin serving another course of lightly grilled fresh water perch from tributary streams feeding the northern Loire River, followed by roasted ortolans, eaten whole, then roast leg of lamb accompanied by a massive cheese board and bread.

As the dinner progresses wine continues to flow. The white Burgundy moves around the table along with the red Bordeaux that so impressed Jefferson when he first dined with Dr. Franklin in Passy. Jefferson received two months earlier his order of 144 bottles of this wine that Bondfield described as "our First Growth."[13]

Working his way through an ortolan Jefferson thinks, *It is perfect with the red Bordeaux.*

"John sailed with Captain Cook on his third voyage in search of the Northwest Passage and personally witnessed Cook's murder in February 1779. John, tell our friends about your fascinating voyage with Captain Cook."

Ledyard sips his wine thoughtfully. "I was in London when Captain Cook was preparing for his third world voyage. My adventurous spirit craved joining the glorious cause, so I enlisted in the British marine service. Captain Cook interviewed me on three occasions before accepting me into his service."[14]

Ledyard cuts into the lamb and sips his wine before continuing. "The *Resolution* and the *Discovery* left London on July 12, 1776. I was aboard the *Resolution* with Captain Cook. The voyage took us all over the globe including New Zealand. In 1778 we discovered the beautiful Sandwich (Hawaiian) Islands. The relationship between the natives and Cook's sailors was friendly. We sailed from the Sandwich Islands to the west coast of North America until we found a safe harbor in Nootka Sound. We sailed along the Alaskan coast looking for inlets that might lead to the Northwest Passage. Eventually we sailed back to the big island of the Sandwich Islands and our reception by the natives was friendly.

"On February 4th after bringing on supplies we weighed anchor and sailed out to sea. The natives lined the shore and gave us an enthusiastic farewell. Four days out we ran into a storm and the *Resolution's* main mast broke. It had to be repaired and we returned to Kealakekua Bay. On our return, for some inexplicable reason, the natives' reception changed. They were hostile and a great deal of stealing occurred including the theft of the *Discovery's* cutter, the ship's largest tender.

"Captain Cook was outraged and led a party ashore to seize King Kalaniopu'u and hold him for ransom in return for the cutter. Cook's party included two lieutenants, a sergeant, two corporals, and six private marines including me.

"Without protest King Kalaniopu'u agreed to return to the ship with us. I got the impression that he was not aware that the cutter had been stolen. But it quickly became clear that the king's subjects were opposed to him leaving with us. As we neared the water a large crowd gathered. Suddenly a shot was fired from one of our ships and a native was killed. This incited the crowd and they surged forward. Captain Cook and several marines fired their muskets. The king's guard charged swinging clubs and iron daggers. Cook was stabbed in the back and the blade went through his body. Cook and four marines were killed and several others wounded. I escaped unhurt."[15]

"It sounds like the theft of the cutter set in motion events that led to Cook's murder," someone says.

"As I mentioned, when we returned to the bay of Kealakekua to repair the main mast, the attitude of the natives toward us had turned hostile. I'm convinced that this hostility led to the stealing of the cutter. If Captain Cook had not made the decision to kidnap King Kalaniopu'u, he would be alive today."

"What caused the natives to become hostile?" Jefferson asks.

"None of us could figure it out, and it remains a mystery.".

"Did Cook's murder end the voyage?"

"No. Charles Clerke took command of the exposition and we sailed north still expecting to discover a northwest passage. Our ships harbored at Kamchatka, Russia for several months and from there we continued the search for the Northwest Passage. We did not find it but our four year exploration charted large tracts of the Pacific and Arctic coasts."[16]

"I look forward to reading you're *Journal of Captain Cook's Last Voyage to the Pacific Ocean, and in Quest of a North-West Passage,*" David Franks says.

Setting: London, April 24, 1786, the Adams residence on fashionable Grosvenor Square

Present are Minister John Adams, 50, wife Abigail, 41, daughter Nabby, 20, Adams's secretary and soon to be Nabby's husband, William Stephens Smith, 30, Lucy Paradise, 35, John Paradise, 43, Thomas Jefferson, 43, John Trumbull, 28.

Everyone is seated in the second floor drawing room around a blazing fire waiting the summons to dinner. Lucy Ludwell Paradise is a beautiful thirty-five year old scatter-brained American heiress who has lived in England since the age of nine. She is also known for a hair-trigger temper. At age eighteen she married John Paradise, a scholar and linguist whose life revolves around scholars, professionals and artists. Theirs is a troubled marriage, financially and otherwise. Jefferson met the Paradises through John and Abigail shortly after his arrival in London on March 11.

"I understand you are going to leave us in two days," Abigail says. "Can't we talk you into staying longer?"

"Yes," Lucy gushes, "we would love for you to stay longer."

"I'd like to but I must get back." Jefferson says.

"Have you enjoyed your stay?" Abigail asks. "John said your six days together traveling through the English country side was very special."

"It was for me too. And, yes, I've enjoyed my seven weeks here."

"What are some of the things you and papa especially enjoyed doing together?" Nabby asks.

"Being with your father six days and nights was special. We enjoyed each other's company, had time to talk about a variety of subjects, but most of our time was spent visiting English landscape gardens which surpass all the earth and far exceeded my expectations. Surprisingly many of these gardens were designed by just two men, William Kent and Lancelot 'Capability' Brown."

"Who were these men?" Nabby says.

"William Kent was a fashionable architect of formal buildings in the Palladian style but, paradoxically, he was the first important pioneer in the creation of the informal English garden. He was opposed to the stiff irregular English garden patterns of the 17th century and was one of the first to eliminate walls or boundaries. He replaced them with sunken fences or what became known as "ha-has" to express surprise at finding a sudden and unnoticed barrier. Kent's guiding principle was that 'nature abhors a straight line.'

"The man who made the greatest impact on English landscape gardens was Lancelot 'Capability' Brown whose nickname derived from his habit of saying of nearly every garden he was asked to improve that it 'has great capabilities.' He worked at Stow under Kent and made it one of the most talked about gardens of that day. Brown was a fervent advocate that gardens should display their natural beauty and give the appearance of freedom. He employed the use of 'ha-has' as a method of disguising boundaries."[1]

"Which gardens impressed you the most?" Nabby says.

"The Stowe gardens," says John Adams. "We climbed to the top of the 115 foot Lord Cobham's Pillar for the view."

"Yes, and the magnificent avenue of elms with the mansion and Corinthian arch in the background," Jefferson adds.

"That evening we traveled to Shakespeare's birthplace, Stratford-Upon-Avon and . . ."

"Papa, I want to hear how Mr. Jefferson experienced his visits. You have already told us about your experiences," his daughter says.

Jefferson smiles, "The inn where we stayed was three doors from the house where Shakespeare was born. They showed us an old wooden chair in the chimney corner where he sat. We cut off a chip according to custom. We saw his gravesite but his name is not on the gravestone.[2]

"At Worchester we visited battle sites, the scene of Oliver Cromwell's final victory in 1651 over Charles II during England's bloody civil war.[3] Leaving Worchester we rode on to Woodstock, a neat little town that served as a convenient stop-over for a visit to the gardens at Blenheim Palace. The next morning we visited Blenheim. The house is colossal and the grounds consist of 225 acres with gardens, lakes, and a park stocked with deer and sheep."

"How did you know what gardens to visit?"

"We both carried copies of *Thomas Whately's Observations on Modern Gardening*, an indispensable guide. At dinner we would decide where we would visit the next day.

"At Oxford we visited several colleges and then went on to High Wycombe and dined at the Antelope Inn on mutton chops with beer and wine."

"I've not traveled in the English countryside," Trumbull says. "What are the accommodations like?"

"We stayed at the best inns and the accommodations were good, but I was disappointed in the quality and cost of the wines. You kept the receipts, Thomas, but as I recall the wine often cost twice as much as our meals," Adams says.

Jefferson nods. "The reason is because of the exorbitant duties the English impose on wines, especially French wines. Your personal wine costs are reasonable, John, but that is because as a diplomat you are not required to pay taxes on the wines you import."

"Was the food also a disappointment?" Abigail asks.

"The food and dining facilities were good. Most of the inns did not have common dining rooms so we usually took our meals in private rooms."

"Where does the common traveler take his meals?" Nabby says.

"In the kitchen," her father replies.

"What were your dinners like?" Trumbull asks

"Chicken, mutton steaks, veal chops, potatoes, tarts, and custards, accompanied by punch, beer, wine or sherry."[4]

"You've been here forty-seven days, Mr. Jefferson. How have you spent your time?" Nabby asks.

Jefferson looks at Smith wryly. "Have you told Nabby about the evening we spent at the Ranelagh."

Nabby's eyes flash and she gives her fiancé a disapproving look. "And what was it that you and William found interesting at the Ranelagh?" she asks.

Everyone in the room knows the Ranelagh is London's main pleasure haunt. Here kings, ambassadors, statesmen, literati, nobility, ladies of fashion and prostitutes mingle at masquerades, banquets, dances, parties, and other fetes.

Realizing that he has set in motion a potential lovers' quarrel, Jefferson retreats. "Nothing specific, it was just a departure in style from my usual evenings at the theatre, opera, concerts and dining with you and your parents and other friends."

Abigail clears her throat. "You have told me how much you enjoyed afternoon sight-seeing visits with John and me to Osterly and Sion House in Brentford, the Tower of London, the British Museum ..."

"And visits with John to booksellers and publishers around Paternoster Row and, of course, shopping." Jefferson pauses. "Probably one of my rougher days was spent traveling to Windsor Castle after spending the evening before at Dolly's Chop House with my erstwhile London guides, William Stephens Smith and Richard Peters."

Nabby, annoyance showing in her voice, says, "Who is Richard Peters?"

"Richard is a friend from the United States who was visiting London. He served in the war as Secretary of the Board of War. We dined on beefsteak and beer, tried our hands at writing poetry, and stayed at Dolly's too long."

"Has your visit brought disappointments?" Abigail asks.

Jefferson thinks for a long moment. "My ostensible purpose in coming to London was to join John in trying to negotiate a treaty of peace with the ambassador of Tripoli. Our diplomatic efforts failed because the price he demanded was too high.

"When John and I asked him under what authority his country was carrying out these criminal acts, he said that it was 'founded on the laws of their prophet, that it was written in their Koran, that all nations who should not have acknowledged their authority were sinners, that it was their right and duty to make war upon them wherever they could be found, and to make slaves of all they could take as prisoners, and every Muslim who should be slain in battle was sure to go to paradise.'"

"How should we respond to such arrogance?" Trumbull asks.

"I'm convinced that the best solution to the Barbary pirates' menace is war. In fact, when I return to Paris, I will try to form an international concert of nations to war against these pirate states."[6]

"I admire your willingness to try to bring a concert of nations against these pirate states, but I suspect most nations will continue to find it easier to pay tribute," John Adams says.

"If it is decided that we shall buy a peace, I know no reason for delaying the operation, and think it ought to be hastened. But I prefer obtaining it by war."[7]

John Adams stands, moves to the fireplace and stokes the fire. "Soon after Thomas arrived in London I took him to the Court of St. James's Palace and presented him to King George III and Queen Charlotte. Our reception from the king and queen was not civil."

"Was I disappointed?" Jefferson says. "I suppose so but not surprised. I'm told that ten years ago the king read in the Declaration of Independence my criticisms of him, and I assume that he has neither forgotten nor forgiven."

"What did he do?" John Paradise says.

"On my presentation to the king and queen at their levee, it was impossible for anything to be more ungracious than their notice of Mr. Adams and myself. I saw at once that the ulcerations in the narrow mind of that mulish being left nothing to be expected on the subject of my attendance."[8]

"The king and queen turned their backs on us, a hint of which, of course, was not lost upon the circle of his subjects in attendance," Adams says.[9]

"And, indeed, it was not, for though I was entertained at dinners by a few Englishmen who are American sympathizers, I've been ignored by members of the British ministry during my stay."[10]

"On a lighter note, Thomas, you will be interested to know that two of the wines that will be served at dinner are wines you heroically tried to save for me."

"What are you talking about?" Abigail asks.

Adams stands. "Don't you remember? During my stays at The Hague and Paris I accumulated a large supply of wines. In fact, just before receiving word I had been appointed America's first minister to England I ordered 500 bottles of French wine. When I arrived in London I was told, to my chagrin, that diplomatic immunity could not save me from paying the English duty of six to eight shillings on every bottle of wine brought into the country. I was in a state of shock and frantically wrote Thomas beseeching him to stop the shipment of all wines except one case of Madeira and the Frontignan adding, 'I am sorry to give you this trouble but I beg you to take the wine, at any price you please. Let your maître d'hôtel judge, or accept it as a present, or sell it at auction, let Petit dispose of it as he will.'"[11]

"Papa, did I hear you say you might give the wine away?" Nabby asks in an incredulous tone. Her father fixes her with scolding stare.

Jefferson catches Nabby's banter and smiles. "I remember a letter from your father pleading, 'For mercy sake stop all of my wine but the Bordeaux and Madeira and Frontenac. And stop the order to Rouen for 500 additional bottles,' saying, 'I shall be ruined, for each minister is not permitted to import more than 500 or 600 bottles which will not more than cover what I have at The Hague, which is very rich wine and my Madeira, Frontenac and Bordeaux at Auteuil.'"[12]

Jefferson chuckles. "It's ironic but the day before receiving your urgent message, I had arranged for the shipment of your wines. On receiving your plea, I immediately dispatched Petit to stop the boat leaving Paris for Rouen but Petit was not in time. The boat had just departed. What happened after that is not clear in my mind but somehow it was resolved in your favor."

"Yes," Adams says, "I was finally told that I could receive my wines without paying duties."[13]

John Adams, standing during the exchange, falls back into his chair in relief.

"When you return to Paris would you like company as far as Greenwich?" John Paradise asks.

"I would be delighted to have your company, John. In Greenwich I would like to see the Royal Observatory and Wren's hospital if that is possible."

"Not just possible but it will be my pleasure to accompany you."

John Adams stands. "I see we are being summoned to dinner."

"What are the two wines you are going to serve that I tried heroically to save?"

"The 60 gallon cask of Gaillac that I have had bottled, and a red wine from vineyards near Montpelier known as St. George d'Orques. It is a quality wine with a good bouquet and not expensive."

"How did you learn about these wines?" John Paradise asks.

"From our consul in Marseilles, Stephen Cathalan. Thomas, Stephen is someone you must get to know. He has a broad range of knowledge about good but little known wines of southern France. And speaking of France, Abigail and I dearly miss French cooking. But today our cook has prepared England's most famous dish—roast beef!" Adams says proudly.

On the trip from London to Dover Jefferson is accompanied as far as Greenwich by his new friend, John Paradise. He stops to see the Royal Observatory and Wren's hospital which is being rebuilt.

He arrives at Dover a little before midnight, but is detained for a day and a half by bad weather and contrary winds. He spends part of the day visiting Dover Castle. Had the weather been better, he would have had a splendid view from Dover Castle of the harbor and the coast of France.[14]

Thinking of his friend on the road alone, William Stephens Smith sends Jefferson a note. "A quarter before four and we are seated as usual round the fire expecting the summons to dinner. The pleasure at it will be lessened by an apprehension that yours today will be rather solitary."[15]

Actually, the winds became favorable and Jefferson crossed the channel to Calais in three hours, had dinner at Pierre Dressin's Hotel d'Angleterre and was on the road between Calais and St. Omer the moment Smith penned his note. Within two days he was at home on the Champs-Elysées.[16]

Setting: Paris, August 12, 1786, Jefferson's residence, Hôtel de Langeac

Present are Thomas Jefferson, 43, John Trumbull, 30, Charles Bulfinch, 23, Baron de Grimm, 63, and William Short, 27.

In October 1785 Jefferson rents a mansion, the Hôtel de Langeac, on the Champs-Elysées. "It is much more pleasant than my old quarters and suits me in every circumstance but the price." The new residence is two stories, twenty-four rooms, in-door plumbing in the form of water closets, a garden, servant quarters, stables, horses, carriages, a cook, and a coachman.[1]

The carriage carrying John Trumbull and his architectural friend from Boston, Charles Bulfinch, turns right off the Champs-Elysées on to a small cobble-stone street and immediately stops in front of the entrance gate to Minister Jefferson's new residence. It is three o'clock and the weather is hot.

It has been a busy day. The two young men in the company of Richard and Maria Cosway visited Versailles to see the royal art collection and the magnificent gardens. Trumbull is staying with Jefferson during his visit to Paris. He knows his host is punctual and he does not want to be late for dinner.

On the right of the gate is a blue sash embroidered with gold grapes. When Trumbull pulls on the sash the tinkle of bells can be heard. Jefferson's maître d'hôtel, Petit, answers and accompanies the two guests across the courtyard to the house.

The entrance foyer is a circular room with a skylight. There are three doorways. One leads to the dining room, another to a small salon, and the third to a large oval salon with the ceiling decorated with a painting of a rising sun.[2]

Petit escorts Trumbull and Bulfinch into the large salon where Jefferson and his secretary and friend, William Short, are seated in armchairs by floor-to-ceiling French doors that look out to a garden.

Trumbull introduces Bulfinch to Jefferson and Short as a friend and an architect "whose work will reflect simplicity, balance and good taste."

Noting Bulfinch's youth, Jefferson says, "I anxiously look forward to seeing and admiring your works. John mentioned that you are in Paris before starting a grand tour of Europe. I asked John to bring you to dinner so that we could meet. I wish I could find the time for a European tour. I feel honored to have you and John Trumbull, an artist whose talents are almost unparalleled,[3] to my dinner table."

"Minister Jefferson, I am honored to meet you and Mr. Short. I understand that you and Mr. Trumbull only recently met."

"Yes. I met John when I was recently in London and immediately became interested in him when I learned of his plan to devote himself to painting the great events of the American Revolution."

Trumbull nods, "Mr. Jefferson encouraged me to persevere in this pursuit and invited me to come to Paris to see and study the fine arts, and to make his home my home during my stay. He has been a gracious host showing me the . . ."

"John, I'm sure Mr. Bulfinch will enjoy the narrative of our Paris activities even more if they are accompanied by a glass of wine." He walks to a side table, lifts a decanter of white wine, and pours four glasses.

"We are going to be joined shortly by an interesting character, Baron de Grimm, minister to France from the Duchy of Saxe-Gotha. 'His forte is belles-letters, painting and sculpture. In these he is the oracle of society, and as such, is Empress Catherine's private correspondent, in all things not diplomatic.' Should he like your paintings, John, it will have a beneficial influence on many of the most important people in Europe."

"What is he like as a person?" Trumbull asks. "He is the most pleasant and conversable member of the diplomatic corps, a man of good fancy, acuteness, irony, cunning and egoism."[4]

Trumbull sips his wine thoughtfully. "It's very good, French?"

The handsome minister nods, "Yes, it is a dry white from the quaint village of Meursault in Burgundy. The village and its adjacent vineyards are surrounded by stone walls, and in my opinion, this is the best wine of Meursault. It comes from the vineyard of Goutte d'Or (drop of gold). It has become one of my favorite table wines."

"John," Bulfinch says, "you were about to tell me about what you have been doing since your arrival in Paris earlier this month."

"It has been a whirlwind of activities. Before our trip today to Versailles, I traveled with Mr. Jefferson to Versailles and I was overwhelmed by the royal art collection, and as you witnessed today the grandeur of the gardens must be seen, they cannot be described. The next day I visited the Louvre and saw another royal art collection, which is 'numberless inestimable things.' I toured the collection of the great sculptor, Jean Antoine Houdon. I visited Jacques Louis David at his apartments in the Louvre. I found the dome of the Invalides one of the most beautiful pieces of architecture in existence. I will take you there. I toured the Luxembourg Palace and its gardens, the King's Gardens, the Sorbonne, and Benjamin Franklin's former residence in Passy from which there is a 'very beautiful' view of Paris."[5]

"I would like to see many of the same things," Bulfinch says.

"And for a different perspective of Paris," Jefferson says, "we climbed to the top of the scaffolding of the new but unfinished church of Sainte Genevieve."[6]

"What a magnificent view of Paris it affords," Trumbull adds. "It was a very fine day, so the eye, without interruption, wandered over the immense extent of the buildings, which lay beneath it, the Tuileries, the Louvre, the Church of Notre Dame, Saint Sulpice, the dome of the Invalides, the Bastille towering above the dwelling houses. The extent of the city, the vast and opulent country, terminating in rough and broken hills, partly in fine Champaign, ornamented with the palaces of Mendon and St. Cloud, the aqueduct of Marly, the Convent of Mount Calvaire, and a number of other splendid buildings formed together a coup d'oeil [view] entirely superior to anything I have seen before. It has been a magnificent visit and Minister Jefferson has been a great guide and gracious host."[7]

"John has been an energetic guest, and through him I met the beautiful, blond, musically and artistically talented twenty-seven-year-old Maria Cosway. And I confess my attention was riveted on Maria from the time we met. In order to be with her I changed my plans for dinner with the Duchesse de la Rochefoucauld and whisked Maria and her husband and John away for dinner at the Palais Royal and a ride to the royal park at Saint Cloud. On our return we saw an elaborate fireworks display. Afterwards we attended a performance by the famous harpist Krumpholtz at the Tuileries Gardens. That first day was a prelude to many spent on trips together without her husband and Trumbull."[8]

Minister Jefferson's rhapsody of his time with Maria Cosway is so unlike the emotionally controlled minister that Trumbull looks at Bulfinch for his reaction. Bulfinch stares wide-eyed back at Trumbull and sips his wine in silence.

"I met Maria today and found her good company. It sounds as though you had a wonderful time together," Bulfinch says.

"We did, indeed."

"I also met her husband today," Bulfinch says. "He is a strange looking man, small in stature, arrogant, flamboyant in dress and manner, and I'm told by John, a womanizer."

"What is his attraction?" Short asks.

"He is a talented miniature artist and a court favorite of the king's debauched son," Trumbull says.

"Still, why would an attractive and talented younger woman marry such an execrable man?" Short says.

"Her mother's inheritance was depleted and she put her daughter up for marital auction . . ." Trumbull shrugs, "Richard made the high bid."[9]

"Do you intend to continue seeing Maria?" Trumbull asks Jefferson.

"Yes."[10]

Jefferson replenishes his glass, walks to the large floor-to-ceiling French doors and stares out at the garden. After a moment he turns back and flashes Trumbull a challenging look. To Bulfinch he says, "I find John's Revolutionary War scenes exciting but I believe his best work is yet to come. He plans on painting the surrender of Cornwallis at Yorktown and that is the painting I most look forward to. John wants to paint the portraits of the French officers who were at Yorktown directly onto the canvas. When John next returns to Paris, I will attempt to get

Rochambeau, Lafayette, Chastellux, Admirals de Grasse and de Barras among others to my house so he can paint them from life.

"John served in our war for independence as an aid de camp to General Washington and is able to empathize with the scenes he paints. He brings realism to his paintings in a way I have rarely experienced."

Jefferson glances at his silver pocket watch. "It appears Baron de Grimm will be late for dinner. Mr. Bulfinch, I hope you find the food to your liking. It is prepared by my twenty year-old cook, James Hemings, who came to France with my daughter and me. James knew nothing about cooking when he arrived two years ago, but he has since been apprenticed to several caterers and has learned the skills of French cooking.[11]

"I do not follow the tradition of the French nobility in offering six and seven course dinners. I serve but two or three courses 'in half Virginian, half French style.'[12] You will have a choice of rice or onion soup, salad, pheasant pie, leg of veal, Rouen duckling, cauliflower with parmesan, green beans with verjuice, artichokes and corn fresh from my garden. For dessert my cook has prepared ice cream in puff pastry and a variety of fruits."[13]

"It sounds very elegant," the young Bostonian says.

"With dinner we will drink a dry red wine from Gaillac known as Cahuzac. I learned about this wine from my friend the Duke of Rochefoucauld who is the Seignor of Cahuzac. The wine is aged in wood six to eight years before bottling and is said to gain in quality with additional bottle age. You will find it very full in color, stout, and spirituous. I am told it is often used as a blending wine in Bordeaux. I think you will like it."[14]

Petit enters and announces that dinner is served.

"John has brought with him the first two paintings of his Revolutionary War series, *The Death of General Warren at the Battle of Bunker's Hill* and *The Death of General Montgomery in the Attack on Quebec.* I have them both on display in the dining room. The famous French painter, Jacques-Louis David, was sufficiently curious about our young American's artistic talents that he came here to see the paintings."[15]

Setting: Beaune, France, March 8-9, 1787

Present are Thomas Jefferson, age 43, and Etienne Parent, a Burgundy merchant and barrel maker.

Jefferson spends three days in Dijon and then begins his journey through the French wine country of Burgundy, the Rhone Valley, Provence, Languedoc, Bordeaux, and the Loire with visits to see the great Roman antiquities of Gaul. He is traveling alone and incognito.[1]

Early on March 8, 1787 Jefferson climbs into his carriage drawn by three horses and heads to Burgundy. Despite a cold beating rain that follows him, it is a two day visit he will remember.

Several miles south of Dijon his carriage enters the heart of the wine country, the Côte d'Or, a series of low hills that serve as home to its best vineyards. Of the vineyards nestled along the hillsides, Chambertin is the first in view, followed by Vougeot, Romanée, Vosne, Nuits. At Chambertin Jefferson "mounts a pony, puts a peasant on another, and rambles through their most celebrated vineyards."[2]

As his carriage approaches the tiny village of Vougeot, named for the stream-like river that runs behind it, he sees in the distance the imposing Renaissance Chateau Clos de Vougeot built by the monks of Citeaux over several hundred years. A stone wall surrounds the 124 acre Vougeot vineyards.

At the entrance to the chateau an elderly monk volunteers to serve as his guide. On entering Jefferson is struck by the sight of four 12th century wine presses that stand nearly thirty feet high and are in perfect operating condition. The guide disappears but quickly returns carrying three bottles of red wine. The bottles are placed on a small table and opened. The old monk explains, "Although we make a small amount of white wine, it is the red that has made our reputation for excellence.

"The annual production is about 50,000 bottles. Hundreds of years of winemaking have honed our skills. But there is a difference in the wines we produce. Wine made from grapes grown in the middle section of the vineyards is the best. It sells for one-third more than that made in the upper part, and for three times as much as that made from grapes at the lower end." The old monk pours with a steady hand from each bottle into three glasses for Minister Jefferson, but he does not indicate which bottle represents the middle, lower or upper sections of the vineyards.[3]

Jefferson tastes the wines, confirms the excellence of the over-all quality, and selects the third wine tasted as the best. "It has a beautiful bright color and exquisite aroma and flavor, combining qualities of lightness and delicacy with richness and fullness of body."[4]

The monk smiles, "Monsieur, your palate agrees with that of our winemaker."

Jefferson observes monks quietly walking about the property but the scene will change in three years. The French Revolution brings radical changes to the Catholic Church, and Chateau du Clos de Vougeot and its vineyards are taken from the monks and sold at public auction.

Continuing on to Beaune Jefferson stops and visits the vineyards of Vosne-Romanée and Nuit St. Georges. In Beaune he lodges at the *Chez Dion à l'Écu de France*. On the recommendation of Abbé Morellet, a Parisian friend, Jefferson hires Etienne Parent, a local barrel maker and wine merchant, as his guide to the vineyards of Pommard, Volnay, Montrachet and Meursault.

Late that afternoon Parent joins Jefferson and at dinner Jefferson gives his opinion of the wines he has tasted since leaving Dijon. "I liked Chambertin best, followed by Vougeot and Vosne because they were the strongest, and will bear transportation. They will live longer and improve with age, and in so doing reach a perfection that most other Burgundies fail to achieve."[5]

In the morning he sets out in his carriage with Parent leading on horseback. The first stop is Montrachet (Maun-rasch-*shay*), a gently sloping vineyard a short distance from Beaune and situated between the communes of Puligny (*Poo*-lean-ye) and Chassagne (Shass-*an*-ya). Parent calls Montrachet "the best dry white wine of Burgundy." Jefferson's tasting confirms Parent's opinion, but at three livres per bottle, the same price as Chambertin, it is expensive. *Why?* Jefferson wonders. *There appears to be nothing that distinguishes this vineyard from its neighbors.* Still, he orders 125 bottles of the 1782 vintage.[6]

Leaving Montrachet Parent mounts his horse and heads northwest in the direction of the quaint village of Meursault (Mere-*so*) surrounded by stone walls and known for its dry white wines. After tasting a series of wines from various vineyards, Jefferson decides that the best wine of Meursault comes from a fourteen acre vineyard with the name Goutte d'Or (drop of gold).

"There is a similarity in bouquet and taste of this wine and Montrachet," Jefferson says.

"There are reasons why," Parent says. "They come from the same grape, essentially the same soil, same exposure, same climate, and the same methods of winemaking."

"What is the difference in price between Montrachet and Goutte d'Or?"

"A *feuillette* (foy-yet) of Montrachet costs 300 livres. A *feuillette* of Goutte d'Or costs 100 livres."

"What is a *feuillette?*"

"It's a Burgundian barrel that holds about 114 liters of wine."

"I like the Montrachet best but at a cost of three times the Goutte d'Or . . ." he shakes his head as though to say, *I will buy the Goutte d'Or.*

"Monsieur Parent, I would like to ensure the authenticity of the wine I buy by having it bottled at the vineyard. Can you do that for me?"

"It will add to the cost, but, yes, I will personally bottle the wines for you."[8]

"When I return to Paris I will order a *feuillette* of Goutte d'Or."[9]

With Parent leading the way they visit the little town of Volnay and its vineyards located southwest of Beaune. Parent advises Jefferson that the wines of Volnay are light in color, have a perfumed bouquet, cherry flavor, and light tannins. "They have," he adds, "the reputation for being the most delicate and the best red wines of southern Burgundy."

Jefferson is impressed with the quality of the Volnay wines. "These wines are softer, lighter, and easier to drink than the wines of Chambertin, Vougeot, and Vosne-Romanée. Why is that?"

"In the Côte de Beaune the time for picking the grapes is strictly regulated. About a month before the grapes are picked, a committee of judges from Beaune begin the first of three visits to the vineyards to examine the maturity of the grapes. On the third visit, the first day for harvesting the grapes is determined. It is the tradition that the vineyards of Volnay are the first to be harvested, followed the next day by Pommard. Thereafter, the other vineyards in the Côte de Beaune are allowed to gather their grapes. Anyone picking even a basket of grapes before the official date is subject to confiscation and a severe fine.[10]

"The vats are brought into the vineyards and filled to the brim with whole clusters of grapes. The weight of the grapes causes some crushing and brings the onset of fermentation, which finishes within 20 to 30 hours.[11]

"It is the early harvesting, retention of whole clusters, short fermentation that combine to produce wines of great charm, soft texture and aromatic flavors that develop sooner than wines from neighboring Pommard and vineyards further north."[12]

"If the weight of the grapes starts the fermentation, how is the final crushing done?

"By the bare feet of men who enter the vats naked."[13]

On the return ride to Beaune Jefferson compares a variable beyond the control of man. "At Pommard and Volnay I observed them eating good wheat bread, at Meursault, rye. I asked the reason of the difference. They told me that the white wines fail in quality much oftener than the reds, and remain on hand. The farmer therefore cannot afford to feed his laborers so well. At Meursault only white wines are made, because there is too much stone for the red. On such slight circumstances depends the condition of man."[14]

Before leaving Beaune that evening, Jefferson and Parent dine at the inn on fresh pike from the Bouzaise River, a beef stew, broiled chicken, an assortment of roasted vegetables, and a local cheese made in the near-by village of Époisses. With the meal Jefferson compares a Volnay and Clos de Vougeot. After tasting the two wines he finds the Volnay the equal of the Vougeot but places it in fourth place behind Chambertin, Vougeot and the wines of Vosne-Romanée.

"Why?" Parent asks.

"Because it is lighter in body, lacks the longevity of its more celebrated northern neighbors and does not bear transportation as well. But it has two distinct advantages over its more famous neighbors. It costs only one quarter as much and is ready to drink after one year."[15]

Pleased with Jefferson's assessment, the Beaune wine merchant smiles and triumphantly lifts the Volnay bottle in the air.

After dinner Jefferson says, "My carriage is ready, and I'm leaving for Chalon. You have been a good guide and enjoyable company. I have learned much, and I carry away the remembrance of great wines—not the 'waterish Burgundy' Shakespeare spoke of in *King Lear*."

Setting: October 12, 1787, The Hermitage, a monastery outside of Paris

Present are Thomas Jefferson, age 44, and three fellow communal Hermitage guests.

One crisp morning in October with the sky clearing, Jefferson leaves his mansion on the Champs-Elysées, mounts his horse and rides through the Bois de Boulogne. On this occasion he does not stop to "survey its beautiful verdure" or "to retire to its umbrage from the heats of the season." Instead, he is "away to my Hermitage."[1]

His Hermitage is the communal retreat of a group of lay brothers known as the "Hermites." To reach the Hermitage Jefferson rides through the Bois de Boulogne to Longchamps where he takes the ferry across the river to the village of Suresnes, and then climbs to the top of Mont Valerien, known also as Mont Calvaire, where the monastery stands.[2]

The Hermitage is an idyllic retreat for the American minister who often feels a compelling need to be alone.[3] The Hermitage is housed in a stately old monastery on top of Mont Valerien with sweeping views of the countryside: the villages of Suresnes, Puteaux, Longchamps, Bois de Boulogne, Paris, Sevres, Saint-Cloud, Bellevue, all connected by the winding Seine.[4]

With silence enjoined, except at dinner, Jefferson relaxes and uses his time for working, reading, walking, thinking or simply resting. At dinner, conversation among guests, who usually know one another, is a welcome addition to meals accompanied by the local wine.

Before going to dinner on this late afternoon Jefferson stands outside the monastery and takes in the magnificent views. The distant towns of Saint Cloud and Bellevue remind him of his recent romantic outings with Maria Cosway. He thinks of the austere life of the Hermites and how they support themselves—*by providing accommodations to paying guests like me, selling wood, honey, and silk stockings from their manufactory, and wine from their vineyards–known locally as vin de Suresnes.*[5] His thoughts remind him that the Hermites silk stockings are favorites of Abigail Adams and he must remember to buy her several pairs before he leaves.

The Hermitage vineyards cover a portion of the lower slopes of Mont Valerien and face southeast toward Paris. Vineyards have flourished on these hillsides for over 900 years. The Hermites' wine has the reputation of a good quality vin ordinaire. It is especially popular with Parisians who by leaving the city can eat and drink for only a fraction of what it would cost them in Paris because of taxes levied on everything entering the city.[6]

As he walks along a dirt path leading to the dining room, he thinks about what a fellow habitué recently said, "The meals can be good when you plan ahead and ask, Brother Joseph, to cook something good. If he is not forewarned, the cuisine lacks variety and is very lean."[7]

The dining room is a long rectangular space furnished with bench-like tables and wooden chairs. The austerity of the room is relieved by a series of windows that afford a picturesque view down the hillside toward Paris.

Three men are seated at Jefferson's regular table whom he knows from prior visits. After the customary greetings a Hermite brother approaches and places a pitcher of white wine on the table.

"*Vin de Suresnes*," Mr. Jefferson says, pouring the glasses. He takes a sip. It is a bit acidic but quite drinkable. His dinner companions wait for his approval. He nods and pours their glasses.

One of the men with big bushy eyebrows tastes the wine with obvious satisfaction and says, "I think we are very fortunate to have the Hermitage as our retreat. The brothers are polite and accommodating, the food is acceptable, and the wine good. Where else can you go and get away like this?"

Jefferson smiles, "There are other places to find solace and quite in and around Paris but I too like it here. My friend John Adams found retreat in the comfort of a warm bath aboard boats that move up and down the Seine for that purpose. Adams told me about boarding such a boat near the Pont Royale and taking a bath in a little room, which had a large window looking out over the river into the Tuileries. He said he was furnished with hot linens and towels, and a bell to ring if he wanted anything else."[8]

Another man at the table says, "In May I had dinner with Marquis de Lafayette and several Americans at the Marquis's mansion, and I enquired about you. The Marquis told me that you were traveling through southern France having left in February. Was it an enjoyable journey?"

"Yes, 'I never passed three months and a half more delightfully.'[7] I left Paris on February 28 with only rain, hail and snow as traveling companions. My nightly custom of gatherings for dinner and conversation I left behind. 'Had they been my objects, I would not have quitted Paris.' I did not return to Paris until June 10."

"Where did your travels take you?"

"Through southern France and into northern Italy."

"I have not traveled the back roads of France, what is it like?"

"There are three methods of travel by road, all of which utilize posthouses. Posthouses are franchises of the king and are way-stations along the roads. The posthouses provide horses, drivers, postilions, guides and, usually, overnight lodging. The distance between posthouses is approximately ten miles and the average speed about seven and a half miles an hour. The safety of the public roads is overseen by the *maréchaussée*, mounted troops engaged by the king for this purpose.

"The usual method of travel is by *diligence* or stagecoach. For a fixed price you are provided a seat in the coach and meals on the road until the final destination. The obvious drawbacks are crowded conditions (usually eight persons to a carriage), the inability to select traveling companions, and being the captive of the stagecoach schedule which often means being hurried out of bed at three o'clock in the morning. Another way is to hire a *voiture* or carriage. This allows you to control your time schedule and traveling companions, but it is more expensive.

"The third method, and the one I used, is to provide one's own carriage and to rely on the posthouses for horses, guides and, when in remote areas, room and board."[9]

"You mention guides. I can see how they can get you from place to place, but did you rely on them to tell you where to eat and where to lodge."

"No. I carried with me a copy of Louis Duetens' *Journal of Travels Made Through the Principal Cities of Europe*. Duetens' *Journal* gives the time and distances between towns, e.g., 'Dijon to Beaune 23 miles, 3 hours 15 minutes.' It recommends the best inns and taverns, e.g., 'Fontainebleau–The Dauphine, in Beaune the Post House with a fine garden.' It provides monetary rates of exchange between countries, a description of the towns and cities and sights to see, and a variety of other useful hints and advice."

"What places did you visit and sights did you see?" an inquisitive table companion asks.

"I traveled to the vineyards of Burgundy, Cote Rôtie, Hermitage, through Provence, over the Alps into Italy, along the French and Italian rivieras, through Languedoc on the Canal-du-Medi, and eventually on to Bordeaux, but wine wasn't my only interest. I visited the great Roman antiquities of Gaul: Glanum, the Pont de Gard, the Maison Carrée, the Theatre at Orange, the Amphitheatres at Nimes and Arles. Along the way I focused on the living conditions of the peasants.

"In this regard I noted that laborers breakfasted on a piece of bread with an anchovy or an onion, and for dinner, bread, soup and vegetables, and their supper the same. But, overall, I found among the peasants less physical misery than I had expected to find. They were generally well clothed with plenty of food, not animal indeed, but vegetables, which are as wholesome."[1]

Jefferson glances across the room. "I see a brother coming with our meals of roasted vegetables and beef, which I trust is not too lean. If you like, I will tell you more about my trip during dinner."

Setting: May 12, 1788, Jefferson's Paris residence, Hôtel de Langeac

Present are Thomas Jefferson, 45, Thomas Lee Shippen, 23, John Rutledge, Jr, 22, and William Short, 29.

During his five years in France, Jefferson extended his assistance to all Americans visiting Paris who asked for it. Two who fell into his sphere of strong attention were Thomas Lee Shippen, son of Dr. William Shippen, Jr. of Philadelphia, and John Rutledge, Jr., son of Governor Edward Rutledge of South Carolina. When these young men arrived in Paris preparatory to starting out on a grand tour of Europe, Jefferson, a friend of their fathers, was quick to extend his friendship and advice.

Rutledge arrived in Paris in November 1787 short of funds, and Jefferson loaned him 600 livres. Rutledge then went to England and returned to Paris in March. Shippen arrived at Jefferson's house in January. Jefferson invited him to dinner twice a week, presented him to court, and introduced him to his social and political friends. He also promised the young travelers that he would go through his travel notes and furnish them with letters of introduction, interesting things to see, places to visit, and where to stay. Unfortunately, a change in circumstances prevented him from making good on his promise.[1]

A cold, beating rain has snarled Paris traffic and Minister Jefferson's guests Thomas Lee Shippen, and John Rutledge, Jr. are late for their three-thirty dinner appointment. When they arrive Petit shows them into the elegant dining room where Thomas Jefferson and his friend and secretary, William Short, are waiting.

Petit places a decanter of white wine on a marble table near the fireplace. Mr. Jefferson pours the wine and hands each young man a glass. "I feel as though I've let you men down . . ."

"Please don't feel that way," Shippen says.

"I feel badly. I promised you letters of introduction and copies of my travel notes of France, Italy and Germany, but because I was called away to Holland on official business, I won't have them ready when you leave Paris in two days.

"I owe you an explanation. Here is what happened. John Adams learned that Congress had granted his request to return home and decided that it was important that he go to Holland in order to tie up any loose ends that existed in financial arrangements between Holland and the United States. I received a letter from Abigail advising that John would be delighted to meet me there. Because I had no experience in financial dealings with the Dutch, and knowing that as the sole minister I might be called upon to conduct future financial negotiations, I found the prospect of such a get-together with John necessary.

"I left Paris on March 4th for The Hague and joined Adams there. Our negotiations for bond loans from the Dutch were successful.[1]

"With the financial business transacted, Adams left for London. I stayed on until the end of March and decided to travel down the Rhine as far as Strasbourg 'in order to see what I have not yet seen.' I did not return to Paris until late April. You waited for my return before starting your tour with the expectation that I would supply you with valuable travel information."

Jefferson shakes his head in disgust. "I've let you down but I promise I will get the information together and send it to you."[2]

"I have a suggestion," Short says. "I also have plans for my own tour of Europe. I think it would be valuable to hear the highlights of your travels through southern France. That will give us guidance on what we can expect to see, eat, drink, and where to stay. "

"That would be splendid," Rutledge says.

Jefferson replenishes his wine and nods. "Very well, I'll cover the southern part of the trip, and if time permits during dinner, perhaps some thoughts on Italy and Germany."

Jefferson makes sure everyone's wine glasses are full, pulls up a chair, and begins. "I arrived at Orange on March 18th, and entered the city through a 'sublime' triumphal arch erected in about 25 A.D. during the period of Marcus Aurelius. After taking lodging at the Royal Palace Hotel, I visited the Roman theatre. Here I was outraged to find that in this 18th century, in France, under the reign of Louis XVI, they were at that moment pulling down the circular wall of this superb remains to pave a road. And that too from a hill which is itself an entire mass of stone just as fit and more accessible."[3]

"Are you saying that the citizenry was demolishing the theater to make a road to it," Rutledge says.

"That is exactly what they were doing. It was absolutely senseless.

"The next morning I was on my way to Nîmes. Nearing Nîmes I detoured to Remoulins and stopped to see the Pont du Gard, a magnificent Roman aqueduct built towards the end of the first century B.C. to carry fresh water from the town of Uzés to Nîmes. As I approached through a plain covered with olive trees on my right and mountains on my left, I saw its three-tier arch construction spanning the Gard River, a distance of 295 yards. Built by slave labor using huge blocks of stone, its six foundation arches support a second tier of eleven arches which in turn support the upper tier of thirty-five arches. When operational the water flows through a covered concrete channel on the top. It is 'a sublime antiquity and well preserved.' An interesting time to visit is between six and seven when the sunrise casts a pink glow across the bridge, its reflection shimmering in the Gard River.[4]

"Approaching Nîmes I could see the remains of a Roman tower, the Tour Magne, on the summit of a hill overlooking the city. During my three days in Nîmes I lodged at the Hotel du Louvre, a commodious and excellent inn."

"What were your meals like?" Short says.

"Bountiful: mutton, poultry, pork, partridge, rabbit, game, ragouts, and sauces heavily spiced with garlic and plenty of vegetables,[5] accompanied by an excellent vin ordinaire called Ledenon that cost only two or three sous a bottle.

Rutledge nudges Shippen. "We must ask for Ledenon wine when we get to Nîmes."

"It is a good wine with an agreeable bouquet. The vineyards are located near Nîmes and consist of about 800 acres. There is a particular best vineyard area of 450 acres called Plane de Paza. It is the most expensive of the wines of Nîmes and is served pure on the tables of the finest rank in France."[6]

"I understand there are many Roman antiquities in Nîmes." Shippen says.

"Yes. Nîmes was first settled as a Roman colony about 50 B.C. and contains more monuments of Roman antiquity than any other city in France, which attests to its former importance within the Roman Empire. I wasted no time investigating its treasures.

"I visited the Maison Carrée, a great Roman remains, gazing at it for whole hours like a lover at his mistress. The stocking-weavers and silk spinners around it considered me a hypochondriac Englishman about to write with a pistol the last chapter of my history. This is the second time I have been in love since I left Paris. The first was with a Diana at the Chateau de Laye-Epinaye in the Beaujolais, a delicious morsel of sculpture by Michael Angelo Slodtz."

"What was the purpose of the Maison Carrée and what does it look like?"

"The Maison Carrée is a Roman temple built in the time of Augustus. It is an oblong windowless structure of stone masonry with a portico and fluted Corinthian pillars that was part of the Forum Complex of ancient Nîmes.[7]

"While in Nîmes I saw the collection of Objects d'Art of the well-known antiquarian Jean Francois Seguier (1703-1784) who supervised the excavations and restorations of the Maison Carrée. One object of antiquity that struck my fancy was a Greek askos (wine pitcher). When I returned to Nîmes I paid a craftsman 18 livres to make a model of this antique vase.

"About five blocks from the Maison Carrée, and in the center of Nîmes, is the Roman amphitheater built in the early first century A.D. Arles has a similar arena built about the same time. I visited both, and thought the arena in Nîmes the best preserved and 'a superb remains.' It consists of 60 arches that continue around the circumference on two levels. It was built without mortar and has withstood the attacks of weather and the worse depredations of the barbarians in the various revolutions of sixteen centuries.[8] In amphitheaters like these throughout the Roman Empire crowds delighted in seeing all types of spectacles including gladiators fighting gladiators, gladiators fighting lions, domesticated panthers pulling chariots, bulls battling rhinoceroses, and chariot races

"I also visited the Jardin de la Fontaine and the Temple of Diana and the Roman baths. The fountain flows from beneath the rocks of Mt. Cavalier into a series of basins constructed in about 1740 together with a series of walks and canals. The Temple of Diana survives only as ruins, and is to the left of the fountain gardens and in front of the Roman baths. Above the fountain gardens at the top of Mt. Cavalier is the Tour Magne. The original function of Tour Magne is unknown but it probably served as a watch tower. From the fountain gardens the Tour Magne is reached by walking up a series of paths that twist through a beautifully landscaped park.[9]

"My next stop was Arles, a Roman colony founded in 46 B.C. At one time Arles competed as an important port with Marseilles. It is here that the Rhone River divides into two branches before emptying into the Mediterranean to the south. I stayed at a detestable tavern located on one of Arles' narrow, winding, cobblestone streets. I will try to remember the name of this place so that you don't make the same mistake. I visited three Roman antiquities that are of interest: the Alyscamps, the Graeco-Roman theatre remains and the amphitheater.

"In the suburbs of Arles at the Church of St. Honorat, I saw hundreds of ancient stone coffins along the road side. These grounds are the Alyscamps or Elysian Fields, the renowned Roman and early Christian burial grounds of Arles. In the Middle Ages Alyscamps was considered sacred and it became a pilgrimage Shrine of the Dead. At the request of the dying, friends would place their bodies, after death, in caskets and float them down the Rhone River to Arles. The bodies were then buried in the Elysian Fields in elaborately sculpted limestone coffins and tombs. When I visited many of the elaborate sarcophagi had been removed, sold or destroyed.[10]

"The country from Nîmes to Aix-en-Provence is covered in vines. Before reaching Aix I stayed the night in St. Remy and lodged at the Cheval Blanc, and if you go there I recommend it. A short distance south of the town I visited a mausoleum and the oldest triumphal arch outside of Italy. It is believed the arch was erected on orders of Julius Caesar to commemorate the Roman capture of Marseilles.[11]

"In Aix-en-Provence I stayed at the Hôtel St. Jacque. My visit to Aix was the *raison d'être* for my trip. Its mineral waters have been famous since Roman times for their healing powers. It was my hope that the mineral waters might restore the strength in my injured wrist. Other considerations also concurred including instruction, amusement, and abstraction from business, of which I had too much in Paris."[12]

"How did you injure your wrist?" Rutledge asks.

"How the right hand became disable would be a long story for the left to tell. It is one of those follies from which good cannot come but ill may."

Jefferson's enigmatic answer perplexes Rutledge but he decides to ignore it. "Did the baths help your wrist?"

Jefferson shakes his head. "I took forty douches without any sensible benefit and thought it useless to continue them.

"I wrote William from Aix, 'The man who shoots himself in the climate of Aix must be a bloody minded fellow indeed. I am now in the land of corn, wine, oil, and sunshine. What more can man ask of heaven? If I should happen to die at Paris I will beg of you to send me here, and have me exposed to the sun. I am sure it will bring me to life again. It is a wonder to me that every free being does not remove to the southward of the Loire. It is true that money will carry to Paris most of the good things of this canton. But it cannot carry Aix's sunshine, nor procure any equivalent for it. This city is one of the cleanest and neatest I have ever seen in any country. The streets are straight, from 20 to 100 feet wide, and as clean as a parlor floor with rows of elms from 100 to 150 years old, which make for delicious walks.'"[13]

"What is this about a man shooting himself?" Rutledge asks.

"It's in reference to a remark Lafayette made to me about Mr. Jefferson being in Aix," Short says. "He said he hoped Mr. Jefferson would not follow the example of Monsieur de Simiane, the husband of the beauty of that name, who put an end to himself by a pistol shot while in Aix."[14]

Jefferson chuckles and says to his two young guests, "You must include Aix in your itinerary. It is a lively town. Beautiful elms provide shade for walks along the Cours Mirabeau, the main street, lined with handsome mansions. There is a steady stream of troubadours, musicians and actors who routinely perform operas, ballets, tragedies and comedies at the Municipal Theatre. Its bread is the equal to any in the world, the best olive oil, and interesting wines."

"We will be sure to visit Aix," Shippen says with enthusiasm.

"My travels next took me to Marseilles. Although the road leading to Marseilles is one of the most traveled in France, it is in a scandalous condition, not wide enough at places for two carriages to pass with convenience. The country is hilly and intersected by chains of mountains of rock with vines, corn, mulberries, almonds and willows growing among rows of olive and fig trees that produce the most delicate figs known in Europe. The vineyards around Marseilles produce wines of good color, body, spirit and flavor. Many of the vineyards make a *vin cuit* or boiled wine that is compared with Tokay and often sold as such.[15]

"My journey to this point was a continual feast of new objects and ideas. In order to make the most of the time available, I avoided good dinners and good company and courted the society of gardeners, winemakers, coopers, farmers and devoted every moment of every day almost to the business of enquiry."[16]

"Tell us about this continual feast."

"I found Marseilles a charming place. All life and activity like London and Philadelphia with an extensive society and an animated commerce.[17] I recommend the Hotel de la Princesse. It is where I stayed from March 30 to April 6.

82

"My stay here was busy with excursions to the Chateau Borely, a boat ride to the Island Chateau d'If, and an evening at the theater. I visited the Chateau Notre Dame de la Gard on a hill with a magnificent view of the city and the Mediterranean that included vine-clad hills, gardens, country houses and clusters of islands, including the Isle d'If, the place of Mirabeau's imprisonment.[18]

"Through a letter of introduction from Chastellux, I made the acquaintance of Henry Bergasse, one of France's great wine merchants. If your travels take you to Marseilles, and I recommend they do, I will give you a letter of introduction to meet Bergasse and visit his wine cellars."

"With your letter of introduction we will certainly visit Monsieur Bergasse. Where did you go next?" Shippen says.

"Over the Alps into Italy."

"I thought from Marseilles your plans were to travel to Bordeaux. Why Italy?"

Jefferson smiles, "Rice was the culprit, but that is another part of the trip I think should be told at dinner. For now I suggest that we drink this wine." Jefferson lifts a decanter of red wine from a side table. "This is the wine I discovered in Nîmes, vin de Ledenon. I am interested in your opinions of it. My cook, James Hemings, has learned the art of French cooking, and I think you will enjoy dinner. The vegetables are fresh from my garden."

"I keep forgetting to ask you, but what is the massive structure across the Champs-Elysées from your place with a huge iron gate barring passage into Paris?" Rutledge asks.

"It is the Grill de Chaillot, one of more than forty tollgates that circle Paris for collecting taxes on all goods coming into the city. They are a great burden to the people but an indispensable source of income to the king. These barriers are operated by appointees of the king. They are called Farmers General, or we would say in America tax collectors."[19]

Jefferson notices Petit standing in the doorway, a signal that dinner is ready. "Gentlemen, I'm told that dinner is ready, so let's adjourn to the dining room."

As they take their seats in Jefferson's spacious dining room the host says, "Dining on the road throughout southern France can be a rewarding experience but only if you stay at the best inns or with private persons through letters of introduction. Posthouse food, at best, is no more than adequate. A plethora of meats, game, fish, vegetables, dairy products, and fruits are available throughout Southern France. Today's dinner will be typical of what you will find available during your travels."

"What might that be?" Rutledge asks.

"Whatever was available at the market. I have not conferred with my cook about what he will serve except for one dish—beef a la mode. Beef is available all year round and that which comes from Piedmont is very good. Other available meats you will find on your travels are veal, lamb, mutton, and all types of sausages.

"For game, especially in autumn, hares, partridges, quails, capons, wild-pigeons, woodcocks, snipes, thrushes, wild boar, and ortolans.

"The Mediterranean yields a wide variety of fish: grey and red mullet, rockfish, sea bass, dory, mackerel, bonita, eels, and fresh anchovies.

"There is an abundance of fresh vegetables including green peas, asparagus, artichokes, cauliflower, beans, French beans, celery, and endive, cabbage, coleworts, radishes, turnips, carrots, sorrel lettuce, onions, garlic, shallots, potatoes from the mountains, mushrooms, and truffles.

"Southern France proliferates in fruits, oranges, figs, apples, lemons, peaches, grapes, salads, olives, pears, cherries and strawberries.

"You will not lack in dairy products: butter, milk, eggs and cheeses are readily available, as are almonds, chestnuts, and walnuts."[20]

Petit enters carrying a decanter of red wine. He places it beside Jefferson who pours and passes the glasses. He lifts his glass. "When I traveled to Bordeaux the first vineyard I visited was Haut Brion, located in the Grave region at Pessac. I walked through its vineyards and noted the soil of sand mixed with round gravel or small stone and very little loam. I tasted the wine and found it representative of the very best Bordeaux wines. I purchased six dozen bottles of the 1784 vintage, the only very fine one since the year 1779."[21]

William Short tastes the wine. "This wine is less than four years old. Has it reached maturity?"

"Perhaps it is a bit young but my experience is that Latour, Haut Brion and Margaux are ready to drink after four years, and Lafite, because it is a lighter wine, after three years. All red wines decline after a certain age, losing color, flavor and body. Those of Bordeaux begin to decline after seven years old."[22]

Jefferson sips his wine and says, "Haut Brion has a certain sentimental attachment for me."

"In what way?" Shippen asks.

"John Locke was, in my opinion, 'one of the three greatest men the world has ever produced.' Locke lived in France for several years after his retirement at age forty-three, and he became interested in wine. A hundred years before my visit, he also visited Haut Brion and waked through its vineyards."[23]

Short tips his glass in the air and says, "a salute to two of the world's great political thinkers who enjoyed the same wine."

Setting: Paris, June 1788, Jefferson's mansion on the Champs Elysées

Present are Jefferson, 45, Lafayette, 30. Jean Antoine Houdon, 47, William Short, 29.

A large iron gate spans the Champs-Elysées at the Grille de Chaillot. The entrance to Jefferson's mansion is around the corner on Rue de Berri. The entrance gate is open. Lafayette's carriage enters and crosses the spacious courtyard. The stables, coach house and servants quarters are on the left, the main entrance to the right. He knocks and is received by Adrien Petit, Jefferson's trusted maître d'hôtel. He enters a circular reception area. There are three doorways, one leading to the dining room, another to a petit drawing room, and a third to a large oval shaped drawing room, the ceiling decorated with a painting of a rising sun.[1] Petit shows Lafayette into the grand salon. A moment later he is joined by Jefferson and his secretary, William Short.

Jefferson is elegantly dressed in a silk front cutaway tail coat. His thick coppery red hair is cut short and his hair powered. The two friends shake hands.

Although not as tall as the six-two Jefferson, Lafayette is only slightly shorter, about six-one. He is trim and broad shouldered with a long face, sloping forehead, aquiline nose and high cheekbones. His face is more than handsome; it reflects his charisma.

Seeing the famous sculptor Jean Antoine Houdon in the garden with Jefferson's secretary, Lafayette says, "I didn't realize that dinner included being at the same table with the world's greatest sculptor."

"Yes. When he arrived he told me that your bust will be finished next month. He also mentioned that he recently returned from a trip to the United States and stayed at Mount Vernon as General Washington's guest."

"Yes, and I'm interested to hear about his trip." Houdon and Short enter the salon. "It is wonderful to see you Jean Antoine," Lafayette says. The two famous Frenchmen shake hands. "How long were you gone?"

"I left France on July 20 on the same packet with Benjamin Franklin, and I didn't get back to Paris until Christmas."

"How is his Excellency George Washington?"

"He appears to be in excellent health. Despite an unfortunate start to our introduction, General Washington was a very gracious host during my fifteen day stay at Mount Vernon."

"Unfortunate start?" Jefferson says.

"Yes, my men and I arrived at Mount Vernon on October 2 at eleven o'clock at night. The general had retired and his staff got him out of bed to greet me." Everyone laughs.

"Despite a bumpy start how were your accommodations?" Jefferson says.

"I stayed in the main house with the general and Mrs. Washington and dined with them nightly. My men had adequate quarters in another building."

"Did you accomplish everything you set out to do?" Jefferson asks.

"Yes. The general's first sitting was on the 6th for his bust. That was completed and I'm pleased with the results. I also took all the general's measurements for his life-size statue and have finished all the preliminary work necessary to complete it. In fact, I am ready to start work on it as soon as I am told what his dress will be—classical or contemporary?"

"Did you talk to General Washington about his preference?" Lafayette asks.

"I did and though he said he was going to leave to others to decide, I came away with the impression that he would prefer contemporary dress."

"When I was in England I met with four American artists, Benjamin West, Mather Brown, John Singleton Copley, and young John Trumbull. I discussed the general's dress issue with them, and to a man they agreed that it should be contemporary. I passed this information on to General Washington," Jefferson says.

"As you know Minister Jefferson, the general has an agricultural background and current agrarian interests. I have brought along a couple of sketches. One shows him wearing sandals, a cloak fastened across his chest, one hand resting on a walking stick, the other holding a fasces with a plough at his feet . . ."

"The symbolic image of agriculture?" Lafayette asks.

Houdon nods. "Another sketch shows him standing regally as a revolutionary officer."

"That, I think, more appropriate," Lafayette says, relief showing in his voice.

"We will study your preliminary sketches at dinner," Jefferson says.

"Has it arrived?" the Marquis asks.

Jefferson notices that Short seems surprised by Lafayette's comment. He chuckles, "The Marquis is referring to the wine. During his time in America, the Marquis acquired a taste for Madeira. Recently we agreed to share the expense of a pipe [110 gallons]. It is my task to buy it, and because it is impossible to get good and genuine Madeira in France, I ordered it from Frances Lewis, a New York wine merchant. I was telling the Marquis that I specified that it be of the nut quality and the very best. I left it to Mr. Lewis whether it would come better in bottles, or in a cask, and if in a cask, whether the precaution of one cask within another cask would be necessary."

"Why would a wine merchant ship a cask of wine within another cask?" Short says.

Jefferson gives his friend a knowing smile. "Because the men who transport wine sometimes break into a cask and drink the wine. Putting a cask of wine inside another cask is an added security measure. If the second cask is broken you can be pretty sure that it did not occur by accident."

Jefferson says to the Marquis, "In you, my friend, I find an echoing voice, sharing memories of the Revolution, an interest in France's political and social structure, and Gallic cuisine and wine. It is a pleasure to have you to dinner."

Petit appears with a decanter of white wine that he places on a side table along with four glasses. Jefferson pours the wine. He lifts his glass and says to Lafayette, "When I was last at your place, I promised to serve you this wine."

"As I recall you said you discovered it on your visit to Champagne, a wine better than the king's Champagne."

Jefferson's face breaks into a broad smile. "Correct. On my travels from Germany I stopped in Champagne staying in Épernay. Monsieur Cousin, the owner of the inn where I lodged, and a vintner, was my guide to the vineyards. In Aÿ he introduced me to a still champagne, that of a Monsieur Dorsay, a prosperous merchant who lives in Paris and owns many vineyards in and around Aÿ. Of all the champagne's I tasted, I thought Dorsay's the best. The Benedictine monks at Hautvillers produce a first quality champagne supplied to the king's table, but upon tasting it I thought Dorsay's better. I bought all of his remaining supply of non-sparkling champagne of the year 1783—sixty bottles at three and a half livres a bottle, about the same price I pay for the best red Bordeaux."[2]

Jefferson holds his glass to the light and examines the color, breaths in the bouquet, and tastes the wine. "It has that silky quality that I esteem."

"During your travels through southern France did you meet any wine people who particularly impressed you?" Short says.

The host looks to Houdon, "Jean Antoine, if we get into a wine discussion, will it bore you? If it will, please say so and we won't start it."

"Not at all, I will be delighted to hear the adventures of a well-traveled man into the world of wine."

"The first wine stop on my trip was Beaune. It was here that I met a barrel maker and wine merchant by the name of Etienne Parent. He served as my vineyard guide and has become my Burgundian wine counselor. Parent showed me through the vineyards of Montrachet, Meursault, Volnay and Pommard.

"He took me to the vineyard of Monsieur de la Tour, and introduced me to the most expensive dry white wine of France—Montrachet, which Parent says is the best white wine of Burgundy. My tasting confirmed his opinion, and I ordered 125 bottles of Montrachet on the spot.

"All of my Burgundy wine purchases are made through Parent. He selects the best vintages and bottles them for me. In that way I know that I am getting wines that have not been adulterated."

Lafayette looking out into the garden says, "Is that corn?"

"Yes, cornstalks, not weeds. I cultivate in my garden Indian corn for the use of my table, to eat green in our manner. I have also planted Burgundy vines that I got on my trip there, and Rheingau vines I brought back from my trip to the German wine country this past spring.[3] Do you like the champagne?"

"It is very good," the Marquis says.

"We will follow this wine at dinner with a Montrachet from Monsieur de la Tour's vineyard."

It is a beautiful late June afternoon. Lafayette, standing beside a floor-to-ceiling French door, stares out at the fading sunlight. "It has been a cold spring. We haven't had many days like this." After a moment he turns and says, "Didn't you tell me about a wine merchant in Marseilles who can make any style of wine from local grapes, and it is impossible to tell the difference between his wine and the real product?"

"Yes, Henry Bergasse. His Claret de Bergasse is made by blending different grapes, so that it is the genuine juice of the grape, and so perfect an imitation of the finest Bordeaux as not to be distinguishable. The Bordeaux merchants buy it from Bergasse paying one livre a bottle and send it to the U.S. as a growth of Bordeaux, charging four livres a bottle.

"Last year when I visited Marseilles I had the pleasure of dining with Monsieur Bergasse at his home. After dinner he took me to his wine cellars where I witnessed in bottles and casks the equivalent of more than 1,500,000 bottles of wine. The temperature of his cellars is a constant 54 degrees."[5]

"Will it be possible to taste Claret de Bergasse?"

"Yes, we will have a bottle with dinner. In addition to Bergasse's wines, I discovered several articles of culture: the best figs, the best grape for drying, a smaller one for the same purpose without a seed, olives, capers, pistachio nuts, almonds. All of these articles may succeed on, or southward of the Chesapeake."

"Can Bergasse produce a wine of the quality and taste of this champagne?" the Marquis says.

"I have not asked him to do that, but he can so perfectly imitate the taste of any kind of wine, by blending a variety of grapes, that even the most experienced wine connoisseur cannot tell the difference. So yes, I believe he could do it. Incidentally, Stephen Cathalan, the American Consul in Marseilles, accompanied me to dinner at Bergasse's. Stephen purchases and ships all the wines I order from southern France."[7]

"From Marseilles where did you next travel?" Short asks.

"It was my intention to head west to Bordeaux, but because I heard about an Italian rice machine that produced better rice than we do, I changed plans and went to Italy."

"I remember receiving a thought provoking letter you wrote me from Nice counseling me to take a similar trip incognito to ferret the people out of their hovels, look into their kettles, eat their bread, loll on their beds under the pretense of resting myself, but in fact to find out if they are soft. You told me that should I do that I will experience a sublime pleasure from being able to apply that knowledge to making their lives better," Lafayette says.[8]

"Yes, I noted that the laborers breakfasted on a piece of bread with an anchovy or an onion, and for dinner 'bread, soup and vegetables. The peasants' houses are chiefly low thatched huts without a single glass window.

"Before traveling over the Alps I spent three days in Nice. It is a handsome city with new houses and new streets being built, good accommodations, a 'gay and dissipated society' heavily populated by the English, and a superb climate. I lodged at the Hotel York, a fine English tavern. Through our mutual friend, Abbé Arnoux, I was introduced to a local wine merchant, André Sasserno. At Sasserno's house I drank the wines of Bellet, white, red and rose, which come from vineyards in the hills above Nice that face the Mediterranean. I was told these vineyards are some of the oldest in France. I found Sasserno's wines of such good quality that I plan on importing them when I return home."[9]

"And from Nice you traveled to Italy?"

"I did but I see Petit is calling us to dinner. I'll continue my travels at dinner."

Jefferson's dining room is a large rectangular room with three windows looking out onto the Champs-Elysées. The windows are hung with blue silk damask draperies. On the far wall is a fireplace, a marble mantel decorated with a series of biscuit figurines, and on each side of the fireplace a marble-topped table. In the center of the room is a fifteen-foot table lined with twenty chairs covered in blue silk.[10]

There are four place settings, two facing the windows that look out onto the Champs-Elysées and two facing into the room. The table is ornamented with three lighted pairs of silver candelabra placed on flat plaques of glass with silver balustrades, and a crenellated porcelain bucket used for cooling wine glasses.

The table is covered with a white table cloth and set with silverware, and glasses. Jefferson says to Houdon and Lafayette, "You are our guests, so please take whatever seats you like."

A moment later Petit enters and places a crystal decanter containing red wine on the table. Jefferson pours four glasses and hands them around. "This is Claret de Bergasse," he says with pride. "At dinner I will serve a 1784 Haut Brion. You will have the opportunity to judge which you like best. Petit tells me that the meal is not quite ready. While we wait, if you've not heard too much already, I can talk some more about my travels through Italy.."

"I've been waiting a year to hear about Italy," Lafayette says.

"But first, do you like the wine?"

Short takes a sip and lets the wine run over his palate. "Yes, I think it's quite good."

Lafayette says, "Is this Bergasse wine of the quality of the best Bordeaux wines? I think not, but it is a wine with good fruit and taste. Now, Thomas, I happen to know that when you started over the Alps into Italy it was your 44th birthday. How did you celebrate?"

As Jefferson begins narrating his travels over the Alps and through northern Italy, servants wheel into the dining room two étagère dumbwaiters, the four shelves filled with food on platters and in tureens. One dumbwaiter is placed between Jefferson and Short and the other between Houdon and Lafayette seated across the table facing the window.

"Gentlemen, let us serve ourselves. In that way our privacy will be respected." On the top shelf of the dumbwaiter is a large Sèvres blue celeste tray containing twenty-four oysters on the half-shell. Jefferson and his guests fill their plates

Petit enters and places a crystal decanter of white wine beside Jefferson who pours four glasses. "The oysters are from Normandy and have the reputation for being some of the best in the world." He removes an oyster from the shell, chews and swallows it, and takes a sip of wine. "Perfect with the wine."

"I agree," Lafayette says. "Where is the wine from?"

"Burgundy. From a small vineyard named Goutte d'Or in Meursault. It is owned and operated by a Burgundian family with roots to the sixteenth century."

While his guests are occupied with the oysters, Jefferson says, "Because no highway exists along the Mediterranean coast from Nice to Genoa, my trip into Italy from Nice required me to cross the Maritime Alps on the back of a mule, a distance of 93 miles, before reaching the town of Coni. The road is probably the greatest work of this kind ever executed in either ancient or modern times, and it did not cost as much as one year's war. The road is a series of twists and turns up and down the mountains, and in good weather wide enough for carriages to pass, but a problem develops when winter snows make the road impassable. Because the snows prevent carriages from passing, I put my carriage in storage, rented mules, and on April 13, I started across the Alps.[11]

"That night I stayed at the village of Tende, surrounded by precipitous walls of rock, in an inn, all black, dirty, stinking, and no glass windows.[12]

"Early the next morning I set out to cross the col de Tende, the mountain range that separates the Maritime from the Ligurian Alps. This was the most dangerous part of the trip. Col de Tende is the highest mountain I had to cross. It was still covered with ice and snow, with high winds or storms within the mountain passes often creating avalanches. Since the wind is 'most quiet' in the early morning hours, I left Tende at dark in order to cross col de Tende as soon after the break of day as possible.[13]

"Halfway up were quarters for a detachment of soldiers posted to prevent smuggling and an inn called La Ca (The House). It was here that I hired several men to assist me and my valet in ascending and descending the mountain. These men, called 'coulants,' use a hoe-like device to break the ice and make steps for the mules. Near the top, I had to get off my mule and climb on foot because, although the mountain mules are sure-footed and frost-shod, the ice is so hard and slippery that the mules often stumble and fall. Although the climb to the top is arduous and dangerous, the way down is the envy of anyone who has ever enjoyed a sleigh ride.

"I went down the mountain in a wooden sleigh called a *Lèze*. One of the coulants sat in the front of the sleigh, I was in the middle, and another coulant stood in the rear. The front coulant used his feet to regulate the speed of the sleigh's descent, which was so rapid that the village of Limone was reached in about an hour.[14] Limone, at the base of col de Tende, is the headquarters for the muleteers. Here I abandoned my mules, and rented post-horses and a carriage for the rest of the trip in Italy until I reached Genoa.

"On reaching the Po River, I crossed on what is called a swinging batteaux, two boats placed side by side with a common platform onto which the horses and carriage are driven."

A servant removes the oyster plates. Petit reappears with four wine glasses and a decanter of white wine that he places beside Jefferson who looks up at Petit and says, "Le Montrachet?" Petit nods, turns and leaves.

Jefferson pours the wine and hands each man a glass. The next dish selected by the host is Macaroni with Cheese. As the guests serve themselves, Jefferson says, "I may have been introduced to this dish when Philip Mazzei lived at Colle, but I am delighted to find that it is fashionable here in France. The best macaroni is made from a particular flour called semolina, from Naples, but in almost every shop a different sort of flour is used, but if the flour is of a good quality, it will always do well."

Jefferson acknowledges his guests praises of the Le Montrachet by smiling, and he continues his travel monologue. "In Turin I stayed two days at the Hotel d'Angleterre, the best hotel. It was here that I first tasted a wine called Nebiule. It was a singular wine, melding three contradictory characteristics. It was about a sweet as silky Madeira, as astringent on the palate as Bordeaux, and as brisk as Champagne. It is a pleasing wine."[15]

"From Turin I took an excursion to the Village of Moncalieri and visited the fifteenth century royal castle. The castle, on a hill above the village, has a view of the Po and the plains, which spreads to a ridge of mountains that form the dutchy of Montferrat.

"In Turin I learned that the exportation of rice in the husk from Piedmont is prohibited and punishable by death. I had come a long way to determine the superiority of Piedmont rice, and I was not to be deterred by a death threat. I filled my coat pockets with rice and possibly risked the life of a muleteer by the name of Poggio by having him smuggle a bagful to Genoa. I succeeded in getting the rice out of Italy and sent it to the South Carolina Society for Promoting Agriculture. Responding on behalf of the society, Ralph Izard found the rice inferior to the South Carolina variety and, fearing that the commingling of the rice could lead to an undesirable hybrid, asked me to send no more.[16]

"From Turin to Vercelli I found the people poorly clothed compared to the people of France, and the women at heavy laboring jobs. I drank 'a wine called Gatina made in the neighborhood of Vercelli, both red and white.' I thought the white Gatina resembled a Carcavelos, a sweet wine from Portugal. I also drank an 'esteemed' light red wine from Salussola.[17]

"From Vercelli to Novaro, the fields are in rice and mostly under water. Milan is so surrounded with vines, corn, pasture, and gardens that I could hardly see it until I was in its streets. I spent one day, from sunrise to sunset, in the town of Rozzano at a dairy, learning the intricacies of Parmesan cheese and examining the local ice houses and the methods of storing snow. I journeyed north to Lake Como, went to a casino, examined another rice-beating machine, visited Villa Simonetta, famous for its echo, and enjoyed an evening at the theater.[18]

"From there I headed south to Genoa, staying along the way in Pavia. I visited the University of Pavia and saw a botanical garden laid out in the Linnaean system.

"Genoa rises above the Mediterranean and is laid out in a semicircle. During my three days in Genoa, I stayed at Le Cerf, an inn more in the French style, with its back windows looking onto the Mediterranean. I made garden tours to some of the country seats of the Genoese nobility at Sestri, Pegli, and Nervi. Prince Lomellino's gardens at Sestri are the finest I have seen outside of England."[19]

Jefferson notices Petit standing in the doorway with a tray holding four wine glasses and a crystal decanter of red wine. Jefferson motions him in. Petit sets the tray in front of Jefferson. Jefferson thanks Petit, lifts the decanter and pours the wine. "I promised you Haut Brion and this is it of the 1784 vintage."

"You have told me that on your visit to Bordeaux last year you drank the four best wines. I believe you said they are called first growths or first crops, and Haut Brion is one of them," Lafayette say.

"Yes, Lafite, Margaux, Latour and Haut Brion."

"How do you compare them in taste?"

Jefferson swirls the wine in his glass. "Lafite is silky with a charming perfume. Latour has fuller body and a considerable aroma but is not as soft as Lafite. Margaux is lighter and has all the delicate qualities of Lafite but not quite the flavor. Haut Brion has more spirit and body than the other three, but rough when new and requires being kept longer in wood."[20]

Petit enters carrying a large beef a la mode on a silver platter. While Jefferson continues his monologue, Petit carves the beef, places heaping portions on the plates with an assortment of roasted vegetables and serves the diners.

"From Genoa, I decided to return to Nice by boat because there are no roads, just paths suitable only for mules and walking that lead through the mountains and along the coast. I arranged passage on a felucca, an open boat propelled by one sail and a crew of twelve sailors: a master, ten rowers, and a boy who called commands. It was a well-built vessel with a wood railing around it over which can be thrown canvas to protect the passengers from rain or the sun. However, because of contrary winds and my own 'mortal seasickness,' I abandoned the sea voyage after two days and set in at the fishing village of Noli.[21] Noli has . . .

Une petite merveille, Lafayette utters from across the table.

Jefferson pauses, takes a sip of wine and says, "Do you mean the beef a la mode or the wine?"

Lafayette smiles, "Both and I am enjoying hearing about your travels."

"Yes, please continue," Houdon says.

"The next morning I hired a guide and three mules and for the next two days clambered across the precipices of the Apennines. Once across, the change of scenery was as abrupt as it was exhilarating: to the horizon extended the blue Mediterranean, white sand beaches, orange and lemon groves, and the silver green of olive trees gilded by the sun. Descending to the coast, I walked along the shore from Louano to Albenga, spending another unpleasant night in the most detestable gite, called a tavern that I ever saw in any part of the earth, and the dearest too. But despite physical discomforts, I was taken by Albenga's natural beauty: a rich plain opening from between two ridges of mountains triangularly to the sea and abounding in olives, figs, mulberries, and wine. I stopped at the seaside towns of Oneglia and Port Maurice, a mile apart, and in a rich country surrounded by vines and olive groves.[22]

"I spent the night in San Remo. The old section of town, with its narrow streets, flights of steps, archways, and crowded houses, occupied a steep hill that sat between two valleys, planted with orange and lemon groves. My room at the Auberge de la Postea looked into a handsome garden with palm trees under the windows. I also had available a very good vin ordinaire that was made in the environs.[23]

"The following morning I continued along the coastline to Nice. From Menton to Monaco, I was surrounded by groves of oranges and lemons, and I mused along the way that a superb road might be made along the margin of the sea from Laspeze to Nice by which travelers could enter Italy without crossing the Alps."[24]

"I'm surprised that there is no coastal highway between France and Italy," Short says. "That is disappointing."

"Such a road would make one's journey a great deal easier. I was exhausted when a reached Nice. Still, I stayed there just one night before retrieving my carriage, renting post horses and heading back through southern France."

"Fascinating," says Lafayette. "I must find the time to take such a trip. But for now let us concentrate on this remarkable wine."

Setting: Paris, Friday, April 8, 1789, Thomas Jefferson's
mansion on the Champs-Elysées

Present are Jefferson, five days short of his 46 birthday, Gouverneur
Morris, age 37, Philip Mazzei, 59, William Short, 30.

It is Good Friday and Gouverneur Morris is invited to dine at
Minister Jefferson's Paris residence. On arrival he notices large
crowds of people dressed in their best apparel on foot, horseback, and
in carriages parading up and down the Champs-Elysées. Morris has
been in Paris four months but he has never seen anything like it. He
reminds himself to ask Minister Jefferson what it is about.

He rings the gate bell and is met by Petit, Jefferson's *maître d'hôtel.*
Petit leads him through the courtyard, into the house. Motioning for
Morris to wait, Petit opens one of the three doors that lead from the
reception area, and with a slight bow indicates that Morris should enter.

Waiting in the main salon are Jefferson, his secretary William Short,
and Philip Mazzei. Morris is younger and shorter than his host, and he
walks with a noticeable limp. Introducing Morris to Mazzei, Jefferson
says, "Gouverneur Morris served as a delegate from Pennsylvania at the
Constitutional Convention and his pen, according to our friend Madison, 'styled' the Constitution."[1]

Morris explains that he arrived in Paris four months earlier on private business.

"What kind of business?" Mazzei asks.

"My friend and sometimes business partner, Robert Morris, wants
me to look into and untangle, if possible, some of his French business
transactions."

"I notice that you walk with a considerable limp," Mazzei says.

"As a young man I was thrown from a carriage and my leg was so
severely injured that it had to be amputated."

"Oh, I had heard a more interesting story," Mazzei says, and waits
for a response. When none comes, he adds, "I've heard that you injured your leg when you jumped from a balcony to escape a jealous
husband."[2]

Petit enters carrying a decanter of white wine. Jefferson pours four glasses.

Morris smiles weakly. "Yes, that is a popular rumor." Morris accepts a glass of wine and takes a sip. "I've heard nice things about you, Mr. Mazzei. What brings you to Paris?"

"King Stanislaus of Poland appointed me his special agent in Paris, so I'm here for an indefinite period."[3]

Morris remembers to ask his host about the activity outside, "What is going on outside?"

"It's the annual Parisian rite of spring, known as the Promenade of Longchamps. Each year on Wednesday, Thursday and Friday in the week before Easter, Parisians parade along the Champs-Elysées and cross the Bois de Boulogne to the little church at Longchamps. The origin of the rite was to enjoy the music of the Tenebrae services at the Abbey de Longchamps, but over time it evolved into a parade featuring Parisians of every walk of life dressed in their Sunday best. John Adams who saw the fete several times said that "everybody who has a splendid carriage, a fine set of horses, or an elegant mistress, sends them out on these days to make a show."[4]

Jefferson sips his wine before continuing. "I have been away from Paris the past three years during the Easter holidays, so this is the first time I will see the fete. I suggest that we take our wine and witness the parade from my balcony overlooking the Champs-Elysees."

From the balcony Morris points to a splendid carriage, "That must be the carriage of some high ranking nobleman."

"Not necessarily," Jefferson says. "John Adams tells the story of a beautiful prostitute whose carriage was so superior to any other that it brought on the wrath of Queen Marie Antoinette. According to Adams she had sold her charms for such profit that she appeared in the most costly and splendid carriage of all, six of the finest horses in the kingdom, the most costly coach that could be built, numerous servants, and richer liveries than any of the nobility. Her show was so audacious to all modest women of nobility and to the national morality and religion that the queen sent her a message warning that if she ever appeared again, she would find herself in the Bastille in the morning."[5]

"It is always a pleasure to dine here with our minister," Morris says to Mazzei. "Since my arrival in Paris in January, I've been a frequent dinner guest at Mr. Jefferson's house. 'He lives well, keeps a good table, with excellent wines, which he distributes freely, and by his hospitality to his countrymen here, he possesses their good will.' We have enjoyed one another's company very much."

"I quite agree," Mazzei says. He has not met Morris before but by reputation he knows he is Jefferson's political opposite, and he mentions that to Morris.

At first Morris seems taken back by the candor of the Italian's remark, but after a moment of reflection a broad smile breaks across his face. "That is true. We are political opposites, but our intellectual respect for one another transcends our political differences. I am confident that we will remain social companions during Minister Jefferson's remaining time in Paris."

"Yes," Mazzei says, "I know Minister Jefferson wishes to return home temporarily."

Wondering how Morris and Mazzei are getting along, Jefferson says to them, "Do you like the wine?"

"Yes," Morris says, "the wine is good, but it is different from any wine I've ever drunk. Where is it from?"

"About two years ago I took a three and a half month trip through southern France visiting the vineyards and Roman antiquities. It was at Avignon that I discovered a white wine I thought the equal of Montrachet and Sauternes – vin blanc de Rochegude. Produced in the rich, reddish countryside near Avignon, I thought it so good I ordered a quantity for my Paris cellar. I like this wine so much I plan to share it with President Washington and John Jay by sending them some. I think it is one of the best white wines of France."

"Who produces it?" Morris asks.

"It is produced by Robert d'Aqueria, the Marquis de Rochegude, the seignor of the tiny village of Rochegude that he owns. His properties and vineyards extended beyond the village of Rochegude and include vineyards at Bedoin, Rières and the Marquis's chateau near Avignon. On my palate the wine resembles a dry Lisbon and reminds me of Madeira. I've been told that the Marquis said that his wine is like sherry (cheres). It has an affinity in taste with fortified wines, especially Madeira. The wine is aged six years in cask, and at 22 sous a bottle it is not expensive."[6]

After viewing the parade activities for about a half hour Jefferson says, "Have you seen enough?" Morris, Mazzei and Short agree that they have. "Then let's go to dinner. Three French friends are going to join us."

"Who?" Mazzei asks.

"Three of your favorites, Marquis de Lafayette, the Duc de Rochefoucauld, and Marquis de Condorcet."

Setting: Saturday, July 4, 1789, Hôtel de Langeac, Thomas Jefferson's mansion on the Champs-Élysées

Minister Jefferson, 46, is hosting a large dinner party that includes, among others, Marquis de Lafayette, 31, Adrienne Lafayette, 29, Gouverneur Morris, 37, John Paradise, 46, Philip Mazzei, 58, William Short, 30, Martha Jefferson, 16, Mary Jefferson, almost 11.

Fourth of July is the one holiday Thomas Jefferson always celebrates. Today he is hosting a dinner party which is on the cusp of the French Revolution. The first spark that sets on fire the revolution occurs in Marseilles in March when Jefferson's friend and favorite French wine merchant, Henry Bergasse, raises his prices. This defiant act in combination with the high price of bread causes the local populace to riot and threaten to destroy the Bergasse wine cellars. Frightened by the mob's violence, Bergasse sells his wine business and flees to his native city of Lyon.[1]

By the end of March the peasant insurrection is spreading throughout France. The people have begun to hunt and kill game. Tithes and other forms of taxation are being ignored, and such feudal rights as *banalité du moulin* and *droit du four*--the obligation of the peasantry to have their corn ground in the seigneur's mills and their bread baked in the seigneur's ovens is being disregarded. Widespread seething disobedience develops into attacks on the nobility and clergy and their property.[2]

The brutally cold winter of 1788-89 has also brought on serious consequences. The price of bread, which even in normal times accounted for half the household budget, has nearly doubled causing peasants and laborers to spend four-fifths of their earnings on bread alone. But hunger and poverty are not the only catalysts to the gathering storm of revolution. By convening the States-General the king has allowed hope to creep into the peasants' lives.

As Jefferson's guests gather in his beautiful garden, revolution is either on the lips or in the thoughts of everyone present.

Despite the political turmoil another type of revolution is well underway in France, a food revolution, and it started before Jefferson's arrival five years earlier. Restaurants are a common scene in Paris, especially in the Palais Royal. French chefs have set the standards for cooking throughout Europe creating a culinary atmosphere of "but one opinion . . . every man in Europe that can afford a great table either keeps a French cook, or one influenced in the same manner."[3]

French culinary talents have been deeply absorbed by Minister Jefferson. Before he turned his Paris kitchen over to his own cook, James Hemings, he had him trained in the art of French cooking. From a personal perspective he has acquired a taste for the best olive oils, delicate figs, oranges, lemons, olives, ortolans, pheasants, partridges, quails, sardines, anchovies, lobsters, pasta, parmesan cheese, capers, almonds, and the incredible bounty of meats, fish, vegetables and fruits available to the wealthy and privileged French nobility, clergy and affluent visitors.[4]

This will be Minister Jefferson's last Fourth of July dinner in France. In less than three months Jefferson, his daughters, Martha and Mary, and slave-servants James and Sally Hemings will leave France and return home to Monticello.

John Paradise, Jefferson's friend from London, sees Jefferson's daughters, Martha "Patsy" and her younger sister, Mary "Polly", huddled together on a bench in the garden. Paradise, a charming but shy and self-effacing linguist in his forties, approaches them and introduces himself. Martha is sixteen, tall and gangly with her father's facial features. Mary is shy and petit with beautiful delicate features and approaching her eleventh birthday.

"Have you enjoyed your time in France?" Paradise asks.

"Yes," Martha answers. "I have been here longer than my sister. I came to France with my father five years ago. My sister arrived just two years ago."

"Do you live with your father?"

"Until recently we resided at Abbaye Royale de Panthemont, a Catholic convent boarding school where I received an excellent education. But Polly and I contacted typhus at the convent, and we have lived with our father for much of the past winter. We finished our Panthemont studies in the spring and now live here until we leave for America."[5]

Paradise has noticed a young, attractive light-skinned black woman attending the needs of Patsy and Polly and helping with the food service. She appears to be about sixteen. He asks who she is.

"Her name is Sally Hemings," Martha says. "She is a slave-servant who accompanied Polly on the voyage from America. She and her brother James are members of our father's staff and household."

Polly says, "How do you know my father?"

"We are friends. I live in London with my wife Lucy who is in London with our daughter." The dinner bell rings. Paradise walks to the dining room with Martha and Mary and sits between them, their chairs facing the windows that look out onto the Champs-Élysées.

"How long have you known our father?" Martha asks.

"My wife and I met Minister Jefferson through Abigail and John Adams during his visit to London in the spring of 1786. We first dined with him at a dinner party my wife and I hosted in honor of the Adamses at our London residence."[6]

The first course consists of roast duck, glazed partridge breasts, stewed veal with garnish of small carrots and onions, baked macaroni with a cheese topping, French beans with sweet herbs, artichokes and brown sauce, peas with hearts of lettuce, and fresh corn from Jefferson's garden. For desserts apple tarts, rice pudding, little sponge cakes, macaroons, oranges, figs, and cheeses.[7]

During dinner the girls learn that John Paradise is a linguist and scholar with an obvious talent for making friends with many important people such as George Washington, Benjamin Franklin, Abigail and John Adams, Samuel Johnson, and James Boswell. They don't learn, however, what others around the table know–his wife, Lucy, though beautiful is imperious, tempestuous, and eccentric with spendthrift habits that have their marriage in ruinous financial condition.[8]

Across the table the outspoken Gouverneur Morris, who has been in Paris since January, says to Jefferson, "Since my arrival here six months ago I have witnessed a break down in law and order. Is the National Assembly, in your opinion, going to be able to bring the situation under control?"

There is no one in France more acutely aware of the gathering storm than Thomas Jefferson. "I don't know. Three weeks ago I witnessed the Third Estate (the common people) request the nobility and clergy to eliminate the distinction of orders and to do the business of the nation.

"The Third Estate has in their chamber almost all the talents of the nation; they are firm and bold, yet moderate. There are indeed among them a number of very hot headed members, but those of most influence are cool, temperate, and sagacious. Every step of this house has been marked with caution and wisdom. The Noblesse on the contrary is absolutely out of their senses. They are so furious they can seldom debate at all. They have a few men of moderate talents, and not one of great in the majority. Their proceedings have been very injudicious. The clergy are waiting to profit of every incident to secure themselves. They have no other object in view. Among the commons there is an entire unanimity on the great question of voting by persons.[9]

"A few days ago the king made matters worse by locking the representatives of the third estate out of their meeting hall. Led by Mirabeau they promptly reassembled on the tennis court at Versailles and bound themselves to each other by an oath never to separate of their own accord until they have established a constitution for the nation on a solid basis, and if separated by force, they will reassemble in some other place."[10]

Lafayette leans in to Jefferson and whispers, "As you know I have been working on a Declaration of the Rights of Man. Although it is still in draft form I've gone about as far with it as I can. I would very much appreciate your observations on my bill of rights before I present it to the National Assembly."[11]

"I will be honored to read it and give you the benefit of my thoughts."

"At some point after it is presented I will need to meet with certain members of the assembly who are sympathetic to my position. For obvious reasons, the meeting will have to be secret. Will you allow us to meet here?"

Jefferson nods, "Yes. Let me know a day or two in advance."

Morris, whose sentiments are clearly on the side of the nobles, urges Lafayette "to preserve if possible some constitutional authority to the Body of the Nobles as the only means of preserving any liberty for the people. The current is setting so strongly against the Noblesse that I apprehend their destruction."[12]

These are troubled times and the author of the Declaration of Independence wonders where it will end.

Secretary of State Jefferson, 1790 – 1794

On September 26, 1789, after five years in France, Jefferson, his two daughters and slave-servants James and Sally Hemings, leave Paris for home and what he thinks will be a six-month leave of absence. Except for a little seasickness their twenty-six day voyage is uneventful and they enjoy "some of the finest autumn weather it is possible to have."

After landing at Norfolk Jefferson learns by reading the newspaper that President Washington nominated him, and the senate confirmed him, America's first Secretary of State.

Before undertaking his new duties he oversees plans for his daughter Martha's marriage to her second cousin, Thomas Mann Randolph, Jr. A week after the wedding Jefferson prepares for his new appointment by again leaving Polly under the "motherly care" of her aunt, Elizabeth Eppes.[1]

His trip to New York is "as laborious a journey as I ever went through, a snow of eighteen inches deep falling, the roads through the whole were so bad that we could never go more than three miles an hour, sometimes not more than two, and in the night but one."[2]

He stops in Philadelphia to visit Benjamin Franklin. Franklin is eighty-three, bedridden, in pain, emaciated but in good spirits. The following month he receives word that Franklin has died.[3]

Jefferson arrives in New York, a city of 33,000, on March 21. Shortly after his arrival he brokers a deal between Alexander Hamilton and James Madison that allows Congress to pass a bill transferring the capital to Philadelphia for ten years, and, thereafter, permanently to the new capital, Washington.[4]

During the less than six months the new Secretary of State lives in New York he dines frequently with President and Mrs. Washington. In fact, it is at a presidential dinner party that Washington gives for his Secretary of State shortly after Jefferson's arrival that he first meets Alexander Hamilton, Secretary of the Treasury.[5] He dines with John and Abigail Adams at their manor house in Richmond Hill. He visits his best friend and fellow Virginian, James Madison, who is serving in Congress.

As Washington's Secretary of State he accepts the duty of guiding the President through other foreign waters, ordering French wines. In a letter to Short he orders for the President 480 bottles of Dorsay's *non-mousseux* Champagne.[6] In an accompanying letter to Joseph Fenwick, the American Consul in Bordeaux, he orders for the President 30 dozen bottles of Chateau Yquem, 20 dozen bottles of Chateau Latour, and 10 dozen bottles of Lambert's Frontignan.[7]

During the transition of moving the capital from New York to Philadelphia, Jefferson and Madison set out for their homes in Virginia.

Setting: Rock Hall, Maryland, September, 10, 1790

Present are Thomas Jefferson, Secretary of State, age 47, James Madison, member of Congress, age 38, and Thomas Lee Shippen, 25.

Their journey from Philadelphia brings the two Virginians to the little fishing hamlet of Rock Hall on Maryland's Eastern Shore where they are waiting for the ferry to take them across the Chesapeake Bay to Annapolis. The ferry is not scheduled to depart for an hour. Waiting for the same ferry is young Thomas Lee Shippen.

Strolling along the dock Shippen notices in the distance two men rowing a boat and engaged in intense conversation. The two men row the boat to a small dock and tie up. The large man steps onto the dock and extends a helping hand to his smaller friend who is not more than five feet six, and slight of build. As Shippen gets closer he realizes that the tall, lanky man is Thomas Jefferson.

Shippen calls out and runs over to where the men are standing on the dock. Jefferson is delighted to see his young friend from Paris and introduces him to his traveling companion, James Madison.

The ferry has been delayed and now won't leave for at least two hours. At Jefferson's suggestion they buy steamed hard shell crabs and eat them sitting at a wooden table on the dock while Shippen tells about his European travels. Shippen would later tell his father, "We talked and dined, strolled, and rowed ourselves in boats, and feasted upon delicious crabs."[8]

On the ferry ride across the Chesapeake Bay, Shippen learns that he and the author of the Declaration of Independence, and the author of the United States Constitution, are spending the night in Annapolis at the same inn, Mann's, considered by some travelers as "the most excellent in the world."

At the Annapolis dock Shippen is met by a friend and local resident, Shaaff, who offers to serve as their guide. Shaaff takes them to the Maryland State House, and they climb the narrow staircase to the top of the magnificent State House dome. For the next three hours Jefferson, Madison, Shippen and Shaaff circle the dome and view "the finest prospect in the world, if extent, variety of wood and water in all their happiest forms can make one so," while Shaaff "opens the roofs of the houses" and tells them the local gossip.

On the carriage ride to Mann's tavern, Madison says to Jefferson, "You will find Mann's changed since you were last there."

"How has it changed?"

"Three years ago Mann put on two additions. The inn now contains three large dining rooms, a barroom, a first floor dressing room, a sitting room, a kitchen, a wash house, a billiard room, eight lodging rooms on the second floor, a garden with and icehouse, a stable for fifty horses, and a garret room for servants."[10]

After settling into his room Shippen joins his friends in the dining hall. The main course at dinner is dressed turtle seasoned with Madeira, a Maryland tradition. Mr. Madison, an avid Madeira drinker, takes from his travel box a bottle of wine. He removes the cork and pours a small amount into a glass. The color is amber. He runs the top of the wine glass under his nose and smells the bouquet. His countenance expresses his satisfaction. Madison pours Shippen's glass and then Jefferson's.

Jefferson sips the wine. "It is of the silky quality," he says.

Shippen tastes the wine. "What do you mean by silky quality?"

"The silky Madeira we sometimes get in this country is made so by putting a small quantity of Malmsey into dry Madeira. The taste of the dry dashed with a little sweetishness is barely sensible to the palate."

Madison says, "Silky, yes, but it also has that nut quality that we both esteem in the best Madeira."

Jefferson turns to Shippen, "It was nearly seven years ago here in Annapolis that General George Washington resigned his commission as commander-in-chief. I was a member of the committee charged with making arrangements for his stay when he arrived late in December 1783. The day before the resignation ceremony Congress hosted a dinner in Washington's honor here at Mann's tavern for over two hundred 'distinguished guests.' After dinner glasses were raised in thirteen toasts beginning with 'to the United States,' and ending with 'to the long health and happiness of our illustrious general.' The Congressional Committee did not quibble over Mann's bill of $644, calling 'the entertainment exceedingly plentiful, the provisions and liquors good in their kind.'"[11]

"As I recall," Madison says, "James Monroe and you were members of Congress and rented a house together."

Jefferson nods. "Yes, it was in February 1783 that Monroe and I moved into Mrs. Dulany's house that we rented until my departure from Congress eleven weeks later. We were there to work and ratify the Treaty of Peace proposed by Benjamin Franklin, John Adams and John Jay. A French chef by the name of Partout prepared our meals that included beef, turkey, duck, veal and oysters. Our wines we purchased here at Mann's."[12]

Madison refreshes their wine glasses as Jefferson continues. "It was at the Maryland State House that Washington resigned. I remember it vividly. The small gallery was jammed with people anxious to witness the historic event. As the clock struck twelve, Thomas Mifflin, President of the Continental Congress, called upon Washington to speak. The spectators all wept. The General's hand shook as he read. Washington reached in his pocket for the commission and handed it to President Mifflin. An era had ended."[13]

Later that day while on the road to Georgetown Shippen looks back on his experience with Jefferson and Madison and thinks, *I never knew two men more agreeable than they were.*[14]

Setting: Philadelphia, Monday, April 11, 1791, Jefferson's
residence on High Street

Present are Thomas Jefferson, two days short of his 48th birthday, Secretary of State, Alexander Hamilton, 36, Secretary of the Treasury, John Adams, 55, Vice-President, Henry Knox, 50, Secretary of War.

When Jefferson arrives in Philadelphia on November 20, 1790 to resume his duties as Secretary of State, it is America's largest and most sophisticated city with a population of 45,000. Although critical of aristocratic pomp, he rents a house on High Street that he remodels with stabling for six horses, room for three carriages, a veranda and a garden house.

With 680 bottles of his wines still in France, Jefferson sets about replenishing his wine cellar. From Henry Sheaff, a grocer and wine merchant at 223 Market Street (next door to the President's House) he buys twelve bottles of Madeira, and from another merchant, John Nancarrow, a twenty-three gallon cask of Madeira. In March he receives from a Lisbon wine merchant 36 bottles of six different types of Portuguese wines. He likes best the oldest Termo and orders a pipe of it.[1]

It is a cold, bleak afternoon when John Adams, Alexander Hamilton and Henry Knox arrive at 274 High Street near Eighth Street. It is a large house and within easy reach of President Washington's mansion on 6th and Market Streets, the State House, the American Philosophical Society, and Jefferson's offices.

A servant answers the door, admits the distinguished guests to a large comfortable drawing room, takes their coats and disappears. A few minutes later Jefferson enters. "Thank you for coming on such short notice. I received a letter from President Washington, now traveling through our southern states, requesting me to call together the heads of departments, and Vice-President Adams to join us in order to determine a measure which requires dispatch. He desires us to act on it, as decided, without again referring it to him."[2]

Hamilton and Jefferson are at opposite ends of the political spectrum and are not friends. Still, Jefferson finds Hamilton an engaging personality when he doesn't let his political thoughts get in the way of what he is saying. The Secretary of State is acutely aware that Hamilton is held in the highest esteem by President Washington.

Jefferson leads his guests into the dining room where a comfortable fire is burning in the fireplace. Dinner preparations are running a bit behind schedule and the host decides to break with tradition and serve wine before dinner.

Should a stranger have entered the room he would not know that the handsome young man standing on Jefferson's right is Alexander Hamilton. He is well-dressed, tall, with light hair and a pleasing countenance. There is an intense energy and confidence in Hamilton's demeanor.

The short, stout man in plain dress on the host's left is Vice-President John Adams. His face is smooth and round, high forehead, blue eyes, a sharp nose, firm chin, and thinning brown hair flecked with gray. His square-shouldered stance gives the impression of a strong-minded, quick tempered, but determined person.[4]

The other guest, seated in a chair, is huge. He is General Henry Knox, Secretary of War. He weighs more than 300 pounds. He looks older than his 50 years.

Jefferson finishes pouring and passes the glasses. "It is a dry sherry and a welcome libation for a cold day."

A solemn moment elapses while everyone sips the wine.

"It's quite good. Is it available in Philadelphia?" Hamilton asks.

"Yes, you can be ordered it from Henry Sheaff. His wine store is next to the President's House."

"I know Mr.' Sheaff. I've been in his store many times."

"I suppose we all have," Knox says with a chuckle.

"I like the wine," Adams says.

"It has that distinct nut flavor, which to me is the hallmark of fine sherry," Knox says and finishes his glass. "What does it cost?"

"The best dry sherry costs at Cadiz from 80 to 90 dollars the pipe [108 gallons]. Henry Sheaff recently asked me for advice on the quality, prices, and sources of European wines and I supplied him with that information. If any of you would like a copy of my 'Notes to Henry Sheaff,' I will be pleased to get you a copy."

A servant enters and announces dinner.

After dinner when the cloth is removed, Jefferson lifts a decanter of red wine and pours four glasses. "This is a Bordeaux wine from the vineyards of Madame de Rozan. It is what I import for myself. I consider it equal to any of the best four crops."

"What are the four crops?" Hamilton says.

"There are four crops of red Bordeaux wines more famous than all the rest. They are Chateaux Margaux, Tour de Segur [Latour], Haut Brion, and de la Fite [Lafite]. They cost 3 livres a bottle, mature, but are so engaged beforehand that it is impossible to get them. The merchants, if you desire it, will send you a wine by any of those names, and you may pay 3 livres a bottle, which is two and a half times the price of Madame de Rozan's wine. But I will venture to affirm that there never was a bottle of those wines sent to America by a merchant. Nor is it worthwhile to seek for them; for I will defy any person to distinguish them from the wines of the next quality, to wit Madame de Rozan, the wine we are drinking."[5]

"Have you drunk these first crop wines?" Hamilton asks.

"Yes."

"What do they taste like?"

"Lafite is known for its silky softness on the palate and its charming perfume. Latour has a fuller body, and, at the same time, a considerable aroma that lacks the softness of Lafite. Château Margaux, on the other hand, is lighter, and possesses all the delicate qualities of Lafite except that it has not quite so high a flavor. Haut Brion has more spirit and body than any of the others, but is rough when new and requires being kept longer in the wood, while the others benefit from bottling in much less time."[6]

"When you next order Madame de Rozan's wine, I would like to make an order," General Knox says.

Jefferson acknowledges the general's request with a nod. The conversation segues "in which a collision of opinion arises between Mr. Adams and Colonel Hamilton, on the merits of the British constitution, Mr. Adams giving as his opinion, that, if some of its defects and abuses were corrected, it would be the most perfect constitution of government ever devised by man. Hamilton, on the contrary, asserts, that with its existing vices, it is the most perfect model of government that could be formed; and that the correction of its so-called vices would render it an impracticable government."[7]

Jefferson thinks to himself *that is the real line of difference between the political principles of these two gentlemen.* He has Colonel Hamilton in mind when he writes Thomas Paine, "It is but too true that we have a sect preaching up and pouting after an English constitution of king, lords and commons, and whose heads are itching for crowns, coronets and miters."[8]

Around the dining room is hung a collection of the portraits of remarkable men, including those of Francis Bacon, Isaac Newton and John Locke. At some point in the conversation Hamilton says to Jefferson, "Who are those three men?"

"They are my 'trinity of the three greatest men the world has ever produced', Jefferson says, naming them.

Hamilton studies the three portraits and after a long pause says, "The greatest man that ever lived was Julius Caesar."[9]

The look on Jefferson's face conveys his thoughts: *Hamilton's remark epitomizes an important difference in our values: he admires the warrior, I, the philosopher and mathematician.*

After another glass of wine Hamilton, Knox and Adams take their leave. Jefferson accompanies his guests out. Standing in the entrance doorway and watching his cabinet colleagues and the Vice-President climb into their waiting carriages, he thinks, *There is a cult among Federalists that believes the English constitution contains all that is 'perfect in human institutions. We have a sect preaching up and pouting after an English constitution of king, lords and commons, and whose heads are itching for crowns, coronets and miters.'*[10] *This is the kind of thinking that offends me because I believe man can be governed by reason, and the use of force and fear are not necessary.*[11] *'Mr. Adams is honest as a politician, as well as a man; Hamilton honest as a man, but, as a politician, believing in the necessity of either force or corruption to govern men.*[12]

President Washington's French Wines

George Washington is inaugurated as the nation's first president on April 30, 1789 in New York City. The following year the national capital is moved to Philadelphia. In November President Washington moves into Robert Morris's three-and-a half-story brick Georgian style mansion at 524-30 Market Street and occupies it as the President's House. Washington lives and works here as President of the United States until March 1797.

In private talks Jefferson tells Washington about his fascinating three and a half month trip through southern France and over the Alps into Italy. Washington, a lifetime devotee of Madeira and Port, is intrigued by the quality of some of the wines Jefferson describes. He asks his Secretary of State to purchase for him four of the best French wines.

Before leaving New York Jefferson writes William Short in Paris and orders for the President 480 bottles of Monsieur Dorsay's Champagne "of the best year he has, for present drinking," and "it is to be *non-mousseux*." Jefferson instructs Short that the "wine should not move from Champagne until the heats are over and that it should arrive in Philadelphia before the spring comes on. It will of course be in bottles ... Call for the best possible, and they may be sure of a continuance of such annual demand as long as it comes of the best."[1]

On September 1, 1790 Jefferson and Madison leave New York for their homes in Virginia. During a stopover in Philadelphia, where Jefferson makes arrangements for his new residence, he remembers that in addition to the Champagne, the President also asked him to order three other wines he had recommended. He writes Joseph Fenwick, the

American Consul in Bordeaux, and orders 360 bottles of Yquem, a Sauternes, 240 bottles of Latour, a first growth red Bordeaux, and 120 bottles of Doctor Lambert's sweet Frontignan.[2]

Jefferson learns that Chateau Latour cannot fill the President's order because there is "no wine on hand that will do justice to the estate." Using good judgment Fenwick substitutes 1786 Lafite and adds, "We hope it will prove perfect and give entire satisfaction."[3]

Jefferson is scheduled to leave Philadelphia on May 17, 1791 to join James Madison in New York for a month tour of upstate New York and parts of New England. Fearing that some of the wines he ordered for President Washington might arrive while he is away and be placed in a warehouse and spoil, Jefferson instructs his clerk, Henry Remsen, Jr. to watch for them. It is well that he does because, during his absence, Remsen receives notice that four boxes and four baskets covered in oil cloth have arrived from France. Presuming correctly that they contain wine (they are President Washington's 40 dozen bottles of Champagne), Remsen places them in Jefferson's cellar. A few days later, fourteen cases of wine from Charleston arrive, which Remsen also cellars.[4]

On his return Jefferson learns that the President's Champagne has arrived. He sends Tobias Lear, Washington's private secretary, a note suggesting that because the day is cloudy it is a favorable time to pick up the President's four hampers of Champagne. With the President expected to return to Philadelphia "about the 1st of December," and mindful of when the wine will be at its best for drinking, Jefferson suggests that Lear open a case of each and place the bottles on shelves so "that they may be settled before the President's return."[5]

Setting: President's House, Philadelphia, February 20, 1792

Present are President George Washington, two days shy of his 60th birthday, John Adams, 56, Alexander Hamilton, 37, Henry Knox, 41, Thomas Jefferson, 48, Tobias Lear, 30, Washington's private secretary.

It is a bitter cold day with the temperature at sixteen degrees Fahrenheit and snow covering the streets and roadways.[6] Secretary of State Jefferson knows the President to be extremely punctual, and he arrives ten minutes before the hour of three. He is received by a servant in red and white livery and immediately escorted to the main dining room situated just beyond the family dining room to the right of the entrance hall.

Hamilton, Knox and Lear are present when Jefferson arrives, and within a few minutes they are joined by the vice-president. Promptly at 3:15 President Washington's tall, manly figure strides into the dining room dressed in a black velvet suit, and warmly greets his guests.[7] Washington's dinners are notorious for being solemn and lacking spontaneity but this evening will be different. He is in the company of men he highly respects, and about to undertake a new adventure—exploring French wines.

The table is laid in linen with silverware displaying the Washington family arms, wine glasses at each place setting, and in the middle of the table a long sectioned mirror framed in silver on which is placed china statuettes.[8]

Washington's dinner steward, Samuel Fraunces, the former proprietor of the tavern where General Washington said farewell to his officers, is dressed in a white apron, white silk shirt and stockings, velvet breeches. Frances and a cadre of servants place uncovered dishes on the table near the President's personal secretary, Harvard educated Tobias Lear.[9]

Lear, seated at the end of the table, does the carving and filling the plates. Servants standby to serve the guest's plates of soups, broiled pork, goose, roast beef, mutton chops, hominy, cabbage potatoes, fried tripe, onions, fish, mince pies, torts, cheeses and a variety of vegetables. The dinner beverages are beer and cider.[10]

As Lear carves and distributes the dinner plates, Washington says, "I told Tobias when he applied for the position as my personal secretary that he will sit at my table, will live as I live, will mix with the company that resort to the house, will be treated in every respect with civility and proper attention." Washington looks over at Lear. "That was eight years ago. Have I kept my word?"[11]

"Yes, you have made me a part of your family and an intimate with all your friends and acquaintances."

The President seated between Hamilton and Knox adds, "Tradition requires that we not drink wine until the cloth is removed following the dessert course. My favorite wines over the years have been Madeira and Port. However, the wines we will drink this evening are different. The Secretary of State has purchased for me some of the finest wines I have ever tasted. I want to share those wines with you."

The dinner conversation segues in many directions including the President's account of how his Mount Vernon cook Hercules ended up in Philadelphia.

"You will note that Fraunces is in charge of dinner service this evening, but my cook Hercules, from Mount Vernon, is in charge of what comes out of the kitchen."

"Wasn't Fraunces responsible for the dinner preparation and service during your time in New York?" Knox says.

Washington nods, "Yes, but we had a falling out before I left New York."

"What happened?"

"I discharged him because the food and the service were not to my satisfaction. At Martha's suggestion I transferred Hercules from Mount Vernon because his cookery has always pleased us."[12]

"I have heard him called a 'celebrated artist' in the kitchen," Adams says.

Looking across the table at Jefferson, President Washington says, "I did something today that I feel sure would please Benjamin Franklin."

"What was that?"

"I signed legislation creating the United States Postal Service."

"Yes," Jefferson says, "that would please Dr. Franklin very much."

The dessert course of chocolate pudding, cream trifle, macarons, and apple pie is finished and the table cloth removed. Vice-President Adams, rubbing his hands together says, "I am looking forward to the wines. I had my baptism in French wines fourteen years ago while dining aboard a vessel in the Bordeaux harbor. I still remember the taste of the champagne and the claret."[13]

A servant enters carrying a tray containing six wine glasses and places it beside Tobias Lear. Fraunces enters carrying a crystal decanter of white wine. He places it to the right of the secretary and announces with a slight bow, "Champagne, Your Excellency."

A look of anticipation is on everyone's face as Lear begins pouring. "Gentlemen, I too am excited. Please, Sir, tell us about this wine," Washington says to Jefferson.

As the wine is served around the table Jefferson, seated across from Washington, says, "After two and a half years in France my duties had become perfunctory and I had excess time on my hands. So in February 1787 with only rain, hail and snow as traveling companions, I set out on a three and a half month educational tour of southern France that included visits to many of the vineyards. During these vineyard visits I got to meet the owners and the peasants working in the fields, and I came away with knowledge and an appreciation of wine that I didn't know existed."

Hamilton, feeling uneasy that Jefferson has become the dinner spokesperson, says with a bite in his voice, "This trip was paid for by our government?"

Jefferson catches the question's import and smiles. "No, Secretary Hamilton, the entire trip was paid for by me."

"Speaking of wine," Secretary of War Henry Knox says, "Did you remember to order Madame de Rauzan's wine for me?"

"Yes, I ordered you the same as I ordered for myself, 250 bottles and also the equivalent of 250 bottles in cask."

"What kind of wine are you talking about?" Hamilton asks.

"It is the wine that Secretary Jefferson served at his house when he had us to dinner this past April," Knox says.

Hamilton nods, "Yes, I remember."

"I liked the wine and asked the distinguished Virginian to include an order for me."

"In any event," Jefferson says, "my vineyard experiences left me with distinct impressions of what I thought were the best wines. Four such wines I ordered for the President."

"We will drink those wines after dinner," Washington says.

The three hundred pound Secretary of War says, "The roast beef was delicious. How does he do it?"

"Hercules's spit roasted and fricasseed meats are prepared in an open hearth kitchen over hickory smoked fires. He is a strict disciplinarian who glories in the cleanliness of his kitchen," the President says.

Hamilton lifts his wine glass to eye level and studies the wine. Without taking a sip he says, "What is this?"

"Champagne," Jefferson says.

"It can't be Champagne. It doesn't have a sparkle."

"The French prefer non-sparkling Champagne," Jefferson says. "Sparkling Champagne is never brought to a good table in France. The still or non-sparkling is alone drunk by connoisseurs."[14] He does not mention that it is also his own preference.

Henry Knox, quietly tasting the wine, says, "I am very fond of Champagne and this wine is excellent."

Knox's comment clearly pleases the President whose face beams with satisfaction.

The next wine is the 1786 Lafite. Jefferson explains the special status of the four great growths of Bordeaux of which Lafite is one. "During my five day stay in Bordeaux in May 1787 I met most of the principal wine merchants including President Nicolas Pierre Prichard, the owner of Lafite. The Lafite estate has been world famous for hundreds of years."[15]

"What is Prichard president of?" Hamilton asks.

"The Bordeaux Parliament."

"What were your impressions of Bordeaux?" Lear asks.

"Bordeaux is a big, rich city with about a third of its export business in wine. Many of the wine merchants are extremely wealthy and have turned the harbor area, called the *Quai des Chartrons*, into one of the most exciting commercial and fashionable residential areas in the world. Their mansions border the wide curving quays lined with stately elm trees. It is an impressive sight."

Five men who changed the world pay close attention to the 1786 Lafite and pronounce it an outstanding wine.

Lambert's sweet Frontignan receives high praise, especially from Tobias Lear, but it fades in significance when followed by and compared with the Yquem Sauternes, a wine that Jefferson says surpasses all other sweet wines in taste and quality. "When I served it in France, it always proved a most excellent wine, and seems to have hit the palate of the Americans more than any other wine."[16] Sipping his Yquem he adds, "I'm glad to see that it has had that same effect on our palates."

Pleased with the wines and the reception they have received from the vice-president and his cabinet, President Washington promises another dinner featuring "these same wines with our wives to enjoy them with us."

Vice-President Jefferson, 1797-1801

Setting: Monticello, June 1800

Present are Vice-President Thomas Jefferson, age 57, Governor of Virginia James Monroe, age 42, Jefferson's two sons-in-law: John Wayles Eppes, 27, Thomas Mann Randolph, 32.

Governor Monroe's carriage stops at the east portico entrance promptly at three o'clock. For most visitors to Jefferson's 35 room house astride a mountaintop outside Charlottesville, Virginia it is a long and arduous ride up the mountain to reach Monticello. But for Monroe, who lives just two and a half miles to the west on his High-land estate, it is a pleasant fifteen minute ride.

As he steps into the reception hall Monroe never fails to notice the cannon-ball clock at the front entrance with the days of the week painted on the wall. The space was not large enough for Saturday so Mr. Jefferson cut a hole through the floor and put Saturday in the basement.

A servant escorts the young governor to the dining room. The table in the adjoining tea room is set for four with tablecloth, napkins, plates, glasses and silverware. On wall pedestals around the room are the famous French sculpture Jean-Antoine Houdon's busts of Franklin, Washington, John Paul Jones and Lafayette.

Mr. Jefferson is standing by the dining room fireplace talking to two tall, trim young men who Monroe has met many times, Jefferson's sons-in-law, Thomas Mann Randolph and John Wayles Eppes.

Jefferson greets his neighbor warmly. "You got here just in time. I was about to tell a Benjamin Franklin story about the French, one which you as a former minister to France will appreciate. It happened when Dr.

125

Franklin was minister to France. It's about an abbé by the name of Raynal. Like so many French intellectuals he was talkative and opinionated.

"At a dinner party given by Raynal he got on his favorite subject, the theory that men and animals in America were degenerate and much smaller than European men and animals. The dinner guests were equally divided, the French seated on one side of the table, and the Americans on the other side. Doctor Franklin did not agree with the abbé's theory and said, 'Monsieur Raynal, let us decide this question by the facts before us. Let us all rise, and we will see on which side nature has degenerated.' Everyone stood up. The Americans were tall and large and the French remarkably short and diminutive, especially Raynal."[1] Everyone laughs.

"With the presidential campaign between President Adams and your father-in-law in full swing, we should feel fortunate to have this time with him," Monroe says. "The vitriol that is being hurled about by both sides is sickening."

"It has not been easy to take," Jefferson admits. "One newspaper warns that my election will lead to civil war, and hordes of Frenchmen and Irishmen will come to America and destroy everything we hold dear. I've been accused of cheating my clients as a lawyer. The old claim that I'm anti-religious has been revised, and people have been told if I'm elected they'll have to hide the family Bible. A respected member of the cloth has slandered me with accusations that I obtained my property by fraud and robbery, and that in one instance, I defrauded and robbed a widow and fatherless children of an estate to which I was executor, both absolute falsehoods."[2] The vice-president shakes his head in disgust.

Mr. Jefferson nods toward the Tea Room and says, "Enough about politics. Let's have a quiet dinner and discuss interesting subjects like music, architecture, gardening, France and wine."

"I always enjoy hearing about your years in France," John Wayles Eppes says.

"Having spent two years there as our minister, Governor Monroe can certainly add to the discussion," Thomas Mann Randolph says.

Monroe shakes his head. "My tenure in France was not easy. I had no problem adhering to President Washington's strict neutrality between France and Great Britain. The complicating factor was the Jay Treaty. The French became irate when they learned about it believing that we had entered into an alliance with Great Britain. Consequently official France became a hostile environment and it made my two years there uncomfortable," he pauses, "even unpleasant."

"I should think that with the revolution in full swing, France was an unpleasant place for everyone." Eppes says.

"Was it Thomas Paine's opposition to the National Assembly's death sentence of Louis XVI that brought on his French imprisonment?" Randolph says.

"That highlighted it, but Paine vocally opposed the death penalty under all circumstances. He stood up in the National Assembly and made an impassioned plea for Louis XVI's life in opposition to the group of fanatics who were sending thousands of people to the guillotine. He exclaimed, 'Kill the king but spare the man.' He did this despite his hatred of tyranny. He had to be silenced and the government decided that prison and the guillotine were the answer."[3]

"How were you able to secure his release from prison?" Eppes asks.

"I have always felt that Thomas Paine rendered an important service to our Revolution as an advocate for liberty and human rights. When I arrived in Paris replacing Gouverneur Morris as minister, I sent him a note saying that 'to liberate you will be the object of my endeavors, as soon as possible.'"[4]

"How did you go about it?" Randolph says.

"Robespierre's execution led to an ease in tensions, ameliorated the thirst for death, and allowed more even-minded people to assume the reigns of the government. I appeared before the Committee for General Surety and continued to demand Paine's release as an American citizen. When he was released ten months and nine days after entering prison, he was a physical and mental wreck. He came and lived with my wife and I, and we nursed him back to health."

"Should I become President, Thomas Paine will be welcome to return to America," Jefferson says.

"What are your best and worst impressions of France?" the youngest son-in-law asks Jefferson.

"There are many of both. I felt that the great mass of the French people suffered under physical and moral oppression and that among my aristocratic friends, conjugal love had no existence, and domestic happiness was utterly unknown. To friends in America I expanded on how the benefits of freedom enriched the lives of Americans as compared to the wretched existence of the vast majority of the French people.

"It is difficult to conceive how so good a people, with so good a king, so well-disposed rulers in general, so genial a climate, so fertile a soil, should be rendered so ineffectual for producing human happiness by one single curse, that of a bad form of government. But it is a fact. In spite of the mildness of their governors, the people are ground to powder by the vices of the form of government. Of twenty millions of people supposed to be in France, I am of opinion there are nineteen millions more wretched, more accursed in every circumstance of human existence, than the most conspicuously wretched individual of the whole United States.'"[5]

"I remember your writing me from France and urging me to come there in order to better appreciate my 'own country, its soil, its climate, its equality, liberty, laws, people, and manners,'" Monroe says.[6]

"On the other hand I have to admit that I wanted words to describe how much I enjoyed their architecture, sculpture, painting, and music. And in the pleasures of the table, they are far before us, because with good taste they united temperance."[7]

"You once mentioned that you had a great deal of free time the first ten months after your arrival in Paris. Why was that?" Eppes asks.

"Negotiations for treaties of commerce with European countries did not go well."

"Why?"

"We were an upstart new nation. Europe was controlled by monarchs, many of whom did not respect us. Others did not want to alienate powerful Britain. Still others worried that by dealing with the United States they might give their own people encouragement for rebellion. So, I was left with free time on my hands."

"How did you spend that time?" Randolph says.

"I explored my new environment. I combed bookstalls along the Left Bank for bargains that would become part of my book collection; I wandered the streets of Paris absorbing its architecture; I took daily walks through the Bois de Boulogne; I sampled the pleasures of the Palais Royal; I attended dinner parties at the homes of fellow ministers and new French friends; I attended concerts, plays, operas; I shopped the elegant stores along Rue Saint-Honoré; and I made almost daily visits to the Tuileries Gardens that stretched toward Place Louis XV and faced the Seine. Here, surrounded by the beauty of its gravel walks, beds of flowers, raised terraces, marble statues, rows of trees and water basin, I viewed the construction of a mansion whose architectural beauty had 'violently smitten' me. Known as the Hôtel de Salm, it was going up directly across the Seine from the Tuileries Gardens.

"Speaking of food," Jefferson says, waving his hand in the direction of a servant wheeling a table with tiered shelves at varying heights containing fricassee of chicken, braised leg of mutton, French roast beef, macaroni with cheese crust, string beans, peas, fried potatoes, and artichokes.

The table is positioned on Jefferson's right. The servant leaves the room and Jefferson begins carving. "I still follow the American tradition of not serving wine at dinner until the cloth is removed. With the meal we have beer, porter, and cider, but rest assured John, we will drink wine when the cloth is removed." Jefferson picks up a serving utensil and says, "What can I serve you gentlemen?"

Later when desserts have been served and the table cloth removed, two bottles of wine are brought to the table with plates of pecans, raisins, walnuts, cheese, butter and crackers.

"This red wine comes from vineyards in the hills above Nice. I was first introduced to this wine in April 1787 while in Nice by a wine merchant by the name of André Sasserno. The man from whom I bought this wine calls it *Vin Vieux Rouge de Nice*. His name is Pierre Guide. He brought a shipload of Mediterranean products to America. This is one of his wine offerings.[8] I purchased three dozen and I think this is the last bottle.

"But I suggest we start with this wine." Jefferson lifts a crystal decanter containing a white wine, pours four glasses and hands each guest a glass. He holds his glass to the light and studies its bright, clear amber color. "I discovered this wine on my trip through the vineyards of southern France in 1787. I was traveling to Cette (Sète) and stopped at the small Mediterranean town of Frontignan where I made the acquaintance of Monsieur Lambert, a physician and vintner. Lambert was a very sensible man with a considerable income in addition to the revenue from his vineyard and thus was able to practice his profession with ease. Over dinner at Lambert's home I sampled his sweet white and red Frontignan wines and immediately ordered 250 bottles of the best white to be shipped to my Paris home.

"I consider it best when drunk young. It is potable the April after it is made, is best that year, and after ten years it begins to have a pitchy taste resembling it to Malaga. It is not permitted to ferment more than a half day, because it would not be so liquorish [sweet]. The best color, and its natural one, is amber. The fermentation is stopped by the addition of a neutral alcohol or brandy, so when the alcohol is added determines the sweetness of the wine."

The two future presidents and two future congressmen studiously sip the wine. From the expressions on their faces Jefferson can tell that they like it. Monroe is the first to speak. "During my time in France I don't recall drinking this wine. It is quite nice." He pauses and looking straight at the vice-president says, "There is a rumor going round that you have had a falling out with John Trumbull. Is there anything to it?"

"I'm afraid there is. Trumbull and I became close friends during my time in Europe and I did everything I could to advance his artistic career. I met him when I visited England in the spring of 1786. I immediately became interested in him when I learned of his plan to devote himself to painting the great events of our Revolution. I invited him to come to Paris and study the fine arts there and stay with me, which he did. I introduced him to my friends, including Jacques-Louis David and Jean Antoine Houdon. David was sufficiently curious about Trumbull's artistic talents by coming to my house to see his *Bunker Hill* and *Quebec* paintings."[9] Jefferson pauses and takes a sip of wine.

"About a year later John returned to Paris and again stayed with me. He brought with him his unfinished painting the *Surrender of Lord Cornwallis at Yorktown*. When he told me that he hoped to paint the portraits of the French officers who were at Yorktown directly on to the canvas, I managed to get the cooperation of the principal French officers, and Generals Rochambeau, Lafayette, Chastellux, and Admirals De Grasse and De Barras among others were painted from life in my house.[10]

"When Trumbull returned to America he took up residence in Philadelphia and aligned himself politically with Hamilton. He became critical of my support of the French Revolution. Toward the end of my term as Secretary of State I had a dinner party that was attended by, among others, Trumbull and William Branch Giles . . ."

"Oh my goodness," Monroe exclaims, "fireworks are about to go off."

"Why do you say that?" Thomas Mann Randolph asks.

"Aside from the fact that Giles is a political and social friend of your father-in-law, he is a staunch Jeffersonian Democrat and an ardent opponent of Hamilton. He has the frothy manners of a Virginia gentleman, and with some good and old Madeira in him, you can expect fireworks."

Jefferson is smiling. "I've learned that Trumbull claims that no sooner had he taken his seat in the drawing room than Giles began to berate him because of his puritanical New England ancestry. I've also heard that Trumbull claims that throughout dinner Giles continued to attack his Christian beliefs and that 'in nodding and smiling assent to all the virulence of Giles,' I appeared to avow Giles's conduct.[11] If Congressman Giles behaved in that manner, I do not recall it. In any event our relationship has become cold and distant."

"Ah, politics," Monroe says. "When are you two young men going to enter the political arena?"

Jefferson's head snaps up and his eyes dart from one to the other with a sparkle that seems to ask, *Well, when?*

President Jefferson, Washington
1801 – 1809

Setting: Monticello, September 21, 1802

Present are Dr. William Thornton, 43, his wife Anna, 28, Anna's mother Ann Brodeau, about 52, William Short, 43, President Jefferson, 59, Martha Jefferson Randolph, 30, her husband Thomas Mann Randolph.

The guests are assembled in Monticello's handsome parlor. The high ceiling and cherry and beech parquet floor attract the attention of Dr. William Thornton, the architect of the United States Capitol building and the newly appointed Superintendent of the Patent Office. The walls are covered in paintings hung in tiers. Many of the portraits are recognizable: Washington, Franklin, Lafayette, Madison, Columbus, Magellan, and in the opinion of Jefferson the "three greatest men who have ever lived," John Locke, Isaac Newton, and Francis Bacon.[1]

Mrs. Thornton is young and quite handsome. She, her mother, Ann Brodeau, and the President's daughter, Martha, are seated at a card table near the fireplace.

President Jefferson is huddled in a corner with Dr. Thornton, Thomas Mann Randolph, and William Short, who recently returned from Europe where he served as Jefferson's private secretary, America's chargé d'affaires in France, and as minister to the Netherlands and Spain.

"I understand congratulations are in order, Dr. Thornton. The President tells me that he recently appointed you Superintendent of the Patent Office," Short says.

"Thank you. It will present many challenges but I'm looking forward to it. Still, I'll miss my daily architectural duties."

"I understand the pull of architecture was so strong that you gave up a promising medical career."

Thornton nods, "Yes, my love of architecture took me away from medicine."

"Architecture has been one of the delights of my life," Jefferson says. "I taught myself by reading books about architecture. Andrea Palladio is the architect that has most influenced me."

"But what was the influence that first got you interested in architecture?" Short says. Jefferson looks at Short with a blank stare. "Have you forgotten so soon? I have frequently heard you say that the germ of a fondness for buildings was developed in you by the accidental circumstance of your purchasing a book on architecture, when a student at the College of William and Mary, from an old drunken cabinetmaker. Who could discover by any course of reasoning that a drunken cabinetmaker, residing near the college and having a book on architecture to dispose of, would have caused this immense pile of building on top of Monticello's height?"[2]

Jefferson's face breaks into a broad smile, "I had almost forgotten but, yes, that is exactly how it happened." The men laugh.

Jefferson sees John Freeman standing in the doorway leading to the dining room, the signal that dinner is ready. "I see we are being summoned to dinner." He walks over to where Anna Thornton and her mother are seated, offers his arms, and escorts them into the dining room.

"I understand Mr. Short that you have spent the past seventeen years in Europe serving our country in various capacities including minister to Holland and Spain," the beautiful Anna Thornton says.

"That is correct."

"Is your return home permanent and, if so, what are your future plans?"

"I'm not entirely sure. I'm a lawyer by profession and practiced for a brief time before I left for France, but I have no interest in starting a law practice. I have some property here in Virginia and in New York, and I will look into developing the properties. I will probably work in finance." Never one to talk too much about himself, he changes the subject. "How do you find living in Washington?"

Anna Thornton rolls her eyes. "It is getting better. I am meeting more people. I have become especially friendly with Dolley Madison whom I like very much."

Jefferson overhears their conversation. "I would like to see William move into the neighborhood. What could be better than a society forming here of Monroe, Madison and Short?"

Anna Thornton purses her full lips and says to Short, "Well?"

Anna's lips remind him of Rosalie Rochefoucauld with whom he has been romantically involved since her husband was stoned to death in the French Revolution. "I haven't decided where I'll eventually reside," he says.

As the conversation flows around the table John Freeman brings the food on stands with shelves and places them between the guests so that they can serve themselves.[3]

The dinner dishes include larded and glazed rabbit with bacon and small onions, baked pike, loin of veal roasted with clear gravy, macaroni with a cheese crust, peas with hearts of lettuce, carrots, and turnips with butter sauce, string beans with sweet herbs, artichokes with white sauce.[4]

To Anna's surprise her mother says, "President Jefferson, I understand that you were witness to the unfolding of the French Revolution. Did the major events that set it off come suddenly or evolve over time?"

"For those perceptive enough to see, the signs and warnings were there before the violence. Fourteen months before the storming of the Bastille, I noted that the times were sad and eventful. Gay and thoughtless Paris had become a furnace of politics. All the world was now political and mad. Men, women and children talked of nothing else, and they talked much, loud and warm. Society was spoilt by it, at least for those who like myself were but lookers on.[5]

135

"The spark that set off the insurrection in Paris was the king's dismissal of his popular finance minister, Jacques Necker. News of Necker's exile to Geneva reached Paris at noon on July 12. Thousands of Parisians flooded the Palais Royal where orators gave the call to arms. That night and the next day, crowds swarmed throughout Paris looking for arms. On the morning of July 14, the mobs shut up all the playhouses.

"The king's foreign troops were advanced into the city. Engagements took place between some of them and the people. The first was at Place Louis XV, where, when a body of German cavalry being drawn up, the people posted themselves behind piles of stone collected there for the bridge, and attacked and drove off the cavalry with stones. Having won the first skirmish, a crowd of more than 7,000 crossed the river and moved on to the Invalides in search of arms and ammunition.[6] They were refused and the people forced the place and got a large supply of arms.

"They then went to the Bastille and made the same demand. The governor, after hoisting a flag of truce and deploying a hundred or two within the outer drawbridge, fired on them. The people then charged the Bastille, captured it, beheaded the governor and lieutenant governor, and armed themselves."

"Were you actually at the Bastille when the people attacked it?" Anna's mother asks.

"I was not an eyewitness to the siege of the Bastille, but I was privy to eyewitness accounts. The tumults in Paris which took place on the change of the ministry, the slaughter of the people in the assault of the Bastille, the beheading of the governor and lieutenant governor, and the provost des marchands, excited in the king so much concern that bursting from the shackles of his ministers and advisors, he went to the States-General with only his two brothers, opened his heart to them, asked them what he could do to restore peace and happiness to his people, and showed himself ready to do everything for that purpose, promising particularly to send away the troops."

"Did the king keep his promise?" Anna Thornton asks.

"Yes, the king ordered away all the troops and came to Paris in procession, having in his coach the most popular characters, the States-General walking on foot in two ranks on each side of it, and the Marquis de Lafayette on horseback at their head. There were probably 60,000 or 80,000 armed bourgeois lining the streets through which he passed.

"Sensing the tumult over, I felt I had seen in the course of fourteen years two such revolutions as were never seen before."[7] He pauses. "I have a confession." All heads turn in his direction. "William was much more prescient than I about the course the French Revolution would take."

Anna Thornton's mother, who has had her eyes on Short ever since she met him, blurts out, "I'm not surprised." Her remark draws harsh stares from her daughter and Dr. Thornton.

Dinner being finished and the table cloth removed, John Freeman, the President's favorite slave-servant, walks to the fireplace and removes a bottle of wine from the right side of the fireplace mantel, brings it to the table, removes the cork, and places it beside Jefferson, who says, "Madeira."

Freeman walks back to the fireplace and removes a second bottle. Dr. Thornton says, "That is very clever. I assume it is some type of pulley device that transports wine in bottles from the basement to the dining room."

"Exactly," Jefferson says.

Freeman hands the second bottle to the President. "This is a Pacharetti, and the third wine we will drink is from Portugal with the name Oreiras."

"I've had Madeira, of course, but not Pacharetti, and I've never heard of Oreiras," William Thornton says. "Will you tell us about the wines?"

"Pacharetti takes its name from an ancient monastery located about five miles from Jeres de la Frontera, near Cadiz. It has a good reputation both as a dry and sweet wine. On my palate it resembles sherry. This Pacharetti is more on the dry side but with a touch of sweetness.[8] Oreiras is a little known wine from vineyards surrounding a town of that name just outside of Lisbon. It is a rich, sweet wine made from the Muscatel grape.[9] I think we should start with the Pacharetti."

John Freeman moves around the table pouring everyone's glass.

Dr. Thornton takes a sip. "I like the Pacharetti. Mr. President, in what way was Mr. Short more perceptive about the outcome of the French Revolution than you?"

"From the inception of the revolution I was a fervent advocate of it. In fact, in a small way I participated in it."

Anna Thornton gives the President a searching look. "How did you participate?"

"In July 1789 the Marquis de Lafayette was drafting his 'Declaration of the Rights of Man and of the Citizen' and he asked me to read it and make suggestions, which I did. Then in August, before he submitted it to the National Assembly, I allowed my home to become a secret meeting place for Lafayette and seven members of the National Assembly's Committee on drafting a new Constitution. The feeling was they had to forge a coalition 'as being the only means to prevent a total dissolution and civil war.'

"As I recall the meeting, 'the cloth being removed, and wine set on the table, after the American manner, the Marquis introduced the objects of the conference. The discussions began at the hour of four and were continued to ten o'clock in the evening, during which time I was a silent witness to a coolness and candor of argument unusual in the conflicts of political opinion–to a logical reasoning and chaste eloquence disfigured by no gaudy tinsel of rhetoric or declamation, and truly worthy of being placed parallel with the finest dialogues of antiquity, as handed to us by Xenophon, by Plato and Cicero.'[10]

"Even when the violence of the revolution increased in 1792, I praised its progress saying, 'Was ever such a prize won with so little innocent blood? My own affections have been deeply wounded by some of the martyrs to this cause, but rather than it should have failed, I would have seen half the world desolated.'"[11]

"That sounds a bit extreme," Anna Thornton says coolly. "Mr. Short, what was your opinion of the course the revolution was taking?"

"I saw the tyranny of the king's regime replaced by the tyranny of the mob, and I was horrified by the continuing excesses that led to the indiscriminate murder of women, children, the clergy, and many of our friends. It became a reign of terror."

"At some appropriate time, William, I would like to know the specifics of how some of our friends met their deaths," Jefferson says.

"It would be interesting to hear how your French friends whose enlightened views sparked the revolution were murdered as their reward," Anna Thornton says.

Jefferson's eyes sweep the room. Sensing avid interest, he says, "What happened to our dear friend, the Duke of Rochefoucauld?"

Short's mouth tightens. He stares at Anna Thornton who stares back at him. "First, some background. The Duke of Rochefoucauld came from a noble family that traces its roots back to the 10th and 11th centuries. He was a great admirer of the United States and our Revolution. Despite his background and enormous wealth, he was quite liberal and felt social reform was necessary. He was elected to the Estates-General by the nobility of Paris but he didn't fit in there. Soon, he and 46 other noble deputies joined the Third Estate and the Duke became one of its most active orators. He supported such liberal changes as a constitution without the king's sanction, the sale of church lands, the suppression of monastic orders, and a law that subordinated the Catholic Church to the French government. With his increasing liberalism he became a Jacobin. But with the growing excesses of the revolution he became disenchanted and left the Jacobin party.

"On August 10, 1792 Jacobin backed mobs attacked and captured the Tuileries Palace signaling the end of Louis XVI's rule. The Duke fled the city. Weeks later he was recognized while riding in a carriage with his wife and mother. He was removed from the carriage by the mob and stoned to death."

"Dreadful," Jefferson says. "I received a letter from the Duke's mother, the charming and regal Duchesse of Rochefoucauld, sometime after his death. I hear her words now. 'You know my son's sentiments. No sacrifice was too great for him that would bring about the well-being and happiness of his country. His reward was assassination before our very eyes. This catastrophe extinguishes all my happiness and delight in life.'"

Total silence grips the room. Jefferson breathes in deeply. "He was a kind, caring and generous man." He hesitates, "What about our friend the Marquis de Condorcet."

"Condorcet was another caring man with a love for human good. He fought for civil rights changes and received in return a death sentence." Anna Thornton grimaces. "Condorcet was a brilliant mathematician, philosopher, social intellectual, and inspector-general of the mint. He too was from an ancient family," Short says.

"When the States-General convened Condorcet worked on the periphery in furtherance of democratic change. After the attempted escape by the king in June 1791, Condorcet became a firm supporter of the republic. Like Rochefoucauld, he too became disillusioned with the more violent direction of the revolution.

"During the trial of Louis XVI he spoke out against the execution of the king. He drafted a conciliatory constitution, which was rejected in favor of a constitution adopted by the radical convention. He was accused of conspiring against the republic, branded a traitor, and an order issued for his arrest." Short pauses and takes a sip of wine.

"Through friends he found refuge in a house in the Left Bank where he hid for eight months. During this time he wrote *Sketch for a Historical Picture of the Progress of the Human Spirit*, the work for which he is best known.

"Sensing the house where he was hiding was about to be searched by government officials, he fled to the countryside and sought asylum with a friend who rejected him. It is perhaps apocryphal but the story is told that he wandered about for several days and, tired and hungry, he entered a tavern and ordered an omelet. When asked how many eggs he wanted he is reported to have said, 'a dozen.' This remark caught the attention of a *sans-culotte* seated nearby who asked Condorcet his trade. He said, 'carpenter.' The interrogator looked at his smooth, soft hands and asked for his papers. He had none. He was arrested and taken to a nearby jail and thrown into a cell. In the morning he was found dead."

"What is a *sans-culotte?*" Anna's mother asks.

"*Culottes* were fashionable knee-breeches worn by the nobility. The working class did not wear such apparel and became known as *sans-culottes*. They were usually radical and militant partisans."

"What caused Condorcet's death?" Anna asks.

"The official cause was listed as apoplexy but many believe he took poison to escape the guillotine."

"Where did he get the poison" Anna asks.

"We don't know. Perhaps it was concealed on his body."[12]

"What happened to the great sculpture Jean Antoine Houdon who came to America to sculpt the life-size statue of George Washington?" Dr. Thornton says.

"Yes, and a friend," Jefferson says.

A smile creases Short's lips. "Houdon survived the violence. Oh, he fell out of favor, but he did not go to prison."

"Why not?"

"Probably because he was born of poor parents and not viewed as an elitist."

"What caused the downfall of your dear friend Lafayette?" Dr. Thornton asks Jefferson.

Jefferson's brow furrows and he pushes back in his chair. "In the beginning of the revolution many thought Lafayette might become a military revolutionary leader like George Washington but ..." He shrugs.

"Why didn't he?"

"He didn't fully commit to republicanism. He favored reform but he refused to advocate abolishing the monarchy. He became the champion of constitutional monarchy. The tide of the revolution rejected monarchy and moved on, and there was no one for him to lead."

Short interrupts. "When the mob stormed the Tuileries on August 10, 1792 and Louis XVI fled into the arms of the Jacobin National Assembly he was effectively deposed. Mob rule had won. His reign was over. Nine days later the National Assembly accused Lafayette of treason and issued a warrant for his arrest.

"Lafayette knew that if he returned to Paris he would be guillotined. That same day he left his post as a commander in the French army and attempted an escape by crossing the border into the Austrian Netherlands. He was captured by Prussian soldiers and imprisoned for five years."

"I don't understand," Dr. Thornton implores. "Lafayette was totally committed to our republican form of government. Why did he not support a similar style government in France?"

All eyes shift to Jefferson and silence falls like a blanket over the room. President Jefferson regards his guests quietly for a moment. "More than once Lafayette told me that a republican government was perfect for our country because we were new and unfettered and the perfect proving ground for it to flourish. Whereas monarchy had always been the nexus of French civilization and the two could not be separated."[13]

"And now France has Napoleon," Anna Thornton says, shaking her head in disgust.

There is a moment of thoughtful silence before Jefferson speaks. "I have ever believed that had there been no queen, there would have been no revolution."

"Why do you say that?" Anna Thornton asks.

"The King had a Queen of absolute sway over his weak mind, and timid virtue; and of a character the reverse of his in all points, disdainful of restraint, indignant at all obstacles to her will, eager in the pursuit of pleasure, and firm enough to hold to her desires, or perish in their wreck. Her inordinate gambling and dissipations, with those of the Count d'Artois and others of her clique, had been a sensible item in the exhaustion of the treasury, which called into action the reforming hand of the nation; and her opposition to it, her inflexible perverseness, and dauntless spirit, led herself to the guillotine, and drew the king on with her.[14]

"Speaking of monarchs, I remember telling George Washington, 'I was much an enemy to monarchies before I came to Europe. I am ten thousand times more so, since I have seen what they are. There is scarcely an evil known in these countries which may not be traced to their king, as its source, nor a good, which is not derived from the small fibers of republicanism existing among them. I can further say, with safety, there is not a crowned head in Europe, whose talents or merits would entitle him to be elected a vestryman by the people of any parish in America.'"[15]

"Have you personal opinions of specific monarchs that you would care to share?" Anna Thornton asks.

"While in Europe, I often amused myself with contemplating the characters of the then reigning sovereigns of Europe: Louis XVI was a fool, of my own knowledge, and in despite of the answers made for him at his trial. The king of Spain was a fool, and of Naples the same. They passed their lives in hunting, and dispatched two couriers a week, one thousand miles, to let each other to know what game they had killed the preceding days. The king of Sardinia was a fool. All these were Bourbons. The Queen of Portugal, a Braganza, was an idiot by nature. And so was the king of Denmark. Their sons, as regents, exercised the powers of government. The King of Prussia, successor to the great Frederick, was a mere hog in body as well as in mind.

"Gustavus of Sweden and Joseph of Austria were really crazy, and George of England, you know, was in a strait waistcoat. There remained, then, none but old Catherine, who had been too lately picked up to have lost her common sense. In this state Bonaparte found Europe; and it was this state of its rulers which lost it with scarce a struggle. These animals had become without mind and powerless; and so will every hereditary monarch be after a few generations. Alexander, the grandson of Catherine, is as yet an exception. He is able to hold his own. But he is only of the third generation. His race is not yet worn out. And so ended the book of kings, from all of whom the Lord delivers us."[16]

"How does George Washington compare against those monarchs?" Dr. Thornton asks.

"Washington was incapable of fear, meeting personal dangers with the calmest unconcern. Perhaps the strongest feature in his character was prudence, never acting until every circumstance, every consideration, was maturely weighed; refraining if he saw a doubt, but, when once decided, going through with his purpose, whatever obstacles opposed. His integrity was most pure, his justice the most inflexible I have ever known, no motives of interest or consanguinity, of friendship or hatred, being able to bias his decision. He was, indeed, in every sense of the words, a wise, a good, and a great man.

"On the whole, his character was, in its mass, perfect, in nothing bad, in few points indifferent; and it may truly be said, that never did nature and fortune combine more perfectly to make a great man, and to place him in the same constellation with whatever worthies have merited from man an everlasting remembrance. For his was the singular destiny and merit, of leading the armies of his country successfully through an arduous war, for the establishment of its independence; of conducting its councils through the birth of a government, new in its forms and principles, until it had settled down into a quiet and orderly train; and of scrupulously obeying the laws through the whole of his career, civil and military, of which the history of the world furnishes no other example. I felt on his death, with my countrymen, verily a great man has fallen this day in Israel."[17]

A dead silence grips the room. Finally, Jefferson says, "We could talk all night about the good and worthy men and women who have sacrificed their lives on the mantle of liberty, and because of them the ball of liberty, I believe most piously, is now so well in motion that it will roll around the globe, at least the enlightened part of it, for light and liberty go together. It is our glory that we first put it into motion."[18]

Ann Brodeau raises her hand. "President Jefferson, these are the most delicious figs I have ever eaten. Where do you get them?"

Like changing masks, the president's face beams with pleasure. "Now that is an enlightened subject worthy of discussion over a glass of Madeira."

Setting: Washington, the White House (then called the President's House), July 3, 1803

Present are Thomas Jefferson, 60, Meriwether Lewis, 29, Lewis Harvie, 25.

A stout young man of medium height leaves his room and walks down the steps that lead from the second to the first floor of the executive mansion and threads his way along a bleak corridor that leaks when it rains to the dining room located at the south front of the building. He is Lewis Harvie, a law student at Georgetown when not working as President Jefferson's personal secretary. Today he will have dinner with the President and the man he replaced, Meriwether Lewis. Hopefully, he will learn from the President's former secretary what his job requires him to know and do. He has been on the job for a month and his duties and responsibilities have not been made clear to him.

Jefferson and a tall young man are engaged in deep conversation when Harvie enters the dining room. The President sees Harvie and says, "Finally I've been able to get you two young men together. Lewis Harvie meet Captain Meriwether Lewis, my former secretary, who is about to begin an exciting adventure."

The two young men shake hands. There is a marked contrast in their appearances. Captain Lewis is nearly as tall as the six feet two and-a-half inch President. He is trim, of a solid build and obviously in splendid physical condition. He looks to be about thirty years old.

"I've been looking forward to getting together with you and talking about my responsibilities," Harvie says.

"I'm sorry I haven't been able to get with you sooner but I've been away and consumed with getting ready for my trip west. I camp out in a little room down the hall, and you're welcome to come by any time."

John Freeman, a man with a perpetual smile and Jefferson's trusted slave-servant, appears at the entrance doorway, a signal to the President that dinner is ready. The three men take their seats at the oval dining table. Freeman brings the dinner on a vertical stand with shelves that hold the food. He places it beside the President.[1]

"With duties as the President's secretary and my law studies, I won't have much free time, but if I should, what do you do in this town for entertainment?"

The President, who is carving and filling the plates is surprised, even amused, by Harvie's question. "I assume that you noticed the roads leading to the new capital are still dirt." He can't suppress a grin. "There are only two hotels and a number of taverns with wretched accommodations but virtually no restaurants or coffee houses. No sidewalks or lamps interrupt the darkness along the few roads in the city.

"Lewis," the President says solemnly, "Washington is a noble concept on paper but in reality not much more than a cluster of about twenty boarding houses grouped around the still-unfinished Capitol building which is encircled by a forest. The boarding houses have as residents a transient society, for virtually none of the members of Congress have built homes in Washington or bring their wives here. They spend only the winter months when Congress is in session.[2]

"For entertainment you have a choice of a race track or a theatre that is astonishingly dirty and void of decoration. As one habitué said, 'one must love drama very much to consent to pass three hours amidst tobacco smoke, whiskey breaths and other stenches mixed up with effluvia from the stables, and the miasmas of the canal, which the theatre is exactly placed and constructed to receive.'[3]

"Senator Gouverneur Morris may have described Washington best when he said, 'All we lack here are good houses, wine cellars, decent food, learned men, attractive women and other such trifles to make our city perfect in the future.'"[4] Harvie's features turn sullen. The President falls silent.

"When I accepted the position as your personal secretary you told me that my principal responsibility would be as your liaison with Congress and to maintain communications between your office and Congress, and occasional conferences.[5] I started as your secretary last month and since Congress is now in recess, I'm at a loss for what I'm to do. To make matters worse you will leave Washington and be at Monticello for August and September and . . ."

"That is true, Lewis. I take two vacations a year to Monticello, a short one in early spring and, because of the capital's stifling heat and humidity, a longer one in late July or early August that normally extends through September.

"Before you accepted the position as my secretary you told me that you wished to pursue your law studies in your free time, and I assured you that you could continue your studies. You will have extra time for study. I will also confer with Secretary of State Madison and other members of my cabinet about utilizing your availability during my absence."

"I think it might be helpful to advise Lewis on what he might expect during the social season and your heavy commitment to dinner parties," Meriwether Lewis says.

Jefferson nods, "I have tried to ease the pain of Washington's ennui by accepting the social leadership expected of me by turning the White House into an interesting social center. There are two dining rooms. The large formal dining room in the northwest corner is used sparingly for the few large dinners and usually when ladies dine, and for public receptions on New Year's Day and the Fourth of July, which we will celebrate tomorrow.

"My favorite place for dining is in this room. The dinners are usually stag and limited to twelve or fewer guests. You will note that the dining table is oval and intended to eliminate any perception of rank. There is never assigned seating.

"The principle with us as well as our political constitution is equal rights of all, and if there be an occasion where equality ought to prevail preeminently, it is in social circles collected for conviviality. Nobody shall be above you, nor you above anybody, pele-mele is our law."[6]

Captain Lewis interjects, "The President's hospitality is extended to political friend and enemy. The two political parties are generally not mixed but entertained separately. In this regard he prepares lists of those members he wants to entertain four times, three times, twice, and only once."

"On what basis are some members invited four times and others just once?" Harvie asks.

"The intension is to bring together people who are compatible and generally foster good conversation and friendship. Although politics are not discussed at the dinner table, it has served as an effective way for members of Congress to get to know me and for me to get to know them, and it promotes opportunities for the explanation of circumstances, which, if not understood might produce jealousies and suspicions injurious to the public interest."[7]

"Washington is a community starved for social amenities and the President's dinners are 'mandatory for all who do not choose to live like bears.'[8] President Jefferson has developed the art of meeting informally with his political friends and foes over good food and fine wines, never talking politics, but dropping a hint here and there of how he feels on a subject," Meriwether Lewis says.

Harvie reflects on Lewis's comment, "A form of legislative lobbying?"

"Or you could say that more power rests in private conversation than in public debate."[9]

"Especially when combined with the President's personality," Harvie adds.

"Yes. President Jefferson seldom dines alone, and an important part of your job will be to see that these dinners come together and function in complete harmony."

"And of course you are invited to dine with me every evening you are in Washington," the President says. "One of my greatest pleasures is the 'easy flow of after dinner conversation,' and wine and the three laws of my table are the essential ingredients for spirited conversation."

"What are the three laws of your table?"

"No healths (toasts), no politics, no restraint."

"Is dinner always at three-thirty?"

"The invitation requests the favor of the guest's company at half after three o'clock but dinner is not served until four o'clock," Captain

Lewis says. "Incidentally, the invitation to dinner is from Thomas Jefferson and not the President of the United States."

Harvie's eyebrows arch, "Why is that?"

"It is intended to be the invitation of a private gentleman. In that way the President need not feel any obligation to invite all members of Congress, and particularly members who abuse him in speeches in Congress, as some do."[10]

"Is it Monsieur Lemaire's responsibility to procure the necessary dinner foods, or do I share that responsibility?"

"That is not your responsibility. It is taken care of by the President's efficient maître d'hôtel. Lemaire shops daily the Georgetown markets for produce, meats, eggs and vegetables including lettuce, asparagus, peas, tomatoes, squash, eggplant, shad, sturgeon, rockfish, oysters, wild game, venison, duck, pigeon, squirrel, poultry, and a variety of fruits, including local currants, strawberries and watermelons."[11]

"Who is responsible selecting what dishes are served?"

"Lemaire in conjunction with French chef, Honoré Julien. A typical dinner might include rice, soup, round of beef, turkey, mutton, ham, loin of veal, cutlets of mutton, fried eggs, fried beef, macaroni, and a great variety of fruits and desserts."[12]

"I select the wines," the President says. "As agreed, you will be paid from my private funds the same as Captain Lewis, $500. I promised Captain Lewis that if he agreed to be my secretary he would know and be known to characters of influence in the affairs of our country and give him the advantage of their wisdom. You will have those same privileges and opportunities."

"As a guest at Mr. Jefferson's table I have met the most accomplished and elegant society that has been anywhere, at any time."[13]

"Other than the servants and some of my family members, Captain Lewis and I have been the only residents living in the White House, rattling around like 'two mice in a church.' For the past two years we have worked and dined together on a daily basis. Consequentially, we have had a lot of time to talk about our ambitions and dreams. Captain Lewis has agreed to fulfill a dream that I've entertained for nearly thirty years. He and his friend, William Clark, will lead an expedition across our continent to the Pacific Ocean."

"Is the expedition a secret?"

"For a while it was but only in the sense that until recently Captain Lewis and I kept the details of our discussions to ourselves. At the beginning of this year I told key Congressmen about our plans and their response was positive. In February Congress provided funds for the expedition, and in the spring Captain Lewis traveled to Philadelphia and studied under some of our leading scientists." The President nods in the direction of Lewis.

"Andrew Elliott taught me map making. The President's friend Benjamin Rush instructed me in medicine. I was tutored in botany by Benjamin Smith Barton and by Casper Wistar in anatomy and fossils. I received math lessons from Robert Patterson."[14]

"Have you really dreamed of exploring the American west for nearly thirty years?" a wide-eyed Harvie asks.

"More than just dreamed about it," the President says solemnly. "Shortly after the Revolutionary War, I asked General George Rogers Clark, the elder brother of William Clark, if he would lead a party in exploring the territory between the Mississippi River and the Pacific Ocean. General Clark declined, so my interest in exploring this vast, unknown territory was put on hold until I met John Ledyard in Paris."[15]

"Who is John Ledyard?"

"He was an American explorer, navigator, soldier of fortune and the greatest walker I've ever known. Broke and living about twelve miles outside of Paris in St. Germain-en-Laye, he was a frequent guest at my dinner table. One evening over wine Ledyard learned of my desire to have the American west explored. He immediately volunteered to explore the western part of our continent and walk from the Pacific Ocean across the continent to Virginia."

"How did he intend to do that?"

"By walking from Paris to Stockholm, on to St. Petersburg, across Siberia to Kamchatka, procuring passage thence in some of the Russian vessels to Nootka Sound, whence he might make his way across the continent to America."

"Are you saying Ledyard planned to walk around the world?" the new young secretary says, shaking his head as though he wants to clear it of what he has heard. "That's preposterous."

"Not for Ledyard. He got within 600 miles of his Russian goal, and would have made it to the American continent had not the Empress had him arrested and expelled from Russia." Jefferson shakes his head sadly.[16]

"What happened to Ledyard?" Meriwether Lewis asks.

"He died while waiting to walk across Africa. I received a copy of a letter Ledyard wrote his mother shortly before his death in which he unwittingly wrote his epitaph, 'Born in obscure little Groton, formed by nature and education . . . behold me the greatest traveler in history, eccentric, irregular, rapid, unaccountable, curious, and without vanity, majestic as a comet. I afford a new character to the world, and a new subject to biography."

Jefferson stares ahead for a long moment, "John Ledyard, was a romanticist of extraordinary determination, fearless courage, uncompromising honesty, and incredible strength of character." He shakes his head sadly.

"Three years after I returned from France, and while serving as secretary of state, I got the American Philosophical Society interested in the exploration of our west. We undertook a subscription to engage the famous French botanist and explorer Andre Michaux to lead an expedition to the Pacific, and we were successful in raising the money. My instructions to Michaux included that he 'take notice of the country you go through, its general face, soil, rivers, mountains, its productions of animal, vegetable and mineral so far as they may be new to us and also may be useful; the latitude of places, the names, numbers, and dwellings of the inhabitants, and such particulars as you can learn of them.'"[17]

"What happened to the Michaux expedition?" Harvie asks.

The President's lips draw tight. "Michaux got started in June 1793, but the expedition was aborted when we learned that Michaux was a

French agent whose chief goal was to liberate Louisiana from Spanish rule by a joint attack by a French naval force and American volunteers he was to raise in Kentucky.[18] But now I have the right man for the task.

"For the past 27 months Captain Lewis and I have dined together every evening that we were in Washington. Our dinner conversations ranged from the exquisite taste of his mother's smoked hams to paleontology, mathematics, anatomy, physics, mechanics, astronomy, meteorology, architecture, botany, gardening, and, of course, wine. But our conversations never strayed far from one overriding subject—the exploration of our western country.

"From the beginning Captain Lewis was an enthusiastic recruit. With his knowledge of the west and Indian dialects, his innate intelligence, and courage, he is the perfect candidate to lead the expedition. Yet he accepted on condition that his friend William Clark be elevated to the rank of captain and given co-equal authority. I, of course, acceded to his wish, and that is how this western expedition was born."

"What is the mission of the expedition?" Harvie asks.

"There are multiple missions and I will provided Captain Lewis with specific written instructions. But generally speaking the most important objectives are to find the best water route to the Pacific, return with unknown species of plants and animals and related information, record the geography of this vast territory, and learn the ways of living of Indian tribes and explore trade possibilities with them."

President Jefferson takes a sip of wine. "Tomorrow is the Fourth of July, the only birthday I commemorate.[19] The executive mansion will be open to the public and the U.S. Marine Band will play patriotic and spirited music in celebration of this historic day. At some point during the celebration I will announce the purchase of the entire Louisiana territory and the Lewis and Clark expedition."[20]

Captain Lewis and Lewis Harvie stand transfixed in stunned silence. Finally, Meriwether Lewis says, "That is fantastic! An incredible accomplishment that without firing one shot doubles the size of the United States. Congratulations, Mr. President."

"Congratulations!" Harvie says.

"Thank you. When I learned that James Monroe and Robert Livingston had signed the treaty with France purchasing 'all Louisiana,' I told my son-in-law that the acquisition removes from us the greatest source of danger to our peace."[21]

Lemaire enters and announces that dinner is ready. The President and his two young secretaries take their places at the oval dinner table. The first course consists of a choice of bean or beef soup, fresh rockfish from the Potomac, braised leg of mutton, and roast wild canvasback duck. As Jefferson carves the duck, he says, "Lewis, you are in for a special treat. No one prepares duck better than my French chef, Honoré Julian. I hope you enjoy vegetables for as you can see there are a variety of them including peas, spinach and squash fresh from the Georgetown market stalls."[22]

The dessert offering is pound cake, ice cream in a puff pastry, and an assortment of cheeses. When the dessert dishes are taken away the cloth is removed and Lemaire enters carrying two decanters of wine– a red and a white. He places them beside the President who pours the white wine, passes the glasses and says, "This is Sauternes from the Bordeaux region of France. I liked it and purchased 540 bottles from my Philadelphia wine merchant friend, Henry Sheaff." Jefferson waits until his two young friends have tasted the wine.[23] "Do you like the wine?"

"Yes," Lewis Harvie says, "It is a very nice sweet wine."

Captain Lewis nods his head in approval. He has been very quiet. "I will miss such pleasures on my western journey."

The new secretary says, "Your expedition will take you into the unknown. Aren't you afraid?"

"Captain Lewis is a man of courage undaunted," the President says. "Now, let me tell you about this red wine ..."

The Ambassador's Wife – A Virago

After a stormy crossing, the British Ambassador Anthony Merry and his recently married, rich, large, somewhat masculine, and pretentious wife arrive on the shores of the Potomac with a coterie of servants and an armada of baggage. Humorless, plain in appearance, and called rather inferior in understanding, Merry will not live up to his name.[1]

The ambassador's immediate welcome to the raw new capital is one of outrage–suitable housing is lacking. The only housing he can secure is two "mere shells of houses with bare walls and without fixtures of any kind, even without a pump or well." He laments, "So miserable is our situation."[2]

This is just the first adverse trial that awaits the new diplomat. Three days after his arrival Merry, dressed in full regalia and accompanied by Secretary of State James Madison, calls on President Jefferson at the White House to present his diplomatic credentials.

His reception is not what he expects. "I found myself introduced to a man as President of the United States, not merely in an undress, but actually standing in slippers down at the heels … both pantaloons, coat, and under-clothes indicative of utter slovenliness and indifference of appearance, and in a state of negligence actually studied."[3]

The next day Ambassador Merry tells Madison that the President's attire was a deliberate charade prepared and intended as an insult to him personally and "to the sovereign I represent." Madison assures Merry that the President received the Danish chargé in similar attire. Merry's response is to call the Dane "a diplomat of the third rank."

The Secretary of the British Legation, Augustus Foster's opinion of the President is less severe. He describes Jefferson as "a tall man, with a very red freckled face, and gray neglected hair; his manners good-natured, frank, and rather friendly, though he had somewhat of a cynical expression of countenance. He wore a blue coat, a thick gray-colored hairy waistcoat, with a red under-waistcoat lapped over it, green velveteen breeches with pearl buttons, yarn stockings, and slippers down at the heels, his appearance being very much like that of a tall, large-boned farmer."

Madison reports Merry's attitude, temperament, and remarks to Jefferson. Three days later Ambassador Merry and his wife receive a dinner invitation to the White House. Believing the dinner is in their honor, Ambassador and Elizabeth Merry accept the presidential invitation.[4]

Setting: White House, December 2, 1803

Ambassador Anthony Merry, 47, and wife, Elizabeth, arrive at 3:30 and are escorted to the drawing-room by a servant in exquisite livery. Also gathered in the drawing room are the Spanish Ambassador Marquis Yjuro and his beautiful American wife, Sally McKean, James and Dolley Madison, Secretary of the Treasury Henry Gallatin and wife, Hannah, French chargé d'affaires Louis André Pichon and his wife, and an assortment of congressmen.

Promptly at four o'clock the White House head steward Etienne Lemaire announces dinner. President Jefferson wearing a plain black suit enters and approaches the ladies. To the surprise of everyone he offers his arm to Dolley Madison and escorts her to the dining room and seats her on his right.

Ambassador Merry is speechless. The President's failure to escort Mrs. Merry, the lady of honor, is a flagrant breach of diplomatic etiquette. James Madison, sensing the Merrys' consternation, offers his hand to Mrs. Merry, which she reluctantly accepts. He places her next to the Spanish ambassador who is seated next to Mrs. Madison.

As the guests enter the dining room and begin taking their seats, it finally occurs to Merry that there is no assigned seating at the President's table. Seeing a vacant chair next to the wife of the Spanish ambassador, he heads for it. Just as he is about to sit down a congressman nudges him aside and takes the seat "without Mr. Jefferson using any means to prevent it, or taking any care that I might be otherwise placed."[5]

He looks around. Everyone is seated. He takes the last available place at the far end of the table. Seething with resentment, he looks across the room and sees the French chargé d'affaires, Louis André Pichon, seated near the President. His blood pressure soars. England and France are at war, and it is a well-established unwritten rule that diplomats from countries at war are never invited to the same event. *Another deliberate act*, he thinks. *Jefferson is an experienced diplomat. He knows not to do this. Why is he so egregiously insulting me, my wife, and my country?*

Dolley Madison is her usual vivacious self. Patting the President's right hand she says with a sheepish grin, "I have heard it said, Mr. President, that Benjamin Franklin had a talisman that caused women to fall in love with him. Is it true?"

The President pushes back in his chair and lets out a hearty laugh, "Yes, Dolley, it is true. So far as I can remember he captivated every woman he ever met. When Dr. Franklin left France for home, I came to see him off. It seemed as if the village had lost its patriarch. His two favorite lady-friends, Madame Brillon and Madame Helvétius, begged him to stay and spend his remaining years with them.[6]

"The ladies smothered him with embraces, and when he introduced me as his successor, I told him I wished he would transfer his lady privileges to me and tell me his secret. At this time Dr. Franklin's gout was so bad that he had great difficulty walking. He was lying on a litter, and he motioned with his hand for me to lean down, which I did. He cupped his hands and whispered, 'You are too young to know.'"[7] Dolley bursts into laughter.

"I know you were sorry to see Dr. Franklin leave, but did your appointment to replace him please you?" she asks.

"I was very pleased with my appointment, but when I'm asked whether I replaced Dr. Franklin, I always reply, 'No one can replace Dr. Franklin, I am merely his successor.'"

The dinner is being held in the large dining room and the food is brought in via a revolving door with shelves on which the food is placed. Servants in white and red livery then bring the food to the table. The first course is soup, mutton chops at the head of the table, loin of veal at the foot, sausages with a rich onion sauce, fowls with oyster sauce, and for vegetables, cabbage, turnips, carrots, and pickles.[8]

Elizabeth Merry sits solemn and distraught. As the food passes around, Dolley becomes aware that she has not said a word since taking her place at the table. In an effort to bring her into the conversation, Dolley says, "Elizabeth, I hope you are enjoying this wonderful meal."

The ambassador's wife levels her gaze at Dolley and says haughtily, "It is more like a harvest-home supper than the entertainment of the President of the United States."

The comment surprises Dolley. She takes a deep breath to control her rising anger, and after a brief moment says, "You will find in America that an abundance of good food is better than a little fancy food."[9]

The second or dessert course consists of stewed apples, jelly and a variety of cakes. When the dessert dishes are cleared, the table cloth is removed and wine is served along with oranges, walnuts, prunes, figs, pecans, raisins, butter and cheese.

Everyone in the room is aware of the President's slight of the British ambassador and his wife. Discretely Dolley mentions to President Jefferson that Ambassador Merry and his wife seem upset.

Jefferson's brow furrows and he pushes back in his chair. "They deserve to be upset. Their arrogant behavior since arriving in Washington just one week ago has caused me to rethink our diplomatic etiquette. Merry and the Spanish ambassador believe they are superior in rank and preference to all in Washington. They expect to be taken into dinner ahead of everyone else and placed at the head of the table.[10]

"Their kind of arrogance has no place at a dinner table. At my dinners and receptions all will be treated equally. The principle with us, as well as our political constitution, is the equal rights of all, and if there be an occasion where this equality ought to prevail preeminently, it is in social circles collected for conviviality. Nobody shall be above you, nor you above anybody, pele-mele is our law." His face breaks into a broad smile and he raises his wine glass. "Does this Madeira measure up to what you drink at home?"[11]

Anthony Merry, the son of a London wine merchant, is so distraught that he does not stay for wine. He and his wife leave early, but his dinner rage does not subside. He reports the incident to his superiors in London saying that the President's insulting treatment of he and his wife reflects his hostility to Great Britain and a preference for France.

Merry seeks out and fills the ears of Federalist senators and congressman with his hatred of the President. During his remaining two and an half years in Washington, Ambassador Anthony Merry and his wife never again accept a presidential dinner invitation.[12]

Setting: The White House, March 5, 1805

Present are Thomas Jefferson, 61, Commodore Edward Preble, 43, Jefferson's personal secretary, William Armistead Burwell, 25, and Secretary of State James Madison, and wife Dolley, Secretary of the Treasury Albert Gallatin, and wife Hannah, Secretary of War Henry Dearborn, and wife Dorcas, Attorney General Levi Lincoln, and wife Martha, Secretary of the Navy Robert Smith, and wife Margaret.

When William Burwell, the President's personal secretary, enters the large dining room located on the northeast corner of the White House, President Jefferson and guests are seated. The President is in conversation with a uniformed naval officer on his right. He is Commodore Edward Preble. Burwell takes his place at the far end of the table.

The President, known for his casual and sometimes even sloppy attire, has made an exception on this day. His red hair, heavily streaked with gray, is powdered, cut short and curled at the hairline.[1] He is wearing a dark pepper-and-salt waist coat, knee-breeches, gray-worsted stockings, and shoes fastened with metal buckles.[2]

The President stands. "Thank you for attending this special dinner in honor of a great naval hero, Commodore Edward Preble. Two days ago Congress approved a resolution authorizing the striking of a gold medal honoring Commodore Preble who commanded the third squadron naval force in attacks against the Barbary pirates at Tripoli last year. The medal is in recognition of 'gallantry and good conduct' of himself and his squadron at Tripoli. Commodore Preble, on behalf of Congress and a grateful nation, we thank you!"[3] Applause spreads around the room.

"I also thank Commodore Preble for a gift of a hogshead of Marsala wine he purchased in Madrid, which I will share with the commodore and my distinguished guests when the cloth is removed.[4] A larger gift from the commodore was his attendance yesterday at my second inauguration."

"I'm sorry, Mr. President, but I'm not entirely familiar with the commodore's valor at Tripoli, and I would like to know more about it," Hannah Gallatin says from the far end of the table.

"I too would like to hear more details," Martha Lincoln says.

"I see an explanation is necessary. Soon after the United States gained its independence, pirates from the Barbary States on the coast of North Africa—Algiers, Morocco, Tunis and Tripoli, all Muslim states—constantly raided our merchant ships and not only stole the cargoes and the ships but also enslaved the crews and held them for ransom. In a letter to James Monroe more than twenty years ago, I suggested that we send half a dozen frigates under the command of John Paul Jones to the Mediterranean to destroy the pirates and their ships.[5]

"When I visited John Adams in England in the spring of 1786, we attempted to negotiate a peace with the Tripolian ambassador. The price he demanded for peace, however, was too high. When Adams and I asked him under what authority his country was carrying out these criminal acts, he said it was 'founded on the laws of their prophet, that it was written in their Koran, that all nations who should not have acknowledged their authority were sinners, that it was their right and duty to make war upon them wherever they could be found, and to make slaves of all they could take as prisoners, and every Muslim who should be slain in battle was sure to go to paradise.'[6]

"I came away convinced that the best solution to the Barbary Pirates' menace was war, and I expressed that opinion in a letter to John Adams a few months later. I was of the opinion that John Paul Jones with half a dozen frigates would totally destroy their commerce. In fact, while in Paris, I tried to form an international concert of nations to war against these pirate states. My efforts failed because most nations, including the United States, found it easier to pay tribute.[7]

"When I became President I did what I thought should have been done twenty years earlier. The pasha of Tripoli, Yusuf Karamanli, issued an edict demanding the United States pay increased tribute to him or he would declare war on us. When I refused to pay tribute, he declared war on the United States. I saw but one answer to the pasha's jingoism. I took it on myself to send a squadron of frigates into the Mediterranean under the command of Commodore Edward Preble with instructions to cruise their waters and cut them to pieces."

"I left for that mission on August 14, 1803," Commodore Preble says. "The situation became more complicated when our frigate the *Philadelphia* under the command of Captain Bainbridge ran aground on an uncharted reef just outside the Tripoli harbor. Karamanli showed his defiance by boarding the *Philadelphia*, capturing and imprisoning Captain William Bainbridge and his crew of more than three hundred men, and demanding a ransom of three million dollars for their release. They then moored the Philadelphia in the bay of Tripoli and turned its forty mounted cannons on us."[8]

"What did you do?"

Commodore Preble thinks for a moment. "We devised a plan to burn the *Philadelphia*. We knew the Philadelphia was unseaworthy and I ordered her destruction by burning her. In my instructions to Lieutenant Stephen Decatur I said, 'The destruction of the Philadelphia is an object of great importance. Be sure to set fire in the gun room berths, cockpit, store rooms forward, and berths on the berth deck. After the ship is well on fire, point two of the eighteen pounders down the main hatch, and blow her bottom out.' All of the men on the mission were to be volunteers."[9]

"Was there any problem in getting volunteers for the mission?" Burwell asks, wondering if he would have volunteered had he been aboard.

An odd sound interrupts the conversation. The noise emanates from the large door-size dumbwaiter turning into the room with the first course. The conversation continues as servants bring to the table soup, mutton at the head with a rich stuffing, beef steaks at the foot, fish, fowls, potatoes, rice, spinach, eggs, pickles and salad.[10]

"When Decatur told the crew the mission he was about to undertake and asked for volunteers, 'Every officer, man, and boy came forward in a body.'"[11]

"On February 16, Lieutenant Steven Decatur and 75 volunteers under the cover of darkness sailed into the Tripoli harbor. His ship was made to look like a merchant vessel. The boarding party was divided into groups with specific tasks. As they approached the *Philadelphia* they called out in Arabic that they had lost their anchors, needed repairs, and gained permission to tie up next to the *Philadelphia*. They caught the Tripolitans by complete surprise and killed or captured those aboard without the loss of a single American life.[12]

"Lord Nelson of the British navy called the burning of the *Philadelphia* 'the most bold and daring act of the age.' We didn't stop there but carried out four additional attacks on the city of Tripoli and its harbor. Six months later Stephen Decatur and his men returned, boarded the anchored Tripolitan fleet, and in hand-to-hand combat defeated them, and captured three enemy gunboats."[13]

"Marvelous!" exclaims Dorcas Dearborn.

"The war doesn't end there," the President says with enthusiasm. "Some months later Captain William Eaton led a land force of Marines and foreign mercenaries 700 miles across the Libyan Desert and, in a surprise attack on Tripoli's second city, Derna, captured it. These victories, together with our continued assaults on their cities and harbors will, I believe, eventually bring these pirates to the peace table. I should add the pasha's attacks on our merchant ships caused me to rethink the need for a well-equipped navy, and Secretary of the Navy Smith and I have taken action to increase the size and effectiveness of our navy."[14]

"What happened to Captain Bainbridge and the 300 crew members of the *Philadelphia*?" Burwell asks.

"We paid $60,000 for the release of Captain Bainbridge and his crew, far less than the $3,000,000 originally demanded."

The cloth has been removed and the wines are circulating.

"What is the name of this wine and where is it from?" Burwell asks.

"It is one of my favorite red Bordeaux, Madame Rozan's, from the commune of Margaux.[15] But wait. I suggest that we first drink the Marsala that Commodore Preble brought from Madrid."

"I have never drunk Marsala. Please tell us something about it," Margaret Smith says.

"Yes, and what on earth is a hogshead?" Dorcas Dearborn calls out.

The President chuckles, "Good question Dorcas. A hogshead is a wooden cask in which wine is shipped. The actual capacity varies somewhere between 54 to 60 gallons depending on the particular wine region. Does everyone have a glass of Marsala?" Heads nod around the table. Jefferson sips the Marsala. "It reminds me of Sherry, or perhaps Madeira."

Madison, a connoisseur of Madeira, says, "This wine is nice but I would never confuse it with a fine Madeira."

"All I'm saying is there is an affinity to Madeira and Sherry. Perhaps that is because like Sherry and Madeira, Marsala has been strengthened with brandy."

"Is Marsala made in the same wine region as Sherry?" someone asks.

"No, it is produced on the Island of Sicily."

"It is confusing," Dolley Madison says. "I like the Marsala, and I thank Commodore Preble for presenting it as a gift, and I thank President Jefferson for sharing it.

Setting: The White House. December 9, 1805

Present are President Jefferson, 62, the Tunisian Ambassador, Sidi Soliman Mellimelli, about 50, his two secretaries, the President's daughter Martha Jefferson Randolph, 33, the President's granddaughter Anne Cary Randolph, 14, Congressman Thomas Mann Randolph, 37, Congressman John Wayles Eppes, 32, Isaac Coles, 25, Senator John Quincy Adams, 38, Congressman John Randolph, 32, Congressman Joseph Hooper Nicholson, 35, Senator Samuel Smith, 53, Congressman John Dawson, 43, Senator George Logan, 52, Senator Samuel L. Mitchill, 41.

President Jefferson explains to Anne Cary Randolph, his 14 year old granddaughter, the reason the dinner time has been changed from the customary time of 'half after three o'clock' to sundown is because "it being Ramadan our Muslim visitors fast while the sun is above the horizon. I changed the dinner time in respect to the religion of our guest of honor, the Tunisian Ambassador, Sidi Soliman Mellimelli."[1]

"Oh, I wasn't aware that the Tunisian Ambassador is here in the United States," Anne says.

"Yes, he arrived ten days ago for a six month visit."

"What is the purpose of his visit?" she asks.

"It involves a piracy dispute. Tunisian ships tried to run through our naval blockade of Tripoli harbor and our warship the *USS Constitution* captured several of them. The Bey of Tunis, he is like their president, threatened us with war, but on further thought he decided to send an ambassador to negotiate retribution and tribute."

"What have you decided?" Anne's mother and the President's daughter Martha says.

"No tribute. My opposition to paying these pirate states tribute goes back twenty years to my days as minister to France. The pasha of Tripoli's demands for tribute is why I sent Commodore Preble and a fleet of frigates to the Mediterranean with instructions to 'cruise their waters and cut them to pieces,' and that is what our navy did. It brought that belligerent nation to the peace table. As for restitution, perhaps something can be worked out."[2]

"What do you have in mind?" Martha says.

"Mellimelli arrived with eleven assistants. They will be our guests for about six months, so their stay will be expensive. If we sell the four horses and other gifts the Bey sent, it will help cover their expenses while they are here."[3]

Anne looks around. The room is filled with unfamiliar faces. Her grandfather sees the uncertainty on her face. "Let me acquaint you with the guests. The young man your dad and Uncle John are talking with is my personal secretary, Isaac Coles." The president's eyes sweep the room.

"The balding gentleman talking to the gentleman in the blue coat looks familiar," Anna says.

"And for good reason; you have met him before," the President says with a chuckle. "He looks like his father. It is Senator John Quincy Adams. The gentleman he is talking with is Senator Dr. George Logan, 'the best farmer in Pennsylvania, both in theory and practice.'"[4]

Jefferson would be amused if he could hear what John Quincy Adams is telling Senator Logan. "It is always a delight to be invited here. Not just for the food, wines and camaraderie but to hear the outlandish stories the President tells," Adams says.

"Really? Can you give me some examples?" Logan says.

"Well, there is the startling one about his time in Paris when the thermometer did not rise above twenty degrees below zero for six weeks."[5]

Logan's eyebrows arch. "Another memorable Jefferson tale concerns preparations for his trip to France in 1784. Before he sailed he said 'he had some ripe pears that he sewed up in tow bags.' When he returned five years later he found them in a perfect state of preservation—self-candied."[6]

Logan gives Adams a questioning look. "You actually heard the President say that?"

"Yes. Sometimes he has strange, even unexpected guests." Logan looks at Adams, his eyes wide in anticipation. "I heard this story from a reliable source. It's about a congressman whose occupation is that of butcher. One evening at the President's table when he was served what he called 'a miserable lean' leg of mutton, he was heard to say, 'at my stall no such leg of mutton should ever have found a place.'"

"I assume that remark ended his White House dinner visits."

"No, on his next visit the congressman approached President Jefferson and said that he had heard that one of the guests had taken ill so he brought along his young butcher son knowing there would be a spare plate . . ."[7]

Jefferson continues identifying the dinner guests for his granddaughter, "Now, moving around the room from left to right we see the irascible Virginia Congressman John Randolph. One of his well-known quotes will give insight into his personality. He proudly said, 'I am an aristocrat. I love liberty. I hate equality.'" Jefferson's eyebrows lift and he rolls his eyes as if to say, *need I say more.*

"The gentleman Randolph is talking to is Joseph Hopper Nicholson, a congressman from Maryland and a true democrat-republican. Nicholson saved the presidency for me."

"How?"

"In February 1801, the House of Representatives were locked in a struggle to determine whether former vice-president Aaron Burr or I would become president. Congressman Nicholson was extremely ill, but he insisted on being carried into the capitol building on a litter where he stayed throughout the balloting, casting his vote for me and locking the Maryland delegates in a tie. Eventually Maryland swung in my favor and on the 36th ballot I was elected president. You and I would not be here today if Congressman Nicholson had not placed his life in jeopardy to vote for me."[8]

Continuing with the identification of guests Jefferson says, "The gentleman on the right of Randolph is Senator Samuel Smith, the brother of my secretary of the Navy, Robert Smith. Congressman John Dawson, also from Virginia, is next, and he is standing beside

Senator Dr. Samuel L. Mitchill of New York, a man of extraordinary learning and knowledge."

Such a remark coming from her erudite grandfather is high praise indeed. Young Anne studies Senator Mitchill. He is about five feet ten inches tall, neither slim nor stout but sturdy in physical stature with gray eyes. "You do mean the gentleman dressed in the blue coat, buff-colored vest, and shoes with buckles?"

Jefferson smiles, "Yes. Doctor Mitchill is a man of multifarious pursuits. He received his medical degree from the University of Edinburgh and set up practice in New York. At some point during his medical career he studied law and became a practicing lawyer. Then, about twelve years ago, his main interests turned to science and he acquired a depth of scientific knowledge that allows him to teach geology, mineralogy, zoology, ichthyology, botany, theology, and a variety of other subjects. Oh, I almost forgot, he is also a poet. He is acknowledged to be our most learned congressman. Even the captious John Randolph calls him the congressional library."[9]

Mitchill, a seasoned and appreciative guest at the President's table, tells Congressman Dawson, "I always like coming here. The dinners are 'neat and plentiful, and no healths are drunk, nor are any toasts or sentiments given after dinner. You drink as you please and converse at your ease.'"[10]

Minutes before sunset, portly Etienne Lemaire, the White House maître d'hôtel, enters the drawing-room. Normally he would call everyone to dinner but he realizes that the guest of honor has not arrived. He checks with the President who advises him dinner cannot not be served until Ambassador Mellimelli arrives.

A half hour later Mellimelli, accompanied by two secretaries and a servant bearing a four-foot tobacco pipe, sweeps into the drawing-room. In appearance and dress he is different looking. He is tall with a flowing black beard and dressed in baggy purple pantaloons under a scarlet jacket with embroidery of gold, and a richly trimmed purple robe. His head is covered with twenty yards of fine white muslin coiled into a turban, and he wears bright yellow silk Morocco shoes.

By contrast President Jefferson is wearing a blue coat, a red waistcoat, green velveteen breeches with pearl buttons, yarn stockings and shoes with buckles.[11]

After paying his respects to the President, Mellimelli proposes that he retire and smoke his pipe. President Jefferson requests him to smoke in the drawing-room. The Tunisian ambassador pulls up a chair, lights his enormous pipe and proceeds to smoke "taking at the same time snuff deeply scented with otto of roses" from a diamond snuffbox.[12]

When Mellimelli finishes smoking the President and guests go to dinner in the large Public Dining Room. Mellimelli takes his place on the right of the president with Dr. George Davis, former American chargé at Tunis, acting as interpreter. The ambassador's two secretaries sit between the President's secretary, Isaac Coles, at the far end of the long rectangular table. The President nods in the direction of Lemaire who announces that dinner is served.[13]

Within minutes of the guests being seated a large dumbwaiter in the form of a revolving serving door turns into the room loaded with the first course of soup, beef bouilli at the head, leg of mutton at the foot, ducks, partridges, cabbage, spinach, potatoes, beans, and salad.[14,15.]

John Dawson, seated on Adams's right says, "I've seen that big dumbwaiter in action before, but it still surprises me when it pops into the room. I wonder where the food is prepared?"

"In the basement on a large coal burning stove. The chef is a Frenchman by the name of Honoré Julian," Adams says.

For dessert President Jefferson's guests have a choice of an omelet, apples a la francaise and jelly cake.

When the dessert course is finished, the tablecloth is removed and the dumbwaiter again swings into the room carrying a variety of nuts, oranges, cheese, butter and crackers. Wine is served for the first time, and President Jefferson provides a buffet of wines including Champagne, Montepulciano (a light red wine from Tuscany), Madeira, and Sherry.[16]

During dinner Ambassador Mellimelli appears to enjoy his meal although he doesn't comment on the cookery. He drinks only coffee.

At the far end of the table, however, the President's secretary is pouring wine into silver goblets placed in front of the ambassador's two secretaries. When Mellimelli is not looking, the secretaries drink the wine.

Senator Mitchill, sitting two chairs to the left of the President, says, "I especially like the red wine. Is it French?"

Jefferson smiles, "Yes and no. If I didn't know what the wine is, I would say it's a Burgundy from Volnay. It has a light bright color, a perfumed bouquet, cherry flavor, and light tannins, characteristics that I associate with the wines of Volnay. Have you been to Burgundy?"

"When I studied medicine at the University of Edinburgh I made a trip to Paris but not Burgundy."

"The wines of Burgundy are exquisite, especially the wines of Volnay. During my five years in France, Volnay became my favorite Burgundy red wine. But the wine we are drinking is not French. It is Italian and comes from the Tuscan region of Montepulciano. I am told that vast amounts of mediocre wines are sold under the name of Montepulciano. I order mine through Thomas Appleton, the American Consul in Leghorn. He is a good judge of Tuscan wines and selects my Montepulciano from 'a particular very best crop of it known to him.' This wine is 'produced on the grounds formerly belonging to the order of the Jesuits whose property was sold for the benefit of the government in 1793.' I consider it in body and taste the equal of the best Burgundy."[17]

Sipping his wine thoughtfully he adds, "I received this wine a month ago in a shipment of 473 bottles. I always have it bottled with the corks well cemented. When shipped in flask, much of it spoils."[18]

"I've notice that Ambassador Mellimelli does not drink wine," Mitchill says.

"As you know the Muslim religion does not allow the drinking of alcohol although..." The President smiles and nods toward the ambassador's secretaries at the far end of the table. "I'm also told the ambassador scrupulously observes fasting and prayer. On the other hand Secretary of State Madison informs me that because the ambassador is traveling without his harem, he has requested that concubines be sent to his hotel room."[19]

The senator from New York feigns an expression of shock. "How are you going to handle that?"

"I am going to leave that in the capable hands of my secretary of state."

"Without guidance?"

"I might have mentioned to Madison that peace with Tunisia may require passing unnoticed the irregular conduct of their ministers."

"What did Secretary Madison say to that?"

There is a twinkle in Mr. Jefferson's eyes, "Madison said he thinks the matter can be taken care of within the *scope of appropriations to foreign intercourse.*[20]

Senator Mitchill chuckles.

The ambassador politely waits until the President's daughter and granddaughter leave the table before excusing himself so that he can smoke. As soon as the Tunisian ambassador leaves, his two secretaries hold their goblets out to Isaac Coles for more wine.[21]

Setting: The White House, April 3, 1807

Present are James Madison, 56, Secretary of State, Henry Dearborn, 56, Secretary of War, Albert Gallatin, 46, Secretary of the Treasury, Robert Smith, 49, Secretary of the Navy, Thomas Jefferson, President of the United States, ten days shy of 64, and Isaac Coles, 27, the President's personal secretary.

Four days earlier Aaron Burr, former Vice-President of the United States, appeared in the U.S. Circuit Court for Virginia in Richmond before John Marshall, Chief Justice of the Supreme Court. At Burr's preliminary hearing, U.S. Attorney General Caesar Rodney and U.S. Attorney George Hay ask the Chief Justice to commit Burr to jail on charges of treason and the misdemeanor of waging war against Spain.

The next day, Chief Justice Marshall rules preliminarily that the evidence does not conclusively show that Burr's alleged treasonable actions had ripened "into the crime itself by levying war against the United States." Marshall does, however, rule that Burr be committed on the misdemeanor charge. Bail is set at $10,000 which Burr posts in the form of friends acting as "securities" bound to pay if he fails to show up at the next session of court in May.[1]

On hearing this news President Jefferson calls an early morning "consultation" meeting with his cabinet to decide what further legal procedures are necessary with regard to the Burr prosecution, and how to handle the failure of the Monroe-Pinckney Treaty with Great Britain to resolve the impressment of seamen issue, concerns he feels that need immediately action. The meeting carries into the afternoon and Jefferson invites his cabinet to stay for dinner.

At dinner the featured dish is a quarter-side of bear. In the center of the table is a ham of bacon, and sausages and cabbages prepared 'in a French way of cooking them,' soup, beef bouilli, turkey, potatoes, rice, spinach, beans, salad, and pickles.[2] Jefferson carves the bear and fills the plates of his guests, a dinner ritual he very much enjoys.

"Is what you are carving what I think it is?" Madison asks.

"What is it that you think I'm carving?" the President says.

"Bear."

Jefferson suppresses a smile. "That is correct. Lemaire purchased it in Georgetown six days ago."

Henry Dearborn says with a chuckle, "Mr. President, I heard a story that at a recent dinner one of your guests had the misfortune of dumping a hot pudding on his head." Jefferson nods solemnly. "How did it happen?"

"Looking back on it, the incident is sort of amusing but at the time it was embarrassing, especially for the Danish chargé d'affaires, Peder Pederson. The special guest at dinner that evening was the South American revolutionary, Francisco de Miranda. His dream is to liberate Latin America from Spanish rule. He came to America to raise money for a war of liberation. I met with him and told him that while our government could not finance such a mission, I would have no objections to his raising private funds.[3]

"During the dessert course the chargé Pederson spread a hot soft pudding on his plate to cool. He dropped his napkin, and in bending down to pick it up, he struck the plate with his head. The plate flipped over and the pudding fell on his bald head. With tears in his eyes he cried out, 'I vis I vere in hell.' I felt very sorry for him."[4]

"As I recall Miranda attempted an invasion of Venezuela soon after visiting Washington?" Secretary Smith says.

"Yes. Eight months after we met with him he led a force of about 500 ashore near the city of Coro but they were repulsed," Madison says. "He was lucky to escape with his life."

"I'm sure you all remember the Tunisian Ambassador Mellimelli," Jefferson says. Everyone nods their heads in recognition of the guest whose servant carried his four foot smoking pipe. "At the time he was visiting Washington, a number of Indian chiefs were also visiting. Mellimelli met with a group of Cherokees and asked them what God they worship. They answered, *The Great Spirit.* He asked them if they believed in Muhammad, Abraham or Jesus Christ. When they said they did not, he asked, 'What prophet do you worship?' When the Cherokee chief said that *The Great Spirit* has no prophet, an outraged

Mellimelli called them 'all vile hereticks.' Soon after, at dinner one evening, Mellimelli asked me how I could prove that American Indians were the descendants of Adam?"[5]

Madison, a large grin on his face, says, "What was your answer?"

"I told him it was difficult."

The dessert course is served and centers around 'a kind of custard with a floating cream on it.' At the bottom of the table is a 'French dish of apples enclosed in a thin toast, and on each side four dishes and three in the middle.' As Jefferson fills and passes the dessert plates, he begins to reminisce about his years in France.

"As events leading to the French revolution began to accelerate two of the most important personalities in France were Necker and Mirabeau. Necker started the evening in high spirits but faded after nine o'clock. Mirabeau, however, started out brooding until the wine 'warmed him into life.' For an hour or two he became the life of the party, pouring out gossip, poetry, and anecdotes, but as the night passed on and the wine 'heated him,' his eyes became dilated, his voice choked, and with his black hair shaking wildly about his face, he would burst into political prophecies. In a more sober moment, Mirabeau suggested to me that if France was to become another America, France would need another Washington, to which I replied: 'Pardon me, Count, but I consider such is the striking originality of your character, you would deign to imitate any man.'"[6] Laughter sweeps the table.

The tablecloth is removed and the third course, or 'wine course', is accompanied by olives, apples, oranges and 'twelve other plates of nuts'. The wines are Madeira, Paccaretta (Pacharetti), Hermitage, Nebouille (Nebbiolo).[7]

The President pours and passes around the red Italian wine and begins another French story. "One afternoon I was talking with Queen Marie Antoinette and she said she had been wondering how it was possible for the people of America to be happy without a court. 'Surely,' she said to me, 'your great deliverer [George Washington] intends to create nobility?' To which I remember replying, 'Your Majesty, the influence of your own is so powerful that it is the general impression that we can do without them.'"[8]

Albert Gallatin sips his wine and says, "I like this wine but it is different."

"In what way is it different?" Jefferson says.

"I don't think I can explain why, but it is."

"I first drank this wine 20 years ago when traveling through Italy. I too found it singular, melding three contradictory characteristics. I thought it 'about as sweet as the silky Madeira, as astringent on the palate as Bordeaux, and as brisk as Champagne.' Still, I found it a pleasing wine and I continue to import it."[9]

"Didn't you bring this wine along on our trip through the Hudson Valley?" Madison asks.

"No, but you've had it before—at my place in Philadelphia."

"When did you and the President travel through the Hudson Valley?" Dearborn asks.

"In the spring of 1791. We spent four weeks walking over battle-grounds, fishing, killing rattlesnakes, shooting squirrels, studying botanical curiosities, and visiting friends—health, recreation and curiosity,"[10] Madison says.

"Don't you remember," Jefferson says to Madison with a chuckle, "hearing that one of Hamilton's political sycophants told him that we 'scouted silently through the country, shunning the gentry, and quarreling with the eatables, nothing good enough for them.'"[11]

Jefferson's cabinet members have been with him virtually from the beginning of his administration and they know that white Hermitage holds a special place in Jefferson's hierarchy of wines; he has been heard to call it "the first wine in the world without a single exception."

With the decanter of Hermitage in his right hand, the President moves around the table filling each guest's glass.

Sipping the wine Madison says to Jefferson, "This wine has that silky quality with a touch of sweetness that you esteem."

The President nods, "By the term silky I do not mean sweet but sweetness in the smallest degree only. Together with Champagne I think white Hermitage is one of the two best wines of France."[12]

Henry Dearborn, a celebrated warrior of the Revolution, says, "Speaking of Champagne, I remember a dinner party at my house when Postmaster General Gideon Granger downed several glasses of Champagne, and Madison gratuitously said that Champagne is 'a most delightful wine when drunk in moderation, but that more than a few glasses always produce a headache the next day." Dearborn pauses and looks at Madison.

Seeing everyone's attention turn to him, Madison says, "I probably said that because it is a fact–too much Champagne produces a headache."

"Then you don't remember Granger's answer. He said, 'This is the perfect time to try the experiment since tomorrow is Sunday and we will have time to recover from its effects.'"[13]

With four wines on the table in front of him, Jefferson says, "Today is Friday and we have finished our work for the week. We too can experiment."

Jefferson in Retirement, Monticello
1809-1826

Jefferson leaves the presidency with a feeling of profound relief. "Never did a prisoner, released from his chains, feel such relief as I shall on shaking off the shackles of power. Nature intended me for the tranquil pursuits of science, by rendering them my supreme delight."[1] He is free to return to Monticello where he will indulge without interruption his interests in family, friends, farming, books, gardening, architecture, and wine.

Throughout his 17 years in retirement Jefferson continues to be involved in the administration and operation of his Monticello estate and his interest in food and wine never lessens. Without his presidential salary, he knows that he cannot maintain his White House staff in retirement. Two of his slaves, Edy and Fanny, were trained under Chef Julian, and in an attempt to maintain the presidential culinary standards, Julian visits Monticello to organize his kitchen and give his "two good girls" additional cooking instructions. Julian spends almost three weeks at Monticello but in the end Jefferson's attempts to replicate French cooking without a French chef fall short of his hopes for he tells a friend, "I envy Dr. Franklin's French friend M. Chaumont nothing but his French cook and cuisine. These are luxuries which can neither be forgotten nor possessed in our country."[2]

Jefferson imports wine from France and Italy throughout his retirement years. Through Stephen Cathalan in Marseilles Jefferson places an annual wine order for about 600 bottles divided among Bergasse's claret, Ledenon, Limoux, Roussillon and Bellet. He establishes a wine liaison with Thomas Appleton, the American Consul in

Leghorn, Italy, for the importation of the wines of Tuscany, especially Montepulciano which Appleton selects from "a particular very best crop of it known to him."[3]

Thirty-seven years have passed since Philip Mazzei entered his life, and though Jefferson's tastes in wine are Gallic, he harbors the dream that "wine being among the earliest luxuries in which we indulge ourselves, it is desirable it should be made here [Virginia] and we have every soil, aspect and climate of the best wine countries ..."[4]

Setting: Monticello, May 6, 1816, Jean David, a young French vintner, and Thomas Jefferson.

Six years into retirement Jefferson receives a letter from Jean David, a young French vintner who offers his services on 'the basis of my usefulness to you' in the cultivation of vineyards and making wine at Monticello. David is convinced that past viticulture failures are not the blame of Virginia's soil and climate but rather lack of knowledge. David points out that vineyards do better on hillsides than in lowlands, and the secret of good and bad wine lies in pruning.[5]

Jefferson confesses that when younger he had been "ardent for the introduction of new objects of culture suited to our climate," but at age 72 he is leaving those pursuits to younger men. He tells David about a "native grape which of my own knowledge produces a wine so nearly the quality of a fine Burgundy, that I have seen at my own table a large company acknowledge they could not distinguish between them, and there is a gentleman [John Adlum] on the Potomac who cultivates it." Clearly interested in utilizing David's winemaking talents, Jefferson offers to recommend David to persons who might employ him, and invites David to Monticello.[6]

David expresses an interest in Adlum's vines and wines and even proposes traveling from Richmond to Washington to examine them. Jefferson, not knowing if Adlum is still alive, tells David that he will write Adlum and "ask him to send me some of his vines." Jefferson also mentions that James Monroe has a fine collection of vines.

On hearing back from Adlum Jefferson again invites David to Monticello for dinner and the opportunity to fill him in on what he has learned about Adlum's viticultural experiments.

David, a solidly built young man of medium height, is excited to hear what the author of the Declaration of Independence has to say about grape growing, wine making, and the enjoyment of wine, and he accepts Jefferson's invitation.

Although it is early spring it is cold and Jefferson has a fire burning in the dining room fireplace. As is usual when he is having just a few people to dinner, the table is set in the Tea Room. An inveterate reader Jefferson keeps books on the mantel above the fireplace and he is reading when David arrives. He greets the nascent vintner with enthusiasm. After some introductory comments David asks his host what he had learned about John Adlum's viticulture activities.

"When I lived in Washington Adlum sent me two bottles of wine he made, one from currants, the other from a native fox-grape. This wine was as good as the best Burgundy and resembled it. Five years ago he sent me here at Monticello grape cuttings. Unfortunately I was not home and I didn't receive them for more than a month of their arrival at the post office. I immediately planted them but having been six weeks in a dry situation none of them lived.[6]

"Adlum has sent me some vines and has promised to send more. In addition, my neighbor, and now the Secretary of State, James Monroe, when he returned from France brought with him a collection of vines and planted them with a view to making wine.[7]

"I wrote Secretary Monroe and told him, 'I have an opportunity of getting some vines planted next month . . . will you permit me to take the trimmings of your vines, it shall be done by John [sic] David so as to insure no injury to them.' I am waiting to hear back from him."[8]

"How do you stay busy in retirement?"

The question brings a big smile to his host's face. "Gardening is my enduring hobby, and when the weather permits I spend time in my gardens. Until recently I spent three to four hours a day riding about my plantation, and I still ride five of six miles daily. I remain a voracious reader. Keeping up with my correspondence is a job in itself. A constant stream of people visit Monticello, and I love entertaining them with wine and food. I wish there were more time in the day."

"Do you drink wine daily, Mr. Jefferson?"

"I do but 'you are not to conclude that I have become a *buveur* [drinker]. My measure is a perfect sober one of 3 or 4 glasses at dinner, and not a drop at any other time. But as to these 3 or 4 glasses I am very fond of."[9]

"Do you have a preference in a style of wine you like best?"

"If a wine is well-made, it can be sweet or dry and I enjoy it. But I admonish you, as I did John Adlum, against the evils of brandying wine. For example, there is 'a wine of remarkable merit made in considerable quantities in a district of North Carolina on Scuppernong Creek. This wine, when it can be obtained unbrandied would be drunk at the first tables of Europe in competition with their best wines. What of it, however, is sent to the general market at Norfolk is so brandied as to be unworthy of being called wine. To get it without brandy requires a troublesome correspondence and a special agent. Until this fatal error is corrected, the character of our wines will stand low.'[10]

"There is this misguided belief in this country that brandy always and sugar sometimes, are necessary for wine. This idea will retard and discourage our progress in making good wine. Be assured that there is never one atom of anything whatever put into any of the good wines of France. It is never done but by the exporting merchants and then only for the English and American markets whereby a vitiated taste, the intoxicating quality of wine, more than its flavor, is required by the palate."[11]

"Thank you for your thoughts about adulterating wines with brandy, sugar, or anything else. I will not do that."

"Good. Returning to your question, do I have a particular style of wine that I especially enjoy? Yes, and we shall drink two such wines at dinner. Ledenon, a red wine from the vineyard regions of Nîmes, is dry and astringent. I also prefer a wine that is sweet and astringent, the sweetness tempered by an agreeable sharpness and astringency. Of this style wine I especially like Montepulciano from Tuscany."[12]

"Do you agree with me that quality wines can be made from grapes grown here in Virginia?" David says.

"Yes. Wine being among the earliest luxuries in which we indulge ourselves, it is desirable it should be made here and we have every soil, aspect and climate of the best wine countries, and I have myself drank wines made in this state and in Maryland, of the quality of the best Burgundy."

"The red wines you are going to serve sound exciting."

The first dish brought to the table is a salad, which is a break with the tradition of serving simultaneously all of the first course foods.

After his young guest has eaten a portion of the salad, Jefferson says, "Do you like the salad, Mr. David?"

"I like it very much, and yet it tastes different from any salad I've ever eaten. Some of the ingredients such as lettuce, onions, grapes, hard boiled eggs, and, of course, the chicken, are common food items in America. But it is the olive oil, capers and anchovies, foods that I have not experienced in America, that give it a distinct taste. "

"It is a salad served at the best tables in Paris. It is called Salmagundi. And you are correct, the olive oil, capers, and anchovies set it apart and must be imported to America. The chicken is roasted and cut into small pieces."[13]

"Are there other foods you import?"

"Yes, from France and Italy, Dijon mustard, pistachio nuts, raisins, almonds, figs from Marseilles, macaroni (pasta), parmesan cheese, tarragon, and vinegar. I have a mold for making macaroni that my secretary purchased for me in Naples."[14]

"How does it work?"

"The best macaroni in Italy is made with a particular sort of flour called Semola, but in almost every shop a different sort of flour is commonly used ... a paste is made and then put, by little at a time, about 5 or 6 tablespoons each time into a round iron box, the under part of which is perforated with holes, through which the paste, when pressed by a screw, comes out and forms the macaroni, which, when sufficiently long are cut and spread to dry. There is a set of plates with various shapes and sizes for the different sorts of macaroni which may be changed at will."[15]

"I would think that either of the wines you mentioned would complement the Salmagundi salad. It seems a shame that we must wait until the cloth is removed before we drink the wines," David says.

"I understand, but it is the American tradition not to serve wine until dinner is finished and the table cloth is removed. When I was in France I served wine before, during and after dinner."

Setting: Monticello, Nov 4, 1824, Lafayette returns to Monticello

Present are Lafayette, 67, Dolley and James Madison, 73, Jefferson, 81, his family, and a crowd of hundreds.

It is a beautiful autumn day. A crowd is assembled on the front portico of Monticello anticipating the arrival of the Marquis de Lafayette. It has been thirty-five years since the two elderly revolutionaries have seen one another and there is a dramatic tension in the air. A bugle sounds and looking down the mountain to the base a train of carriages and about 50 men on horseback are seen winding their way up the mountain.

It is clearly Lafayette's cortege, and the air is charged with excitement. At length the first carriage moves on to the lawn and stops. The carriage door slowly opens and out steps the Marquis de Lafayette. He is heavier and older but Lafayette's persona and charisma are still present.

As Lafayette leaves the carriage Jefferson moves down the portico steps and shuffles across the lawn until they meet. They fall into each other's arms with the words, 'My dear Jefferson! My dear Lafayette!' and burst into tears. It is a memorable moment in time.[1]

Jefferson leads the general through the crowd, finds his daughter Martha and introduces them. Lafayette last saw Martha when she was a school girl in Paris. Martha is now the mother of 11 children. Jefferson searches through the crowd for former president James Madison and wife Dolley but he cannot find them. *Madison promised to be here*, he thinks.

Everyone wants to meet the affable Lafayette, and he wishes to meet everyone and introductions and pleasantries continue on the portico and in the parlor long into the afternoon. Finally, Jefferson leads the way into the dining room. He sits at a large table with General Lafayette, his daughter, Martha, and the general's son, George Washington Lafayette. Other members of Lafayette's entourage and the Jefferson family are seated at tables throughout the dining room.

Addressing General Lafayette, Jefferson says, "When I learned that President Monroe extended an invitation to you to tour America, I wrote him and warned that you would be in danger of the American people killing you with kindness."

"That has nearly happened, and I still have months to go," a laughing Lafayette says. "Thank you, Mr. Jefferson, for the generous invitation to visit you here at beautiful Monticello and to stay as long as I like. Being with you is the apogee of my incredible American reception."

A bountiful meal of meats, poultry, game, vegetables and desserts is served. It is after sundown and desserts are being served when James and Dolley Madison enter the dining room. Jefferson, whose chair is facing the entrance, immediately sees them. "My dear general, look what the wind has blown in, James Madison and his charming wife, Dolley."

The Marquis and the former president warmly greet one another. As James and Dolley take their places at the table, Jefferson says, "President Madison's timing, as usual, is perfect, first dessert and then wine."

"I'm sorry to be late. Dolley and I fully intended to be here in time for your arrival, general, but we had carriage trouble on the way here."

"You honor me with your presence," the Marquis says.

Directing his remarks to Lafayette, Jefferson says, "The two red wines for tonight you drank on numerous occasions at my Paris residence. That was some thirty years ago, and I wonder if you remember what they are?"

"I drank so many good wines at your place on the Champs-Elysées there is no possibility of me remembering, but I will say this, let's drink them."

Four decanters of wine are lined up on a side table next to Mr. Jefferson: a white, two reds, and an amber. Lifting the white wine decanter the sage of Monticello says, "Six years ago I mounted on a hobby, which indeed I should have better managed some 30 or 40 years ago, but whose easy amble is still sufficient to give exercise and amusement to an Octogenary rider. This is the establishment of the

University.² Tomorrow, General Lafayette, Charlottesville will hold a dinner in your honor."

Martha says proudly, "As I'm sure most of you know, my father is the architect of the University in concept, design, construction and organization."

"As its first guest, your presence, General Lafayette, will bring all the more honor to the University. But now, before we retire for the evening, we have these wines to enjoy. They have been favorites of mine throughout my retirement. The white wine comes from vineyards near the village of Limoux, near the ancient city of Carcassonne. This red wine," holding the bottle in the air, "is Claret de Bergasse . . ."

Recollection flashes through Lafayette's mind and he calls out, "I remember, the wine merchant from Marseilles who could make any style of wine from local grapes."

Madison whispers to his wife, "I've heard this story so many times."

Dolley pats her husband's hand and smiles, "Yes, and I have too."

"Ah, you remember! Bergasse combined different grapes so that it was the genuine juice of the grape, and so perfect an imitation of the finest Bordeaux as not to be distinguishable," the host says. "The other red is Ledenon from vineyards near Nîmes. And to aid us with our sleep, a nut flavored Madeira."

The next morning Lafayette, Madison, and Jefferson slide into a landau and set out down the mountain for Charlottesville. Later that afternoon on the top floor of the still unfinished Rotunda, the three revolutionaries are joined by 400 joyous local citizens for a three hour dinner celebrating the nation's guest.

Thirteen toasts honoring the original thirteen states are followed by a toast in honor of Jefferson whose tribute to Lafayette follows: "I joy, my friends, in your joy, inspired by the visit of this ancient and distinguished leader and benefactor. His deeds in the war of independence you have heard and read. They are known to you, and embalmed in your memories and in the pages of faithful history.

"His deeds in the peace which followed that war are perhaps not known to you; but I can attest them. When I was stationed in his country for the purpose of cementing its friendship with ours and of advancing our mutual interests, this friend of both was my most powerful auxiliary and advocate. He made our cause his own, as in truth it was that of his native country also. His influence and connections there were great. All doors of all departments were open to him at all times, to me only formally and at appointed times. In truth I only held the nail, he drove it. Honor him, then, as your benefactor in peace as in war."[3]

Lafayette stays at Monticello for another nine days. Their conversations are filled with reminisces of the American and French Revolutions, slavery problems, political turmoil in Europe, and Jefferson's passionate belief that wine is the beverage of temperance and health.

"A few years ago among the proposed tariff reforms being considered by Congress 'none was proposed on the most exceptionable article ... I mean that of wines. I thought it a great error to consider a heavy tax on wines as a tax on luxury. On the contrary it is a tax on the health of our citizens. It is a legislative declaration that none but the richest of them shall be permitted to drink wine, and in effect a condemnation of all the middling and lower conditions of society to the poison of whisky, which is destroying them by wholesale, and ruining their families."

"Are you doing anything about the situation?" Lafayette asks.

"Yes. I wrote to William H. Crawford, Secretary of the Treasury, and pointed out to him that it is not from the necessities of our treasury that we undertake to debar the mass of our citizens the use of not only an innocent gratification, but a healthy substitute instead of a bewitching poison. The truth is that the treasury would gain in the long run by the vast extension of the use of wine. The government should therefore be for encouraging the use of wine by placing it among the articles of lightest tax. But be this as it may, take what rate of duty is thought proper, but carry it evenly through the cheap as well as the highest priced wines.'[4]

"No nation is drunken where wine is cheap, and none sober where the dearness of wine substitutes ardent spirits as the common beverage. It is, in truth, the only antidote to the bane of whiskey. Fix but the duty at the rate of other merchandise, and we can drink wine here as cheap as we do grog; and who will not prefer it?"[5]

"Was your argument successful?

"Apparently my letter had some impact because a month later I learned that Congress was considering a reduction of the duties on wine."

Between Jefferson, Lafayette and their dinner companions so much wine is drunk that when Lafayette and his party depart on November 15, Jefferson's cellar is almost depleted. Although expecting any day his annual wine supply from southern France, he becomes fearful of running out and places an emergency order explaining, "In the meantime I must buy from hand to mouth in the country, and for the present must pray you to send me a box of claret of about two dozen by the first wagon. I would refer its quality to your own taste rather than price, which is no test at all, and generally a mere imposition."[6]

Epilogue

Jefferson remained remarkably active during his seventeen years of retirement, but along the way he felt that old age was depriving him of some of the sensual enjoyments of life. To Abigail Adams he wrote, "To see what we have seen, to taste the tasted, and at each return, less tasteful o'er our palates to decant, another vintage."

In 1826, on the Fourth of July, the 50th Anniversary of The Declaration of Independence, Thomas Jefferson died.

Appendix A

Thomas Jefferson's Favorite Wines— Available Today

Thomas Jefferson was the most knowledgeable wine connoisseur of his age, and his favorite wines continue to be favorites of wine enthusiasts today.

FRANCE

Red Burgundies

Chambertin – Jefferson rated Chambertin the best of Burgundy's red wines. He imported 100 bottles of Chambertin during the third year of his presidency.

Clos de Vougeot – When Jefferson visited Clos de Vougeot in 1787 it was still owned by the monks of Citeaux. Its annual production was 50,000 bottles and the wines had a reputation for excellence. Jefferson rated it second in quality behind Chambertin. During the French Revolution the monks were evicted and the vineyards and chateau were sold at public auction. A loss of quality was soon reported following the divestiture. The reason for the loss of quality is clear. The monks knew that the quality of Clos de Vougeot's wines varied depending on the part of the vineyard from which the grapes came, and they priced their wines accordingly. "The wines made from those in the middle selling for one-third more than that made in the upper part, and three time as much as that made from those at the lower end." The new owners of Clos de Vougeot did not follow the monks' practice but blended the wines together.

Vosne-Romanée – Jefferson did not designate the order of rank but one did exist. Alexander Henderson writing during Jefferson's time singled out Romanée-Conti, La Tache, Richebourg, and Romanée St. Vivant for "their beautiful color and exquisite flavor and aroma, combining ... qualities of lightness and delicacy with richness and fullness of body," a remarkably accurate description of these wines today.

Volnay – Jefferson considered Volnay the equal in flavor to Chambertin but relegated it to fourth place because it was lighter in body, lacked longevity, and did not bear transportation as well. However, it had two advantages over the wines of Chambertin and Clos de Vougeot; it cost only one-quarter as much and was ready to drink after one year. Jefferson never identified a particular vineyard from which he purchased his Volnay wines but vineyards of special recognition then were Cailleret and Champans.

Pommard – Clos de la Commaraine. This wine was sent to Jefferson in fulfillment of an order for Volnay. He was not told that it was from neighboring Pommard, and not a Volnay, just that it was of the "best element."

White Burgundies

Montrachet – Jefferson was first introduced to Montrachet when he traveled to Burgundy in March 1787. He called it the best white wine of Burgundy, a distinction it still retains. It sold then at a price that was equal to the best Bordeaux, i.e., Lafite, Haut-Brion, Latour and Margaux.

Meursault – Jefferson thought the best wine of Meursault came from the vineyard of Goutte d'Or (Drop of Gold). Other Meursaults of equal reputation at the time were Les Perrières, Les Combettes, Les Charmes, and Les Genevrières. These five vineyards continue to make outstanding dry white Burgundies and along with ten other Meursault vineyards enjoy Premiers Crus classification. The main exporters of Goutte d'Or today are Arnaud Ente, Bouchard, Buisson-Charles, Comtes Lafon, Francoise Gaunoux, Louis Jadot, Louis Latour, René Emanuel, Vincent Bouzereau.

Rhone Valley

Côte Rôtie – Although the red wines of Côte Rôtie were recognized for their color, strength, bouquet, taste and ability to age, Jefferson made the comment that they were not yet of such high "estimation to be produced commonly at the good tables of Paris." Eighteenth century winemakers recognized their merit, however, often blending them with Bordeaux and Burgundy wines to add strength and character.

Chateau Grillet – Jefferson called Grillet the best white wine of the northern Rhone, a distinction that is in dispute today.

Hermitage – Although Jefferson did not single out the red wines of Hermitage for special praise, he did acknowledge their high quality. He listed the owners of the best vineyards, and the great red Hermitages of today come from those same vineyards.

White Hermitage – Jefferson so esteemed white Hermitage "marked with a touch of sweetness" that he called it the "first wine in the world without exception." During his presidency he purchased 550 bottles of white Hermitage from the House of Jourdan. The Jourdan vineyards were eventually inherited by the Monier family who, because of their ancestry, revived the name Chastaing de le Sizeranne. The Jourdan vineyards presently belong to M. Chapoutier who calls his red Hermitage La Sizeranne. Chapoutier produces two white Hermitage wines, Chante-Alouette (Lark's Song) and the more expensive Ermitage de l'Orée. A sweet white Hermitage was also made during Jefferson's time.

Provence and Languedoc

Bellet (near Nice) – Jefferson was first introduced to these wines before starting over the Alps on the back of a mule on his 44th birthday. He found Bellet wines good "though not of the first quality." He later called them "remarkably good." Later in retirement in a letter to President James Monroe Jefferson said, "This is the most elegant everyday wine in the world." Robert M. Parker, Jr. describes the wines of Bellet as "Nice's best-kept secret." Red, rosé and white wines are made in this small appellation, but the whites are the wines that excel today. The best white wines are made from the Rolle grape. Most of the wines of Bellet are consumed at restaurants along the French Riviera but some are exported and can be found in major U.S. wine markets.

Saint-George d'Orques – Jefferson discovered this wine at Montpelier and he imported and drank it with friends at Monticello and the White House. It had a reputation as a quality wine with a good bouquet. Today the vineyards of Saint-George d'Orques have Languedoc AOC status and are made predominately from Grenache, Syrah and Mourvedre grapes.

Frontignan – A fortified sweet white dessert wine made from the white Muscat grape. Jefferson first tasted this wine on the spot over dinner at the home of Monsieur Lambert, a physician and vintner. Jefferson remarked, "It is potable the April after it is made, is best that year . . . It is not permitted to ferment more than half a day, because it would not be so liquorish [sweet]. The best color, and its natural one, is amber." Lambert also made a red wine. The sweet Muscat wines of Frontignan were enjoying their greatest popularity at the time of Jefferson's visit to this small Mediterranean town. Although still available, there aren't many Lamberts making Muscat de Frontignan today. Its production is now dominated by cooperatives.

Costieres de Nimes – In Nimes Jefferson drank an "excellent" red vin ordinaire from nearby vineyards called Ledenon, and according to Jefferson "served pure at tables of the finest rank in France." Known for its agreeable bouquet, it was considered the equal in quality and taste to the wines of Chateauneuf-du-Pape. It was one of his favorite wines in retirement. The wines from this region are known today as Costieres de Nimes and are reasonably priced and generally available.

Vin Blanc de Rochegude – A sweet fortified white wine, probably the ancestor of today's Beaumes-de-Venise. Jefferson thought highly of this wine and sent it as a gift to President George Washington.

Muscat de Rivesaltes – A variety of wines were produced (and still are) in Roussillon, but those Jefferson liked best were the sweet wines of Muscat de Rivesaltes. They were considered "lighter on the stomach than Frontignan." In his seminal wine treatise (1816), André Jullien ranked Muscat de Rivesaltes "first" of all Vins de Liqueur. Jefferson first drank this wine when he traveled on the Canal du Midi in May 1787. Its taste lingered on his palate because he continued to import it until the last year of his life.

Blanquette de Limoux – From vineyards around the town of Limoux near the medieval city of Carcassonne. Jefferson spent a night in Carcassonne and it was probably here that he became acquainted with the wines of Limoux that he imported in retirement. Blanquette de Limoux, made from the mauzac grape, was sweet and sparkling, the same as it is today.

Red Bordeaux

Chateaux Haut-Brion, Lafite, Latour, Margaux – Jefferson drank all four of these wines and referred to them as "first growths." He also mentioned for special recognition Rozan (Rauzan-Segla), Larose (Gruard-Larose), Dabbadie, ou Lionville (now three chateaux:

Leoville-Las-Cases, Leoville-Poyferre, Leoville-Barton), then owned by Monsieur d'Abadie, Quirouen (Kirwan), Durfort (Durfort-Vivens), followed by a "third class" of wines consisting of Calons (Calon-Segur), Mouton (Mouton-Rothschild), Gassie (Rauzan-Gassies), Arboete (LaGrange), Pontette (Pontet-Canet) de Terme (Marquis de-Terme) and Candale (d'Issan). Madame Rauzan's was his favorite. He wrote Madame Rauzan, "I had the opportunity on a tour I made during my stay in Paris of visiting the canton of the best Bordeaux wines, among which was de Rozan, your cru, of excellent quality." In a letter of wine advice to a friend he said, "Rozan-Margaux which is made by Madame de Rozan. This is what I import for myself, and consider it equal to any of the four crops [growths]."

White Bordeaux

Carbonnieux – The story is told of the Turkish sultan who because of his religion did not drink alcoholic beverages, but members of his staff surreptitiously imported Carbonnieux labeled as spring water. One day the sultan drank a bottle and said, "French water is so delicious I wonder why they bother making wine." Several other white Bordeaux wines that Jefferson mentioned no longer exist having been lost to urban development.

Sauternes

Chateau d'Yquem – Jefferson praised Yquem as the best. On his return to Paris he ordered 250 bottles of Yquem. While secretary of state he ordered it for himself and 360 bottles for President Washington. When he became president he served Yquem at White House dinners. Two other Sauternes he mentioned were President du Roy's vineyards, now known as Chateau Suduiraut, and President Pichard's, now Lafaurie Peyraguey and Haut-Peyraguey. While president he served 150 bottles of Filhot.

Champagne

Monsieur Dorsay's Champagne in Aÿ – Jefferson preferred non-sparkling Champagne. There is evidence that Monsieur Dorsay's vineyard in Aÿ is now owned by Bollinger.

GERMANY

Mosel

Brauneberg, Wehlen, Grach, Piesport, Zelting, Bernkastel –Jefferson did not visit the Mosel. He was told of this ranking of its wines by a "gentleman well acquainted with the vineyards and the wines of the Moselle."

Rheingau

Schloss Johannisberg – He also singled out for praise the wines of Rudesheim and Hochheim. To a German friend who accompanied him on this part of his German vineyard trip he wrote, "I take the first moment to inform you that my journey was prosperous: that the vines which I took from Hochheim and Rudesheim are now growing luxuriously in my garden here [Paris] and will cross the Atlantic next winter, and that probably, if you ever revisit Monticello, I shall be able to give you a glass of Hock or Rudesheim of my own making." There is no evidence that Jefferson took these vines with him when he left France.

ITALY

Piedmont

"Nebiule" – Jefferson's phonetic spelling of the Nebbiolo grape which makes many of Italy's best wines, Barolo, Barbaresco, Gattinara and Ghemme. He found the "Nebiule" wine singular, melding three contradictory characteristics. "It is about as sweet as the silky Madeira, as

astringent on the palate as Bordeaux, and as brisk as Champagne. It is a pleasing wine." The full-bodied, dry, tannic Barolos and Barbarescos of today are not sweet and do not effervesce because the style of the wines has changed. Throughout the 18th century, and well into the 19th century, in the Piedmont region of Italy, the fermentation was not allowed to finish, leaving the wines sweet. The incomplete fermentation also left them frizzanti, which probably explains Jefferson's "brisk as Champagne" comment.

Tuscany

Montepulciano – also Chianti, Carmignano, Artimino and Pomino. Jefferson's "very favorite" Tuscan wine, which he sometimes referred to as a Florence wine, was Montepulciano. He described Montepulciano as a high-flavored, light bodied wine "equal to the best Burgundy." It was Montepulciano that inspired Jefferson to write, "…this being a very favorite wine, and habit rendered the light and high flavored wines a necessary of life with me." TJ to Thomas Appleton, Jan 14, 1816.

SPAIN

Dry Sherry – "if I should fail in the means of getting it, it will be a privation which I shall feel sensibly once a day." Jefferson's taste in Spanish wines ran from Malaga and Pedro Ximenes, both sweet, to pale and dry sherry and dry and sweet Paxarete. Paxarete (also spelled Pacharetti) was made from the Pedro Ximenes grape at an ancient monastery about fifteen miles from Jerez. Pedro Ximenes made sweet and dry wines that resembled sherry in taste. Its name comes from a grape said to have been imported from the Rhine by a man named Pedro Simon (corrupted to Ximenes). Jefferson also drank a sweet red wine made from the muscadine grape called Tinto di Rota, which was known in England as Tent, and was made near the village of Rota north of Cadiz. Jefferson imported substantial amounts of these Spanish wines during his eight years as president.

PORTUGAL

Madeira – Like most of the Founding Fathers, Jefferson was a Madeira enthusiast. While in Paris, Jefferson and Marquis de Lafayette agreed to share a pipe (110 gallons) of Madeira "of the nut quality and of the very best."

Appendix B

Notes to Henry Sheaff

Henry Sheaff, a Philadelphia wine merchant, asked Jefferson for guidance on the quality, prices, and sources of the best European wines. Jefferson's "Notes to Henry Sheaff", with but few exceptions, has left a legacy of wine advice that has, for those wines that still exist, stood the test of time.

Lisbon wines. "The best quality of the dry kind is called Termo, and costs 79 Dollars the pipe at about 2 years old. At 5 years old it is becoming a fine wine; at 7 years old it is preferable to any but the very best Madeira. Buckeley and Son furnish it from Lisbon.

Sherry. The best dry sherry costs at Cadiz, from 80 to 90 Dollars the pipe. But when old and fine, such as is sent to the London market it costs £30 sterling the pipe. Mr. Yznardi, the son, Consul of the US. at Cadiz, at this time in Philadelphia, furnishes it.

The following facts are from my own enquiries in going thro' the different wine cantons of France, examining the identical vineyards producing the first quality of wines, conversing with their owners and other persons on the spot minutely acquainted with the vineyards, and the wines made on them, and tasting them myself.

Burgundy. The best wines of Burgundy are Montrachet, a white wine. It is made but by two persons, to wit Monsieur de Clermont, and Monsieur de Sarsnet. The latter rents to Monsieur de la Tour. This costs 48 sous the bottle, new, and 3 livres when fit for drinking.

Meursault. A white wine. The best quality of it is called Goutte d'Or. It costs 6 sous the bottle new. I do not believe this will bear transportation. But the Montrachet will in a proper season.

Chambertin, Vougeot, Veaune, are red wines, of the first quality, and are the only fine red wines of Burgundy which will bear transportation, and even these required to be moved in the best season, and not to be exposed to great heat or great cold. These cost 48 sous the bottle new and 3 livres old. I think it next to impossible to have any of the Burgundy wines brought here in a sound state.

Champagne. The Mousseux or Sparkling Champagne is never brought to a good table in France. The still, or non-mousseux, is alone drunk by connoisseurs.

Aij [Aÿ]. The best is made at Aij, by Monsieur d'Orsay, who makes more than all the other proprietors of the first quality put together. It costs 3 livres the bottle when of the proper age to drink, which is at 5 years old. The Red Champagne is not a fine wine. The best is made by the Benedictine monks at Hautvillers.

The wines of Burgundy and Champagne being made at the head of the Seine are brought down that river to Havre from whence they are shipped. They should come down in the month of November so that they may be brought over seas in the winter and arrive here before our warm spring days. They should be bottled on the spot where they are made. The bottle, bottling, corking, and packing costs 5 sous a bottle, Capt. Cuttery, Consul of the U.S. at Havre, is a good person and well informed to supply the wines of Burgundy and Champagne.

Bordeaux red wines. There are four crops of them more famous than all the rest. These are Chateau-Margau [Margaux], Tour de Segur [Latour], Hautbrion [Haut-Brion], and de la Fite [Lafite]. They cost 3 livres a bottle, old: but are so engaged beforehand that it is impossible to get them. The mer-

chants, if you desire it, will send you a wine by any of those names and may you pay 3 livres a bottle: But I will venture to affirm that there never was a bottle of those wines sent to America by a merchant. Nor is it worthwhile to seek for them; for I will defy any person to distinguish them from the wines of the next quality, to wit: Rohan-Margau [Rauzan-Margaux now, known as Rauzan-Ségla], which is made by Madame dc Rohan. This is what I import for myself, and consider as equal to any of the four crops. There are also the wines of Dabbadie [the three Léovilles], la Rose [Gruaud-Larose], Quirouen [Chateau Kirwan], and Durfort [Durfort-Vivens] which are reckoned as good as Madame de Rozan's. Yet I have preferred hers. These wines cost 40 sous the bottle, when of the proper age for drinking.

Bordeaux white wines. Grave. The best is called Pontac, and is made by Monsieur de Lamont. It costs 18 sous a bottle.

Sauterne. This is the best white wine of France (except Champagne and Hermitage) the best of it is made by Monsieur de Lur-Salus, and costs at 4 years old (when fit to drink) from 20 to 24 sous the bottle. There are two other white wines made in the same neighborhood called Prignac and Barsac, esteemed by some. But the Sauterne is that preferred at Paris, and much the best in my judgment. They cost the same. A great advantage of the Sauterne is that it becomes higher flavored the day after the bottle has been opened than it is at first.

Mr. Fenwick, Consul of the US. at Bordeaux, is well informed on the subject of these wines, and has supplied the President and myself with them genuine and good. He would be a proper person to endeavor to get from the South of France some of the wines made there which are most excellent and very cheap, say 10 or 12 sous the bottle. Those of Roussillon are the best. I was not in Roussillon myself, and therefore can give no particular directions about them.

At Nimes I drank a good wine, stronger than claret, well flavored. The tavern price of which was 2 sous the quart. Mr. Fenwick might perhaps be able to get these brought through the Canal of Languedoc. A good correspondent at Amsterdam might furnish the following wines:

Moselle. The best of these is called Brownberg, being made on a mountain of that name adjoining the village of Dusmond, 15 leagues from Coblenz, to which last place it is brought and stored for sale. The best crop of Brownberg is that of Baron Breidbach Burreasheim. It costs 22 sous the bottle when old enough to dink; it is really a good wine.

Hock. There has been discovered within these 30 years, a finer wine of this quality called Johannisberg, now decidedly preferred to Hock. They both cost 5 sterling a bottle when of the oldest and best quality. It is to be observed of the Hock wines that nobody can drink them but Germans, or the English who have learnt it from their German kings. Compared with the wines of more southern climates they are as an olive compared with a pineapple.

Observe that whenever the price of a wine by the bottle is mentioned, it means to include the price of the bottle, which is 5 sous deduct that sum therefore, and it leaves always the price of the wine.

Appendix C

Thomas Jefferson's Affordable Wine Favorites

When James Monroe was elected to the "splendid misery" of the presidency in 1817, the sage of Monticello spent all but five lines of his letter of congratulations discussing the wines he recommended for the new President's wine cellar.

"I shall not waste your time in idle congratulations. You know my joy on the commitment of the helm of our government to your hands. I promised you, when I should have received and tried the wines that I ordered from France and Italy to give you a note of the kinds which I should think worthy of your procurement; and this being the season for ordering them, so that they may come in the mild temperature of autumn, I now fulfill my promise. They are the following:

"Vin Blanc, Liqoureux d'Hermitage de M. Jourdan à Tains. This costs about 821/2 cents a bottle put on ship-board. Vin de Ledenon (in Languedoc) something of the port character but higher flavored, more delicate, less rough. I do not know its price, but probably about 25 cents a bottle. 'Vin de Roussillon. The best is that of Perpignan or Rivesaltes of the crop of M. Durand. It costs 72 cents a gallon, bears bringing in the cask. If put into bottles then it costs 11 cents a bottle more than if bottled here by an inexplicable and pernicious arrangement of our tariff.

"Vin de Nice. The crop called Bellet, of M. Sasserno, is the best. This is the most elegant everyday wine in the world and cost 31 cents the bottle. Not much being made it is little known at the general markets.

"Mr. Cathalan of Marseilles is the best channel for getting the first three of these wines and a good one for the Nice, being in their neighborhood and knowing well who makes the crops of best quality. The Nice being a wine foreign to France occasion some troublesome forms. If you could get that direct from Sasserno himself at Nice, it would be better. And by the bye, he is very anxious for the appointment of consul for the United States at that place. I knew his father well, one of the most respectable merchants and men of the place.

"I hear a good character of the son, who has succeeded to his business. He understands English well, having passed some time in a counting house in London for improvement. I believe we have not many vessels going to that port annually and yet as the appointment brings no expense to the United States, and is sometimes salutary to our merchants and seamen, I see no objection to naming one there. There is still another wine to be named to you, which is the wine of Florence called Montepulciano, with which Appleton can best furnish you. There is a particular very best crop of it known to him and which he has usually sent to me. This cost 25 cents per bottle. He knows too from experience how to have it so bottled and packed as to ensure it bearing the passage which in the ordinary way it does not. I have imported it through him annually 10 or 12 years and do not think I have lost one bottle in 100. I salute you with all my wishes for a prosperous and splendid voyage over the ocean on which you are embarked, and with sincere prayers for the continuance of your life and health."

Appendix D

Thomas Jefferson's Tastes in Wines

In a letter to Stephen Cathalan (American Consul in Marseilles), May 26, 1818, Jefferson defines his tastes in wines:

"I will explain to you the terms by which we characterize different qualities of wines. They are:

1. *Sweet* wines, such as Frontignan & Lunel of France, Pacharetti doux of Spain, Calcavallo of Portugal, le vin du Cap &c.

2. *Acid* wines, such as the Vins de Graves, du Rhin, de Hocheim &c.

3. *Dry* wines, having not the least either of sweetness or of acidity in them, as Madere sec, Pacharetti sec, vin d'Oporto, &c. and the Ledenon which I call a dry wine also.

4. *Silky* wines, which are in truth a compound in their taste of the *dry* wine dashed with a little *sweetness*, barely sensible to the palate: the silky Madeira which we sometimes get here is made so by putting a small portion of Malmsey into the dry Madeira.

5. There is another quality of wine which we call *rough* or *astringent*, and you also, I believe, call it *astringent*, which is often found in both the dry & silky wines. There is something of this quality for example in the Ledenon, and a great deal of it in the vin d'Oporto, which is not only dry, but astringent approaching almost to bitterness.

Our vocabulary of wines being thus explained, I will observe that the wine of Nice sent me by Mr. Spreafico in 1816 was silky and a little astringent and was the most delicious wine I ever tasted, and the most esteemed here generally. That of 1817 was entirely dry, moderately astringent and a very good wine; about on a footing with Ledenon. That of 1818 last received, has its usual astringency indeed, but is a little acid, so much so as to destroy its usual good flavor. Had it come in the summer I should have suspected its having acquired that acidity by fretting in the hold of the ship, or in our hot warehouses on a summer passage, but it was shipped at Marseilles in October, the true time for shipping delicate wines for this country.

I will now say why I go into these details with you. In the first place you are not to conclude that I am become a *buveur* (drinker). My measure is a perfectly sober one of 3 or 4 glasses at dinner, & not a drop at any other time. But as to these 3 or 4 glasses *Je suis bien friand (I am very fond of)*. I go however into these details because in the art, by mixing genuine wines, of producing any flavor desired, which Mr. Bergasse possesses so perfectly, I think it probable he has prepared wines of this character also; that is to say of a compound flavor of the rough, dry, and sweet, or rather of the rough and silky; or if he has not, I am sure he can.

The Ledenon, for example, which is dry and astringent, with a proper proportion of wine which is sweet and astringent, would resemble the wine of Bellet sent me in 1816 by Mr. Spreafico. If he has any wines of this quality, I would thank you to add samples of 2 or 3 bottles of each of those he thinks approaches this description nearest. . . .

I have labored long and hard to procure the reduction of duties on the lighter wines, which is now effected to a certain degree. I have labored hard also in persuading others to use those wines. Habit yields with difficulty. Perhaps the late diminution of duties may have a good effect. I have added to my list of wines this year 50 bottles of vin muscat blanc de Lunel. I should much prefer a wine which should be *sweet* and *astringent*, but I know of none. If you know of any, not too high priced I would thank you to substitute it instead of the Lunel."

Author's comments:

Henry Bergasse was a Marseilles wine merchant that Jefferson met in March 1787 on his tour through southern France. Bergasse had Jefferson to dinner, introduced him to his friends, provided him with information, and took him to his wine cellars where Jefferson saw in bottles and casks the equivalent of 1,500,000 bottles of wine. The wine cellar temperature was a constant 54 degrees. Jefferson claimed that Bergasse could replicate the taste of any wine by blending local grapes and even connoisseurs could not tell the difference. Jefferson was an aficionado of Bergasse's Claret de Bergasse that Jefferson said was as good as the best red Bordeaux wines. Jefferson imported Claret de Bergasse during his retirement years on an annual basis.

Ledenon was produced from vineyards near Nîmes and was considered the best wine of the region. It was a wine Jefferson also imported on an annual basis during his seventeen years of retirement.

During Jefferson's time, wines from the wine regions surrounding the Douro River known as vin d'Oporto were dry natural wines. It was later that the adulteration of port wines by blending them with elderberry juice, sugar, and brandy became common practice. It was Joseph James Forrester (Baron de Forrester) who opposed the practices of adulteration. Forrester's position was that port should always be a natural wine and should not be adulterated in any fashion. Forrester's fight against these abuses contributed to changes instituted prohibiting the blending of elderberry juice with port. Perhaps it is fortunate that he lost on the issue of brandy being added to halt the fermentation of port, or we would have a wine dissimilar to what we enjoy as port today.

Appendix E

Thomas Jefferson's Favorite Foods

Jefferson's tastes in food were eclectic. He is reported to have grown 300 varieties of vegetables. In his garden at Monticello he grew a wide variety of vegetables and a variety of the same vegetable. For example, he grew more than 30 kinds of peas, at least 25 kinds of beans, 30 varieties of cabbage. In retirement he wrote a friend, "I have lived temperately, eating little animal and that as a condiment for the vegetables which constitute my present diet."

VEGETABLES: artichokes, asparagus, green beans, lima beans,, snap sugar, beans, red and white beets, broccoli, Brussels sprouts, cabbage, capers, carrots, cauliflower, cayenne pepper, celery, collards, corn, cress, cucumbers, endives, chick peas, eggplant, fennel, kale, leeks, lentils, lettuce, mushrooms, okra, olives, onions, orache, parsley, parsnips, peas, peanuts, peppers, potatoe pumpkins, potatoes, sweet potatoes, radishes, rhubarb, rutabaga, salsifies, savory, sea kale, sesame, shallots, sorrel, spinach, sprouts, squashes, tea onion, tomatoes, turnips.

MEATS: bacon, beef, chicken, duck, game, geese, guinea fowl, ham (fresh and smoked), lamb, mutton, pork, sausages, turkey, veal.

SEAFOOD: anchovies, clams, crabs, lobsters, mussels, oysters, shrimp, fish (fresh and salted): bass, carp, chub, eels, herring, shad, speckled trout, salmon trout. He loved oysters. One evening in Amsterdam he dined alone and ate 50 oysters before dinner.

DAIRY: butter, cheeses, eggs, ice cream.

FRUITS: apples, apricots, blackberries, blueberries, cantaloupes, cherries, cranberries, currants, figs, gooseberries, grapes, lemons, melons, mulberries, nectarines, peaches, pears, pineapples, plumbs, pomegranates, prunes, pumpkins, quinces, raisins, raspberries, strawberries, watermelons.

NUTS: almonds, chestnuts, chinquapins, hazelnuts or filberts, pecans, peanuts, pistachios, walnuts.

HERBS: balm, chicory, marjoram, mint, lavender, rosemary, sage, tarragon, thyme.

Appendix F

Franklin's Secretary-Edward Bancroft-Master Spy

In the words of a noted historian, Edward Bancroft was "destined to become one of the most remarkable spies of all time, achieving the astonishing feat of serving simultaneously as an intelligence agent for two nations at war while serving himself first of all, and mastering the art of duplicity so consummately as to conceal his treasons from some of the most astute men of his time and from historians for six decades after his death."[1] His work as a spy was considered by the British Secret Service a valuable treasure to government.

Why did he betray the American cause? Here is the answer in his own words: "I had then resided near ten years, and expected to reside the rest of my life in England; and all my views, interests and inclinations were adverse to the independency of the Colonies, though I had advocated some of their claims, from a persuasion of their being founded in justice. I therefore wished, that the government of this country might be informed, of the danger of French interference, though I could not resolve to become the informant. But Mr. Paul Wentworth, having gained some general knowledge of my journey to France, and my intercourse with Mr. Deane, and having induced me to believe that the British Ministry was likewise informed on this subject, I at length consented to meet the then secretaries of state, Lords Weymouth and Suffolk, and gave them all the information in my power, which I did with the most disinterested views."[2]

What was the scope of his treachery and espionage? In a memorandum to the British government he sets it out: "I went to Paris, and during the first year, resided in the same house with Dr. Franklin, Mr. Deane, etc., and regularly informed this Government of every transaction of the American commissioners; of every step and vessel taken to supply the revolted colonies with artillery, arms, etc.; of every part of their intercourse with the French and other European courts; of the powers of instruction given by Congress to the commissioners; and of their correspondence with the Secret Committees, etc."[3]

By Bancroft's own confession everything that took place between Franklin and his fellow commissioners, all of their negotiations and agreements with the French, all of their correspondence with Congress, were reported to the chief of the British secret intelligence, William Eden and his superiors. Worse still, the British admiralty learned about sailings, and their warships were able to intercept and capture shipments, dispatches, and men. Bancroft claimed that when Franklin and fellow commissioners, Lee and Deane, signed the Treaty of Alliance with France on February 6, 1778, he reported it to the British government within forty-two hours. He also routinely used intelligence information he learned through the American commission for personal gain by successfully speculating in stocks."[4]

Who was Edward Bancroft? He was a mirror image of his friend and mentor Benjamin Franklin. He was born and raised in Massachusetts of poor parents, his father died when he was two, and his mother married a tavern owner. He grew up living with his mother and stepfather above the tavern. As a youngster he studied briefly under Silas Deane after Deane graduated from Yale, but he was mostly self-taught. He learned early that he had a natural aptitude for science. When fifteen he was apprenticed to a physician, but became discontented and did what Franklin had wanted to do, run off to sea.

He spent several years practicing medicine without a license on plantations in Dutch Guiana, South America. Before coming to London in about 1767, he spent a year traveling between North and South America. He intended to study for his medical degree at the University of Edinburgh, but it was too distant from London. He studied medicine at Aberdeen, became a physician and was eventually elected a member of the College of Physicians.

Edward Bancroft was a man of many talents, interests, and identities including physician, scientist, novelist, stock speculator, and eventually Franklin's secretary in Paris.

Franklin first met Bancroft a year or so after he returned to England in 1767.[5] Bancroft was about twenty-five and had already lived an exciting life. About the time Franklin met him, Bancroft had written and published a book titled *Natural History of Guiana*. He later wrote a novel, a biography of Sir Charles Wentworth, and was a book reviewer for the London Monthly Review. Franklin and young Bancroft (he was thirty-eight years Franklin's junior) took an immediate liking to one another. Franklin took him under his wing, introduced him to his friends, and because of his many achievements including experiments with vegetable dyes, Franklin sponsored his election into the Royal Society in 1773.

Franklin left England in March 1775 and arrived in America in May. He was greeted warmly by his fellow Philadelphians and the next day chosen by the Assembly to be one of Pennsylvania's delegates to the Second Continental Congress that was meeting in Philadelphia in four days.

Over the next two years Franklin served on dozens of Congressional committees including the Committee of Secret Correspondence. When the Committee appointed Silas Deane America's agent in Europe, Franklin thought that Bancroft would be the perfect source for informing Deane on the political climate in England. Franklin wrote to Deane and suggested that he contact Bancroft by writing to him, under cover, to Mr. Griffiths, at Turnham Green, near London, and to ask Bancroft to meet him in either France or Holland, on the score of "old acquaintance."[6]

From Paris Deane sent Bancroft a letter requesting that he come to Paris. Deane enclosed thirty pounds to defray Bancroft's travel expenses. A month later they met in Paris. Deane was impressed with Bancroft, and so eager for his help that he told him the real purpose of his mission—to establish a secret relationship with the French and obtain money and military aid for the Colonies."[7]

In December 1776 Franklin was sent by Congress to France as a commissioner to serve on a three person commission charged with securing from the French government military and economic aid for the colonies. Another goal was to obtain, if possible, an alliance with France.

Shortly after Franklin's arrival in France he hired Bancroft as his personal secretary and Bancroft lived with Franklin during most of his time in Paris.

There was an ease of manner in everything Bancroft did including how he communicated his perfidy. He frequently went to London, sometimes on missions for Franklin and the Commission. While there, he would stop by the Office of William Eden, the head of British intelligence, and make verbal reports, and sometimes turn over copies of documents.

In Paris he used a more clandestine and ingenious method of supplying information to the British. He wrote his reports in invisible ink and placed them in a sealed bottle which he concealed in the hollow of a plane tree located on the south terrace of the Tuileries Gardens. A messenger picked up his messages at half-past nine every Tuesday evening and left in another bottle messages to him."[8]

Franklin's indifferent attitude toward spies, and his contempt of fellow commissioner Arthur Lee blinded him of the opportunities he had to discover Bancroft's treachery.

Three weeks after Franklin's arrival in France, he received a letter from a woman warning him that he was surrounded by spies. His blasé response to her was the advice he followed in his daily conduct. "It is impossible to discover in every case the falsity of pretended friends who would know our affairs; and more so to prevent being watched by spies when interested people may think proper to place them for that purpose. I have long observed one rule, which prevents any inconvenience from such practices. It is simply this: to be concerned in no affairs that I should blush to have made public, and to do nothing but what spies may see, and welcome. If I was sure, therefore, that my valet de place was a spy, as he probably is, I think that I should not discharge him for that, if in other respects I liked him."[10]

At one point Franklin and fellow commissioners Deane and Lee, learned that the British minister to France had in his possession original documents taken from Deane's lodging. They demanded that Bancroft return all the documents. Bancroft promptly sent them his resignation."[11]

It was a calculated gamble on Bancroft's part because if his resignation was accepted his spying days were over. He surely knew this possible consequence when he submitted his resignation, but his bluff worked. Franklin refused to accept his resignation.

Bancroft's spy activities fooled everyone except Arthur Lee, and Lee's pursuit of him was unrelenting. Bancroft had another scare. He heard a rumor that Lee was accusing him of having divulged information to the Privy Council soon after meeting Deane in Paris. He tracked the rumor down, and when satisfied that there was nothing to it, he made new financial demands on the British intelligence service. These were precarious times for this master spy, but he managed to survive, and to come out with Deane and Franklin's confidence in him stronger than ever.[12]

Ralph Izard, a friend of Lee's and a wealthy southern planter, came to Europe as the envoy to Tuscany. He was not received there and ended up staying in Paris. Izard berated Franklin for not sharing with him information about the Treaty of Alliance with France, saying that members of the British Parliament knew about it before it was signed.[13]

His accusations to Franklin were specific. "How extraordinary will it appear to the public, if it can be proved, that notwithstanding your great kindness, and attention to me, speculations of various kinds to a very considerable amount have been constantly carried on by persons residing under your own roof; that one of the gentlemen engaged in these speculations was himself a commissioner; that you were informed of Lord North's having boasted of his lenity in not apprehending a friend of yours who was in London speculating in the funds for the benefit of the commissioners; and that after having been informed of this, you yourself communicated the treaty to that gentleman, at the very time when you refused to make such communication to Mr. William Lee and myself, in defiance of the express instructions of Congress." Izard is, of course, referring to Silas Deane and Edward Bancroft.

Izard continues, "It will appear still more extraordinary if it can be proved, that a friend of yours was in the month of January made acquainted with the very day the Treaty was to be signed; that this information was transmitted to London, and in consequence of it, that insurances to a great amount were made; for whose benefit I will not take upon me to say. If these things can be proved, the world will judge by what motives you have been actuated. I have been confidently assured that they can be proved; and I beg that you will let me know if my information is true or false."[14]

Franklin did not ask Ralph Izard the source of his information because he did not believe him. If Franklin had investigated Izard's source he would have found that Izard based his accusations on Musco Livingston, a Jamaican sea captain.

Livingston came to Paris from London. He told Franklin that he had seen in London a letter written by Bancroft to John Wharton dated January 27, announcing that the treaty would be signed on February 5 or 6, and urging Wharton to speculate accordingly. In addition Livingston signed a statement to this effect. Izard knew about Livingston's charge against Bancroft from his friend Arthur Lee."[15]

Arthur Lee continued his pursuit of proving Edward Bancroft a spy. Early the next year, Arthur Lee wrote a letter to John Adams and Franklin objecting to their having appointed Bancroft to transact business for the Commission in England. Lee's objections centered on his claims that Bancroft was a notorious stockjobber (speculator), lived with a woman to whom he was not married, and his enmity to Lee. Lee was also upset that they had not consulted him about Bancroft's appointment. Lee claimed that he had evidence that Bancroft was a criminal with regard to the United States, and that he would have him charged if he ever entered the jurisdiction of the United States.[16]

Franklin turned a deaf ear to Lee's allegations. Why? Because he placed very little credence in anything Arthur Lee said. Again, given the choice between Lee and Bancroft, Franklin chose to believe Bancroft, and he remained in Franklin's confidence throughout their time in France. John Adams, who personally did not like Bancroft, did not consider Lee's charge of treason of sufficient worth to do anything about it.[17]

The enmity that Franklin and Arthur felt for one another made it impossible for them to work together. Lee constantly complained that Franklin failed to consult him. He resented being left out.[19] His incessant backbiting and mean temper provoked the angriest letter Franklin ever wrote (he didn't mail it), but it summarizes what he thought of Lee. "It is true that I have omitted answering some of your letters. I do not like to answer angry letters. I hate disputes. I am old, cannot have long to live, have much to do and no time for altercation. If I have often received and borne your magisterial snubbings and rebukes without reply, ascribe it to the right causes: my concern for the honor and success of our mission which would be hurt by our quarreling, my love of peace, my respect for your good qualities, and my pity of your sick mind, which is forever tormenting itself with its jealousies, suspicions, and fancies that others mean you ill, wrong you, or fail in respect for you. If you do not cure yourself of this temper it will end in insanity, of which it is a symptomatic forerunner, as I have seen in several instances. God preserve you from so terrible an evil; and for His sake pray suffer me to live in quiet."[20]

Bancroft's influence as a British spy may have saved England from being invaded. At one point during the war, the French foreign minister, Count Vergennes, was considering a plan of raising a rebellion among Irish Presbyterians as a diversion for a planned Franco-Spanish invasion of England. Lafayette and Franklin recommended Bancroft for the mission of traveling to Ireland and evaluating whether the project had merit. Bancroft undertook the mission, and his report to the French foreign minister discouraged any hope of an Irish rebellion. The invasion never took place.[18]

In 1821 Bancroft died a respected scientist. His treachery as a spy was not discovered until seventy years later when it was revealed by the British government.

Appendix G

Jefferson's Wine Glasses

The volume measurements were not taken with scientifically precise equipment and should be considered approximate:

Object: Two Wine Glasses
Date: Late 18th century
Description: Funnel-shaped champagne flutes with plain foot. Both glasses have a band of narrow oblong cuts around the rim. One glass (a) has broad petal-like cuts around the base of the bowl and hexagonal stem. (b) has plain round stem.
Dimensions: Height: 6" and 5 3/4"
Volume: 105 ml and 90 ml filled to the brim; 85 ml and 75 ml filled to 3/8" from top
Provenance: Items descended through family of Jefferson's granddaughter Virginia Jefferson Randolph Trist and was probably owned by Jefferson.
Location: Visitors Center Exhibition

Object: Two Wine Glasses
Date: 1810-1840
Description: Both glasses have squat wafered stems, and bowls with a nine-sided base and cut roundel and ray design.
Dimensions: Height: 4 3/8"
Volume: 95 ml at brim; 70 ml at 3/8" from top
Provenance: Items descended through family of Jefferson's grandson, Thomas Jefferson Randolph.
Location: Tea Room

Object: Wine Glass
Date: 1770-1780
Description: Glass has trumpet bowl and double wafered stem with a heavy plain foot.
Height: 4 3/4"
Volume: 90 ml at brim; 65 ml at 3/8" from top
Provenance: Items descended through family of Jefferson's grandson, Thomas Jefferson Randolph.
Location: Tea Room

Object: Wine Glass
Date: 1760-1770
Description: Glass has trumpet bowl with eight petal-shaped cuts around the base; double wafered stem with a heavy plain foot.
Dimensions: Height: 4 4/5"
Volume: 75 ml at brim; 55 ml at 3/8" from top
Provenance: Items descended through family of Jefferson's granddaughter, Virginia Jefferson Randolph Trist.
Location: Tea Room

The wine glass information was furnished by Lucia Stanton, former Director of Research at Monticello.

Purchases of glassware are recorded in *Jefferson's Memorandum Books* between 1767-1821. Monticello website, "Wine Glasses," Research and Collections Menu.

Appendix H

Game, Poultry, Meats, Fish, Vegetables, Fruits Available During Thomas Jefferson Travels in Southern France.

Thomas Jefferson tells us a great deal about the wines he drank, the things he saw, the places he visited during his travels through southern France and northern Italy, even what the peasants ate, but he says very little about what he ate or what foods were available to the traveler. The following excerpts on the subject are from *Travels Through France and Italy* by Tobias Smollett, an English writer who lived and traveled through France and Italy about twenty years before Jefferson's travels. Smollett leaves us with this detailed account of the bounty of foods that were available. The spelling and punctuation have not been changed.

Letter XVIII: Nice, September 2, 1764,

I have likewise two small gardens, well stocked with oranges, lemons, peaches, figs, grapes, corinths, salad, and pot-herbs … It is very difficult to find a tolerable cook at Nice…. The markets at Nice are tolerably well supplied. Their beef, which comes from Piedmont, is pretty good, and we have it all the year. In the winter, we have likewise excellent pork, and delicate lamb; but the mutton is indifferent.

Piedmont, also, affords us delicious capons, fed with maize; and this country produces excellent turkeys, but very few geese. Chickens and pullets are extremely meager. I have tried to fatten them, without success. In the summer they are subject to the pip, and die in great numbers.

Autumn and winter are the seasons for game; hares, partridges, quails, wild-pigeons, woodcocks, snipes, thrushes, beccasicas, and ortolans. Wild boar is sometimes found in the mountains; it has a delicious taste, not unlike that of the wild hog in Jamaica; and would make an excellent barbecue, about the beginning of winter, when it is in good case: but, when meager, the head only is presented at tables. Pheasants are very scarce.

The hares are large, plump, and juicy. The partridges are generally of the red sort; large as pullets, and of a good flavor: there are also some grey partridges in the mountains; and another sort of a white colour, that weigh four or five pounds each. Beccasicas are smaller than sparrows, but very fat, and they are generally eaten half raw. The best way of dressing them is to stuff them into a roll, scooped of its crum, to baste them well with butter, and roast them, until they are brown and crisp. The ortolans are kept in cages, and crammed, until they die of fat, then eaten as dainties. The thrush is presented with the trail [entrails], because the bird feeds on olives. They may as well eat the trail of a sheep, because it feeds on the aromatic herbs of the mountain. In the summer, we have beef, veal, and mutton, chicken, and ducks; which last are very fat and flabby. All the meat is tough in this season, because the excessive heat and great number of flies will not admit of its being kept any time after it is killed.

Butter, and milk, though not very delicate, we have all the year. Our tea and fine sugar come from Marseilles, at a very reasonable price.

Nice is not without variety of fish; though they are not counted so good in their kinds as those of the ocean. Soals, [soles, flounder] and flat-fish in general, are scarce. Here are some mullets, both grey and red. We sometimes see the dory, which is called St. Pietro; with rock fish, bonita, and mackerel. The gurnard appears pretty often; and there is plenty a kind of large whiting, which eats pretty well; but has not the delicacy of that which is caught on our [English] coast. One of the best fish of this country, is called 'le loup' [Mediterranean seabass], about two or three pounds in weight; white, firm, and well-flavoured. Another, no-way inferior to it, is the 'moustel', about the same size, of a dark grey colour, and short, blunt snout, growing thinner and flatter from the shoulders downwards, so as to resemble a soal at the tail. This cannot be the mustela of the antients, which is supposed to be the sea lamprey. Here too are found the vyvre, or, as we call it, weaver; remarkable for its long sharp spines, so dangerous to the fingers of the fishermen. We have abundance of 'soepie', or cuttlefish, of which the people in this country make a delicate ragout; as also of the 'polype de mer', which is an ugly animal with long feelers, like tails, which they often wind about the legs of the fishermen. They are stewed with onions, and eat something like cow heel. The market sometimes affords the 'ecriviesse de mer', which is a lobster without claws, of a sweetish taste; and there are a few rock oysters, very small, and very rank.

Among the fish of this country, there is a very ugly animal of the eel species, which might pass for a serpent: it is of a dusky black colour, marked with spots of yellow, about eighteen inches, or two feet long. The Italians call it 'murena'; but whether it is the fish which had the same name among the ancient Romans, I cannot pretend to determine. Antient murena was counted a great delicacy, and was kept in ponds, for extraordinary occasions. Julius Caesar borrowed six thousand for one entertainment: but I imagined this was the river lamprey. The murena of this country is in no esteem, and only eaten by the poor people.

Letter XIX, Nice, October 10, 1764

I shall now take notice of the vegetables of Nice. In the winter, we have, green peas, asparagus, artichoaks, cauliflower, beans, French beans, celery, and endive; cabbage, coleworts, radishes, turnips, carrots, betteraves, sorrel lettuce, onions, garlic, and chalot. We have potatoes from the mountains, mushrooms, champignons, and truffles. Piedmont affords white truffles, counted the most delicious in the world: they sell for about three livres the pound.

The fruits of this season are pickled olives, oranges, lemons, citrons, citronelles, dried figs, grapes, apples, pears, almonds, chestnuts, walnuts, filberts, medlars, pomegranates, and a fruit called azerolles, [The Italians call them Lazerruoli.] about the size of a nutmeg, of an oblong shape, red colour, and agreeable acid taste. I might likewise add the cherry of the Laurus cerasus, which is sold in the market; very beautiful to the eye, but insipid to the palate. In summer we have all those vegetables in perfection. There is also a kind of small courge, or gourd, of which the people of the country make a very savoury ragout, with the help of eggs, cheese, and fresh anchovies. Another is made of the badenjean, which the Spaniards call berengena: [This fruit is called Melanzana in Italy and is much esteemed by the Jews in Leghorn. Perhaps Melanzana is a corruption of Malamsana.] it is much eaten in Spain and the Levant, as well as by the Moors in Barbary. It is about the size and shape of a hen's egg, enclosed in a cup like an acorn; when ripe, of a faint purple colour. It grows on a stalk about a foot high, with long spines or prickles. The people here have different ways of slicing and dressing it, by broiling, boiling, and stewing, with other ingredients: but it is at best an insipid dish. There are some caper bushes in this neighborhood, which grow wild in holes of garden walls, and require no sort of cultivation: in one or two gardens, there are palm-trees; but the dates never ripen.

In my register of the weather, I have marked the seasons of the principal fruits in this country. In May we have strawberries which continue in season two or three months. These are of the wood kind; very grateful, and of a good flavour; but the scarlets and hautboys are not known at Nice. In the beginning of June, and even sooner, the cherries begin to be ripe. They are a kind of bleeding hearts; large, fleshy, and high flavoured, though rather too luscious. I have likewise seen a few of those we call Kentish cherries which are much more cool, acid, and agreeable, especially in this hot climate. The cherries are succeeded by the apricots and peaches, which are all standards, and of consequence better flavoured than what we call wall-fruit. The trees, as well as almonds, grow and bear without care and cultivation, and may be seen in the open fields about Nice, but without proper culture, the fruit degenerates. The best peaches I have seen at Nice are the amberges, of a yellow hue, and oblong shape, about the size of a small lemon. Their consistence is much more solid than that of our English peaches, and their taste more delicious.

Several trees of this kind I have in my own garden. Here is likewise plenty of other sorts; but no nectarines. We have little choice of plumbs. Neither do I admire the pears or apples of this country: but the most agreeable apples I ever tasted, come from Final, and are called pomi carli. The greatest fault I find with most fruits in this climate, is, that they are too sweet and luscious, and want that agreeable acid which is so cooling and so grateful in a hot country.

This, too, is the case with our grapes, of which there is great plenty and variety, plump and juicy, and large as plumbs. Nature, however, has not neglected to provide other agreeable vegetable juices to cool the human body. During the whole summer, we have plenty of musk melons.

The markets of Montpellier are supplied with fish, poultry, butcher's meat, and game, at reasonable rates. The wine is strong and harsh and not drunk unless mixed with water. Plenty of game.

Bibliography and Works Consulted

Adams, Charles Francis, ed. *Letters of Mrs. Adams, The Wife of John Adams*, Boston: 1848. [Hereafter cited as *Letters of Mrs. Adams.*]

Adams, Charles Francis, ed. *The Works of John Adams*, 10 vols., Boston: 1851. [Hereafter cited as *Works.*]

Adams, John Quincy. *Memoirs*, edited by Charles Francis Adams, 12 vols., Philadelphia: Lippincott & Co., 1874. [Hereafter cited as *Memoirs.*]

Ambrose, Stephen E. *Undaunted Courage: Meriwether Lewis, Thomas Jefferson, and the Opening of the American West*, New York: Simon & Schuster, 1996. [Hereafter cited as Ambrose.]

Beaglehole, J.C. *The Journals of Captain Cook*, 1967.

Bear, James A. Jr. and Lucia C. Stanton, eds. *Jefferson's Memorandum Books: Accounts, with Legal Records and Miscellany 1767–1826*, 2 vols., Princeton, NJ: Princeton University Press, 1997. [Hereafter cited as *Jefferson's Memorandum Books.*]

Bernard, John. *Reflections of America, 1791–1811*, New York: 1887. [Hereafter cited as Bernard.]

Betts, Edwin Morris. *Thomas Jefferson's Garden Book*, Philadelphia, 1944. [Hereafter cited as Betts.]

Boswell, James. *Boswell on the Grand Tour: Italy, Corsica, and France, 1765–1766*, New York: McGraw Hill, 1955. [Hereafter cited as Boswell.]

Boyd, Julian P., ed. *The Papers of Thomas Jefferson*, Princeton, NJ: Princeton University Press, [Hereafter cited as PTJ.]

Brands, H.W. *The First American: The Life and Times of Benjamin Franklin*, New York: Doubleday, 2000. [Hereafter cited as Brands.]

223

Brodie, Fawn M. *Thomas Jefferson: An Intimate History*, New York: W.W. Norton & Company, 1974. [Hereafter cited as Brodie.]

Brown, Everett Somerville, ed. *William Plumer's Memorandum of Proceedings in the United States Senate, 1803–1807*, New York: 1923. [Hereafter cited as Plumer.]

British Library Board, 3rd Voyage Timeline.

Burke, Thomas. *Travel in England*, London: 1942. [Hereafter cited as Burke.]

Butterfield, L.H., ed. *Diary and Autobiography of John Adams*, 4 vols., Cambridge, MA: 1961. [Hereafter cited as Butterfield.]

Chastellux, Francois Jean, Marquis de. *Travels in North America in the Years 1780, 1781 and 1782*, 2 vols., Chapel Hill, NC: 1963. [Hereafter cited as Chastellux.]

Dion, Roger. *Histoire de la Vigne et du Vin en France*, Paris: 1959. [Hereafter cited as Dion.]

Dumbauld, Edward. *Thomas Jefferson: American Tourist*, Norman, OK: 1946. [Hereafter cited as Dumbauld.]

Fowler, Damon Lee, ed. *Dining at Monticello*, Thomas Jefferson Foundation, Inc., 2005.

Franklin, Benjamin. *Autobiography*. [Hereafter cited as ABF.]

Franklin, Benjamin. *Franklin Papers*, American Philosophical Society, Philadelphia. [Hereafter cited as the *Franklin Papers*.]

Franklin, Benjamin. *The Papers of Benjamin Franklin*. Labaree, Leonard, Ed. [Hereafter cited as PBF.]

Gabler, James. *An Evening with Benjamin Franklin and Thomas Jefferson: Dinner, Wine, and Conversation*, Palm Beach, FL. Bacchus Press Ltd., 2006. [Herein cited as Gabler.]

Gabler, James M. *Passions: The Wines and Travels of Thomas Jefferson*, Baltimore, MD: Bacchus Press Ltd., 1995. [Hereafter cited as *Passions*.]

Gabler, James M. *Wine into Words: A History and Bibliography of Wine Books in the English Language*, Baltimore, Bacchus Press Ltd., 2004.

Garlick, Richard Cecil, Jr. *Philip Mazzei, Friend of Jefferson: His Life and Letters*, Baltimore: The Johns Hopkins Press, 1933. [Hereafter cited as Garlick.]

Gifford, Bill. *Ledyard: In Search of the First American Explorer*, 2007.

Gray, Edward G. *The Making of John Ledyard: Empire and Ambition in the Life of an Early American Traveler*, 2007.

Henderson, Alexander. *The History of Ancient and Modern Wines*, London: 1824. [Hereafter cited as Henderson.]

Idzerda, Stanley J., ed. *Lafayette in the Age of the American Revolution: Selected Letters and Papers, 1776–1790*, 2 vols., Ithaca, NY: Cornell University Press, 1977–1983. [Hereafter cited as Lafayette.]

Isaacson, Walter. *Benjamin Franklin: An American Life*. New York: Simon & Schuster, 2003. [Hereafter cited as Isaacson.]

Jefferson, Thomas. *Autobiography*. [Hereafter cited as ATJ.]

Jefferson, Thomas. *The Papers of Thomas Jefferson*. See Boyd, Julian.

Jewish Virtual Library, David Franks, 1740-1793.

Johnson, Hugh. *Vintage: The Story of Wine*, New York: Simon & Schuster, 1989.

Jullien, André. *The Topography of All Known Vineyards*, London: 1824. [Hereafter cited as Jullien.]

Kay, Bill and Cailean Maclean. *Knee Deep in Claret*, Edinburgh: Mainstream Publishing, 1983. [Hereafter cited as Kay.]

Kimball, Marie. *Thomas Jefferson's Cookbook*, University Press of Virginia, 1976. [Hereafter cited as Kimball.]

Library of Congress. *Thomas Jefferson Papers*. [Hereafter cited as LCTJP, Reel number.]

Lopez, Claude-Anne and Eugenia W. Herbert. *The Private Franklin: The Man and His Family*, New York: W.W. Norton, 1975. [Hereafter cited as Lopez & Herbert.]

Malone, Dumas. *Jefferson and His Times*, 6 vols., Boston: Little Brown and Company, 1948–1977. [Hereafter cited as Malone and volume title.]

Mazzei, Philip, translated by Howard R. Marraro. *Memoirs of the Life and Peregrinations of the Florentine Philip Mazzei, 1730–1816*, New York, 1942. [Hereafter cited as Mazzei, *Memoirs*.]

McCullough, David. *John Adams*, New York: Simon & Schuster, 2001. [Hereafter cited as McCullough.]

Monticello website, www.monticello.org.

Olver, Lynne, ed. The Food Time Line.

Peterson, Merrill. D. *Thomas Jefferson and the New Nation*, New York: Oxford University Press, 1970. [Hereafter cited as Peterson.]

Peterson, Merrill D., ed. *Visitors To Monticello*, 1989.

Randolph, Sarah N. *The Domestic Life of Thomas Jefferson*, 1978.

Redding, Cyrus. *A History and Description of Modern Wines*, London: 1833. [Hereafter cited as Redding.]

Rice, Howard C., Jr. *Thomas Jefferson's Paris*, Princeton, NJ: 1976. [Hereafter cited as Rice.]

Roof, Katherine Metcalf. *Colonel William Smith and Lady: The Romance of Washington's Aide and Young Abigail Adams*, 1929.

Roosevelt, Theodore. *Gouverneur Morris*, American Statesman Series, vol. III, Boston: 1899.

Scofield, Merry Ellen. *The Fatigues of His Table: The Politics of Presidential Dining During the Jefferson Administration*, 2006, 457.

Seale, William. *The President's House*, Washington, D.C.: 1986. [Hereafter cited as Seale.]

Smith, Margaret Bayard. *The First Forty Years of Washington Society*, 1906. [Hereafter cited as Smith.]

Sparks, Jared. *Memoirs of the Life and Travels of John Ledyard*, New York: 1828. [Hereafter cited as Sparks.]

Stanton, Lucia C. "Wine and Food at the White House, The Presidential Table," from *Jefferson and Wine*, edited by Treville Lawrence Sr., The Plains, VA: 1976. [Hereafter cited as Stanton.]

Stein, Susan. *The Worlds of Thomas Jefferson*, New York: Harry N. Abrams, Inc., 1993. [Hereafter cited as Stein.]

Thomas, Evan. *John Paul Jones: Sailor, Hero, Father of the American Navy*, New York: Simon & Schuster, 2003. [Hereafter cited as Thomas.]

Smollett, Tobias. *Travels Through France and Italy from the Miscellaneous Works of Tobias Smollett*, London: 1856. [Hereafter cited as Smollett.]

Trumbull, John. *The Autobiography of Colonel John Trumbull*, 1756–1843, New Haven, CT: 1953. [Hereafter cited as Trumbull.]

Van Doren, Carl. *Benjamin Franklin*, New York: Viking Press, 1938. [Hereafter cited as Van Doren.]

Wandell, Samuel H. and Minnigerode, Meade. *Aaron Burr*, New York: G.P. Putnam's Sons, vol. 1, 1927. [Hereafter cited as Wandell.]

Weld, Isaac, Jr. *Travels through the States of North America and the Provinces of Upper and Lower Canada during the years 1795, 1796 and 1797*, 2nd ed., London: 1799. [Hereafter cited as Weld.]

Wheelan, Joseph. *Jefferson's War: First War on Terror 1801–1805*, New York: Carroll & Graf, 2003. [Hereafter cited as Wheelan.]

Whipple, A.B.C. *To the Shores of Tripoli: The Birth of the U.S. Navy and Marines*, Annapolis, MD: Naval Institute Press, 2001. [Hereafter cited as Whipple.]

Young, Arthur. *Travels During the Years 1787, 1788 and 1789*, London: 1792. [Hereafter cited as Young.]

Ziff, Larzer. *Return Passages: Great American Travel Writing 1780–1910*, New Haven: Yale University Press, 2000. [Hereafter cited as Ziff.]

Dinner Source Notes

Introduction

1. TJ to William H. Crawford, Nov 10, 1818.
2. *Eating In America, A History*, by Waverley Root and Richard de Rochemont, 1975, 120-24.
3. *Passions*, 177-78 and authorities cited therein.
4. Colonial Foodways," by Ed Crews, *Colonial Williamsburg Journal*, Autumn 2004; "Colonial and early American fare, FoodTimeline.org; Thomas Jefferson: America's Pioneering Gourmand, by Laura Schumm, history.com.
5. *Jefferson's Memorandum Books; Maryland Historical Magazine*, Vol. 41, 1946, "Thomas Jefferson in Annapolis," 115-23; TJ to William Short, May 7, 1784; PTJ, VII: 229. Fowler, Damon Lee, ed. Dining at Monticello, 2005, "Thomas Jefferson's Place in American Food History," 2-3
6. Henry Lee, son of Revolutionary General Light-Horse Harry Lee, visited Monticello on Thursday, June 29, six days before Jefferson's death. He wrote of his visit in a letter to the *Richmond Enquirer*, Aug 19, 1826. The letter is reproduced in *Visitors To Monticello*, Merrill D. Peterson, ed., 1989, 107-10.
7. *Passions*, 199-200.
8. Seale, 104-05, 108.
9. Kimball, 17.
10. *Passions*, 212-13.
11. TJ to Cathalan, July 3, 1815

Citizen Jefferson, Monticello

1. Randolph, Sarah N. *The Domestic Life of Thomas Jefferson*, 1978.
2. Bear, James A. and Stanton, Lucia. *Jefferson's Memorandum Books*, Vol., I.
3. Malone, Dumas. *The Virginian*, 1948, 157-8. Martha's son, John, died the summer before her marriage to Jefferson.

Monticello, November 1773, Philip Mazzei, vintner.

1. Monticello website. "Design and Décor – Convenience," Thomas Jefferson Menu.
2. Monticello website. "Design and Décor – Convenience," Thomas Jefferson Menu. Jefferson employed three types of dumbwaiters for the service of food and wine: 1. At Monticello a large revolving door with shelves on which food was placed from outside the dining room and then rotated into the dining room. He also used this revolving door- style dumbwaiter in the large White House dining room. 2. In Paris he became accustomed to the French practice of using an étagère of four tiers of shelves on casters which could be rolled into the room and placed beside the individual diners. He owned five such dumbwaiters. When he returned to the United States he employed this type dumbwaiter at both the President's House and Monticello. See Monticello website, "Dumbwaiters." Margaret Bayard Smith who dined with President Jefferson left this account: "When he had any persons dining with him, with whom he wished to enjoy a free and unrestricted flow of conversation, the number of persons at the table never exceeded four, and by each individual was placed a dumbwaiter, containing everything necessary for the progress of the dinner from beginning to end, so as to make the attendance of servants entirely unnecessary, believing as he did, that much of the domestic and even public discord was produced by the mutilated and misconstructed repetition of free conversation at dinner tables, by these mute but not inattentive listeners." Smith, *First Forty Years*, 387-88. 3. At Monticello Jefferson employed a pul-

ley-type dumbwaiter built into both sides of the fireplace mantel for the service of wine. It consisted of a box into which a slave in the wine cellar, located directly below the dining room, would place a bottle of wine and pull it up to the dining room. When not in use, the doors were shut and the dumbwaiters concealed. It is not clear when this dumbwaiter was first placed in use.

3. Garlick, Jr., Richard Cecil. *Philip Mazzei, Friend of Jefferson: His Life and Letters*, Baltimore, 1933, 14-22, 26; Gabler, James . *Passions: The Wines and Travels of Thomas Jefferson*, Baltimore, 1995, 5. [Hereafter cited as *Passions*.]

4. *Passions*, 3-5.

5. Garlick, 27-9.

6. *Memoirs of the Life and Peregrinations of the Florentine Philip Mazzei, 1730-1816*, Howard R. Marraro [trans.], 1943, 191. [Hereafter cited as Mazzei, *Memoirs*.]

7. Mazzei, *Memoirs*, 118.

8. TJ to John Dortie, October 1, 1811.

9. Mazzei, *Memoirs*, 124.

10. Mazzei, *Memoirs*, 192-3.

11. Café Le Procope is the oldest continuously operated restaurant in Paris.

12. Mazzei, *Memoirs*, 206-7.

13. TJ to Albert Gallatin, Jan 25, 1793; PTJ, 25: 92.

14. Weld, Isaac, *Travels through the States of North America during the years 1795, 1796 and 1797*, 2nd ed., London, 1799, 206-9. There are presently more than 250 wineries in Virginia.

15. Three famous French intellectuals and friends of Jefferson and Mazzei who played major roles in sparking the French Revolution, which they paid for with their lives.

Passy, August 12, 1784 Benjamin Franklin's residence

1. At White House dinners Jefferson frequently told the story of how he taught himself Spanish in twenty days with the use of a

dictionary and reading *Don Quixote*. John Quincy Adams after hearing Jefferson tell the story added to his diary entry, ". . . and Mr. Jefferson tells tall tales."

2. *Passions*, 15-8.

3. TJ to James Currie, January 14, 1785; *Passions*, 25.

4. *Passions*, 59; Young, Arthur, *Travels during the Years 1787, 1788, and 1789*, London, 1792.

5. Benjamin (Benny) Franklin Bache (1769 – 1798) went on to become a successful Philadelphia printer, publisher and liberal journalist. His career was cut short when he came down with yellow fever and died in 1798 at age 29.

6. PTJ, VII: 443; Chastellux to TJ, August 24, 1784.

7. An excellent book about the life and times of Jacque-Donatien Leray de Chaumont is *France and America in the Revolutionary Era: The Life of Jacque-Donatien Leray de Chaumont 1725-1803*, by Thomas J. Schaeper, 1995.

8. Isaacson, 421-2; Van Doren, 702. The Montgolfier brothers launched the first manned flight in a hot-air balloon on November 21, 1783 from Chateau de la Muette, near the Bois de Boulogne and within view of Franklin's residence.

9. PBF, 28, 455-6; *Franklin Papers*, American Philosophical Society, 38u 2.

10. Van Doren, Carl. *Benjamin Franklin*, Viking Press, 1938. [Hereafter cited as Van Doren.]

11. Kay, Bill and Cailean Mclean, *Deep Knee in Claret*, 1983. [Hereafter cited as Kay.]

12. Kay, 6.

13. Kay, 99-101.

14. Kay, 63, 140-51.

15. Thomas Livezey to BF, Nov 16, 1767; PBF, 14: 309; BF to Livezey, Feb 20, 1768; PBF, 15: 54.

16. BF & TJ, 81, PBF, 28: 455-6.

17. Thomas O'Gorman to BF, Jan 4, 1773. BF&TJ, 80; Thomas Livezey to BF, Nov 16 1767, PBF, 14: 309; BF to Livezey, Feb

20, 1768, PBF, 15: 54.

18. PBF, 27: 455. Although there is no specific mention of fish in Franklin's account, we know Franklin served fish from letters of persons who dined with him in Paris.

19. Van Doren, 577, 588.

20. Brands, 583-4.

21. Edmund Burke to BF, August 15, 1781.

22. BF to Burke, Oct 15, 1781; *Works*, 9: 84-5.

23. TJ to Patrick Henry, March 27, 1779; PTJ, II: 242; Malone, *Jefferson the Virginian*, 293.

24. *Passions*, 141, 146-7. Geismar befriended Jefferson years later when Jefferson traveled down the Rhine visiting the German vineyards.

25. TJ to Charles Bellini, Sept 30, 1785.

26. TJ to John Bondfield, Dec 19, 1784; Bondfield to TJ, April 19, 1785.

Auteuil, December 31, 1784, John and Abigail Adams's residence

1. Abigail Adams to Mary Cranch, May 8, 1785.

2. Abigail Adams to Mary Cranch, May 8, 1785.

3. Abigail Adams to John Adams, Nov 5, 1775.

4. *Letters of Mrs. Adams, Wife of John Adams*, 208, 243-5.

5. Roof, Katherine Metcalf. *Colonel William Smith and Lady: The Romance of Washington's Aide and Young Abigail Adams*, 1929, 61

6. Roof, Katherine Metcalf. *Colonel William Smith and Lady: The Romance of Washington's Aide and Young Abigail Adams*, 1929, 61. Bizardel, Yvon, Rice, Howard C., Jr., "Poor in Love Mr. Short," *William & Mary Quarterly*, 1964, 5-16.

7. Abigail Adams to Mary Cranch, Dec 9, 1784 and April 15, 1785. The exclamations are Abigail's.

8. TJ to Francis Lewis, Feb 9, 1786; *Passions*, 32.

9. *Letters of Mrs. Adams, The Wife of John Adams*, 1848, 240-1.

10. Butterfield, L.H. *The Diary and Autobiography of John Adams*, II, 292

11. Butterfield, L.H. *The Diary and Autobiography of John Adams*, II, 293-4. The "mountain wine" referred to by Adams is known today as Malaga. It was called mountain wine in the 18th century because the grapes were grown in the mountainous regions surrounding the town of Malaga. It is a sweet wine made principally from the Pedro Ximenes grape. Henderson, Alexander. *The History of Ancient and Modern Wines*, 1824, 193.

12. JA to TJ, Aug 7, 1785, JA to TJ, PTJ, IX: 25. The cask of Gaillac wine was ordered by Adams from John Bondfield and held 215 bottles of wine.

13. Butterfield, L.H. *The Diary and Autobiography of John Adams, 1771-1778*, Vol. 2, 370-1.

Franklin's Passy residence, March 1785

1. *Letters of Mrs. Adams*, 61.

2. *Works*, III: 134.

3. BF to Elizabeth Partridge, Oct 11, 1779; PBF, 23: 292.

4. Aldridge, Alfred Owen. *Benjamin Franklin: Philosopher and Man.* Philadelphia: J. B. Lippencott, 281.

5. Smyth, Albert Henry, ed. *The Writings of Benjamin Franklin*, New York: 1905–07. [Hereafter cited as *Writings*, X: 431.]

6. BF to Brillon, March 10, 1778; Writings, X: 437-8.

7. Tise, Larry E., ed. *Benjamin Franklin and Women*, University Park: The Pennsylvania State University Press, 2000, 75.

8. Isaacson, Walter. *Benjamin Franklin: An American Life*. New York: Simon & Schuster, 2003, 363-5; [Hereafter cited as Isaacson.] Van Doren, Carl. *Benjamin Franklin*, New York: Viking Press, 1938, 646. [Hereafter cited as Van Doren.]

9. Van Doren, 647; Wood, 208. For a more complete account of Franklin's relationships with Madame Brillon and Madame Helvétius, see Lopez, particularly pages 29-121, 243-301.

10. Isaacson, 366-7.
11. Van Doren, 650-1.
12. Van Doren, 651-2.
13. Butterfield, 4: 74.
14. Butterfield, 4: 74.
15. Butterfield, 4: 74.
16. During the entire time Bancroft served as Dr. Franklin's personal secretary he was a spy for the British government. See Appendix F for a detailed account of "Franklin's Secretary, Edward Bancroft, Master Spy."
17. *Letters of Mrs. Adams,* 61.
18. BF to John Paul Jones, March 14, 1779; Thomas, Evan. *John Paul Jones: Sailor, Hero, Father of the American Navy,* 2003, 153. [Hereafter cited as Thomas.]
19. Thomas, 154.
20. Lafayette to Comte d'Estaing, Sept 21, 1778.
21. BF to Lafayette, March 22, 17789; PBF, 29: 185-7.
22. Lafayette to BF, March 31, 1779; PBT, 29, 239-40, 382; BF to Jones, April 27, 1779; PBF, 29, 383-4.
23. JPJ to BF, May 1, 1779; PBF, 29: 405-06; Lafayette to JPJ, April 27, 1779.
24. BF instructions to Jones, April 28, 1779; Jones to BF, May 1, 1779
25. Jones to BF, May 26, 1779; PBF, 29, 549, note; BF to Jones, June 2, 1779; PBF, 561-2, 563, note 9.
26. Thomas, 186, 192; Brands, 580.
27. Thomas, 194-5; Brands, 580.
28. Jones to BF, Oct 3, 1779.
29. JPJ to BF, Oct 3, 1779; PBF, 29: 444-62; Thomas, 195-96.

Paris, Sept 20, 1785, Jefferson's residence, John Ledyard, etc.

1. PTJ, VII: 452; Rice, 37-42; Thomas Barclay to TJ, Nov 17, 1784.
2. "Dancing here and there like a Merry Andrew" is an expression

used by Abigail Adams to describe such activity.

3. Rice, 39-41; *Jefferson Memorandum Books*, 1: 570, 673, 680.

4. Gifford, Bill. *Ledyard in Search of the First American Explorer*, 2007.

5. Gifford, Bill. *Ledyard in Search of the First American Explorer*, 2007.

6. Gifford, Bill. *Ledyard in Search of the First American Explorer*, 2007.

7. GW to TJ, June 5, 1784. David Humphreys (1753–1818) was born in Derby, Connecticut and graduated from Yale in 1771. He joined the Continental Army, and in 1778 was an aide-de-camp to General Putnam, and two years later an aide-de-camp to George Washington. He became a close friend of George Washington and lived for a period with the Washington at Mt. Vernon after his return from France. In 1790 President Washington appointed him minister to Portugal. Four years later he was appointed minister plenipotentiary to Spain. In 1797, he married John Bulkeley's daughter in Lisbon. One of the first acts that Jefferson performed as president was to recall Humphreys and replace him because of his Federalist leanings. His literary accomplishments included poetry and the biography of General Putnam.

8. Jewish Virtual Library, David Franks, 1740-1793; Gray, Edward G. *The Making of John Ledyard: Empire and Ambition in the Life of an Early American Traveler*, 2007.

9. Monticello website, "Dumbwaiters," House and Gardens Menu.

10. "Ledyard to TJ, August 16, 1786; PTJ, IX: 259-61; PTJ, XII: 159-60; PTJ, XIV: 616; ATJ.

11. ATJ; Ziff, 50.

12. Ledyard to TJ, Aug 16, 1786; PTJ, X: 259061; PTJ, XII: 155-60; PTJ, XIV: 616.

13. Bondfield to TJ, April 19, 1785.

14. Sparks, Jared. *Memoirs of the Life and Travels of John Ledyard*, 1828, 212, 227.

15. Sparks, Jared. *Memoirs of the Life and Travels of John Ledyard*, London: Henry Colburn, 1828, Chapter 2.
16. Sparks, Jared. *Memoirs of the Life and Travels of John Ledyard*, London: Henry Colburn, 1828, Chapter 3; Hough, Richard, *The Murder of Captain James Cook*, p 203; Beaglehole, J.C. *The Journals of Captain Cook*, 527-8.

London, April 24, 1786, John & Abigail Adams's residence

1. Turner, W.J. *The Englishmen's Country*, 1935, 238-42. At age 35, Brown was appointed Royal Gardener at Hampton Court.
2. *Diary of John Adams*, III: 184-185.
3. PTJ, IX: 374-5.
4. Tavern bills, UVA; *Jefferson's Memorandum Books;* PTJ, IX: 379-1; Thomas Burke, *Travels in England*, 56-89.
5. Thomas Jefferson and John Adams to John Jay, March 28, 1786; PTJ, IX: 258.
6. TJ to J. Adams, July 11, 1786; PTJ, X: 1`23-5.
7. TJ to J. Adams, July 11, 1786.
8. TJ, *Autobiography*: Vol: 1, 94
9. Adams, C.F. *The Works of John Adams*, Vol: 1, 420.
10. PTJ, IX: 399.The king's conduct was in sharp contrast to his cordial reception of John Adams on June 1, 1785 - *Diary of John Adams,* Vol: 3, 180-1.
11. J. Adams to TJ, May 27, 1785.
12. J. Adams to TJ, June7, 1785.
13. PTJ, VIII: 175; J. Adams to TJ, June 7, 1785; TJ to Abigail Adams, June 21, 1785; J. Adams to TJ, July 16, 1785.
14. TJ to Paradise, May 4, 1786.
15. William Smith to TJ, April 28, 1786.
16. TJ to Smith, May 4, 1786; TJ to John Paradise, May4, 1786, PTJ, IX: 542.

Paris, August 12, 1786, Hôtel de Langeac, Jefferson's new residence, John Trumbull

1. Rice, Howard C. *L'Hotel d'Langeac: Jefferson's Private residence*, 1947, 15, 17; Monticello website, "Paris Residences," Research & Collections Menu.
2. Hôtel de Langeac was demolished in 1842, and is now represented by a plaque on a commercial building located half way up the Champs-Elysées on the right. The house was located just inside the city limits on the Champs-Elysées and rue de Berri. Jean F.T. Chalgrin, a popular architect of that time, designed it in 1768. Jefferson rented it for 7,500 livres a year. Stein, Susan, *The Worlds of Thomas Jefferson*, 1993, 22–23. Jean-Simon Berthelemy was the artist of the rising sun painting.
3. TJ to Ezra Stiles, September 1, 1786.
4. TJ to J. Adams, April 8, 1816. Jefferson reported that Grimm "came often to my house in Paris while Colonel Trumbull was with me to see his paintings" and "gave him the decided preference" over other contemporary artists.
5. Trumbull, *Autobiography*, 106
6. During the French Revolution the name Saint Genevieve was changed to the Pantheon, and its purpose changed from a church to a burial place for famous French writers, poets, and scientists and includes Voltaire, Rousseau, Marie Curie, Victor Hugo, Emile Zola.
7. Trumbull, *Autobiography*, 106-8. The church was completed in 1790 and the National Assembly voted in 1791 to turn the church into a pantheon for the burial of distinguished men. Voltaire, Rousseau, Mirabeau and Hugo are buried here. Trumbull's *Autobiography* and Jefferson's accounts do not specifically record that Jefferson accompanied Trumbull to the Invalides and climbed to the top of the scaffolding at Saint Genevieve, but given the fact that Trumbull was in Paris at Jefferson's invitation and staying with Jefferson, it is likely that Jefferson would have

served as his personal guide. Trumbull mentions in his *Autobiography* that Jefferson joined him nearly every day.

8. TJ to Maria Cosway, Oct 12, 1786, "My Head and My Heart."

9. Commonwealth Books, LLC website; *The Cosway Affair*, by James C. Thompson, II.

10. Jefferson's romantic outings with Maria ended when he laid himself up with a dislocated wrist. Although he knew Maria and her husband were leaving Paris for Antwerp on October 5, he sent a note to her that morning saying, 'I have passed the night in so much pain that I have not closed my eyes. It is with infinite regret therefore that I must relinquish your charming company for that of the surgeon whom I have sent for to examine into the cause of this change. I am in hopes it is only having rattled a little too freely over the pavement yesterday. If you do not go today I shall still have the pleasure of seeing you again.' Maria replied by return messenger that she would be leaving that morning, and said she was 'very, very sorry for having been the cause of your pains in the night.' TJ to Maria Cosway, Oct 5, 1786; Maria Cosway to TJ, Oct 5, 1786. The precise cause of Jefferson's dislocated wrist is not known. Attempting to jump over a fence in the Cours-la-Reine is the romanticized version. For a more detailed account of how it might have happened, see *William & Mary Quarterly*, January 1948, "Jefferson's Earliest Note to Maria Cosway with Some New Facts and Conjectures on His Broken Wrist," by L.H. Butterfield and Howard C. Rice Jr. Despite the wrist pain, he accompanied the Cosways as far as St. Denis, and "having performed the last sad office of handing Maria into her carriage at the pavilion de St. Denis, and seeing the wheels of her carriage get actually into motion, I turned on my heel and walked, more dead than alive, to the opposite door, where my own carriage was awaiting me." TJ to Maria Cosway, Oct 12, 1786. The letter has become known as "My Head and My Heart."

11. Rice, 39-41; *Passions*, 19.

12. Daniel Webster dined with Jefferson at Monticello and reported that dinner was served at about four o'clock "in half Virginian, half French style, in good taste and abundance." *Papers of Daniel Webster, Correspondence I*, 370-80, Wiltse, Charles M. and Moser, Harold D., eds.

13. Jefferson did not leave menus of dinners served at Monticello, the White House, and his Paris residence, but there is ample evidence of the meats, fish, vegetables and fruits that were served and available at these venues during the late 18th and early 19th centuries. Leading sources for such information are *Dining at Monticello*, Damon Lee Fowler, ed., Thomas Jefferson Foundation, Inc., 2005, an earlier work by Marie Kimball, *Thomas Jefferson's Cook Book*, University Press of Virginia, 1976. See also the Appendix A, B, C, herein. Appendix A lists "Thomas Jefferson's Favorite Foods:" vegetables, meats, seafood, dairy products, fruits, nuts, herbs, spices, grains and beverages extracted from Jefferson's Account Books, Farm Book, Garden Books, letters, and memoranda. See also Stanton, Lucia C. "Wine and Food at the White House, The Presidential Table," *Jefferson and Wine*, 1776, 202-12, Treville Lawrence, Sr. editor; "Mid-18th Century Foods in France As Seen By Tobias Smollett," The Historic Foodie's Blog, August 12, 2012; "Colonial America & 17th/18th Century France: French Revolution Foods", Lynne Olver, editor, The Food Timeline, January 3, 2015. Also the Diary of President Jefferson's secretary, Isaac A. Coles, and the diaries and letters of Senators William Plumer, John Quincy Adams, Samuel l. Mitchill, Manasseh Cutler.

14. *Passions*, 115, 206, and Chapter Ten, notes 1-3, 260.

15. *Passions*, 51.

Burgundy, March 8-9, 1787, Jefferson visits the vineyards - Etienne Parent

1. Papers, XI: 415-16; *Jefferson's Memorandum Books*; TJ to Short, March 15, 1787; TJ to Short, March 27, 1787.

2. TJ to William Short, March 15, 1787; PTJXI: 415-6.

3. Henderson, Alexander. *The History of Ancient and Modern Wines*, London: 1824, 163-4 [Hereafter cited as Henderson.] Jullien, vii-viii. During the Revolution the house of Tourton and Ravel bought Clos de Vougeot for a million livres and indiscriminately blended the wines resulting in an immediate loss in quality. This blending in combination with French inheritance laws has resulted in today's chaotic web of nearly 80 persons owning and producing wine from the original 120 acres.

4. Henderson, 164. These are not Jefferson's words but those of Alexander Henderson, a contemporary, describing the best red Burgundies of Vosne-Romanée.

5. PTJ. XI: 417.

6. Parent told Jefferson that Montrachet's fifty acres produced about 30,000 bottles of wine, and was owned by only two proprietors, Monsieur Clermont, and the Marquis Sarsnet from Dijon, whose vineyard-part was farmed by Monsieur de la Tour. Today there is only 19.76 acres of Le Montrachet producing a scant 15,000 bottles, and it is owned by at least seventeen persons or organizations. The difference in size and production is explained by the fact that Jefferson did not distinguish between the three vineyards entitled at that time to use the suffix "Montrachet" in their names, i.e., Montrachet (now known as Le Montrachet), Chevalier-Montrachet (18.1 acres) and Bâtard-Montrachet (29.3 acres) Two other vineyards have since been allowed to use the suffix Montrachet: Bienvenues-Bâtard-Montrachet (9.11 acres) and Criots-Bâtard-Montrachet (3.87 acres). Le Montrachet remains the most expensive dry white wine in the world.

7. *Passions*, 65, 67.

8. On his return to Paris, Parent advised Jefferson that he had bottled a *feuillette* of Montrachet at a cost of 339 livres 'to wit, 279 for the wine, 30 for the bottles, 6 for baskets, 8 for packing, bottling 4, string, corks and straw 3, and 3 misc." Having the wine bottled added to the cost (in this case 17%), but Jefferson considered bottling

necessary to assure its authenticity, to keep it from being pilfered by the wagoners and, of course, to keep it longer and in better condition. Late 18th century Burgundy wine bottles were broader at the shoulder than at the base and had tall graceful thin necks. Just below the lip was a band of glass called a "string rim." As a method of keeping the corks in, a string went over the cork and was tied round the glass rim. Straw was used as packing material and placed between the bottles to keep them from breaking. Gruber, Anna and Shay, Hal. "Archaeology and Wine," Paper of the Thomas Jefferson Memorial Foundation, Inc., Monticello: c. 1985.

9. On his return to Paris in June of 1787, Jefferson wrote Parent and ordered one *feuillette* (the barrel equivalent of 125 bottles) each of Volnay and Goutte d'Or of the best vintage available for drinking. Jefferson asked Parent to bottle the wines before shipment and deliver them to the gate at the Champs-Elysées which "my house touches." His wine supply was so low he urged Parent to ship the wine in the warm weather. TJ to Parent, June 14, 1787. Goutte d'Or became a favorite Jefferson dry white wine during his remaining two and a half years in France.

10. Shannon, R[obert], M.D., *Practical treatise on brewing, distilling and rectification, ... of making wines, ... With an appendix on the culture and preparation of foreign wines, . . .* London: 1805, 126-127. Shannon's section on the wines of Burgundy is plagiarized word for word from a work by Claude Arnoux, *Dissertation Sur La Situation de la Bourgogne,* written in 1728, 122-3.

11. Fisher, S.I. *Observations on the Character and Culture of the European Vine,* Philadelphia: 1834, 225; Correspondence with Warren Winiarski, former proprietor of Stag's Leap Wine Cellars, Napa, California.

12. Barry, Edward. *Observations, Historical, Critical and Medical on the Wines of the Ancients and the Analogy between them and Modern wines,* London: 1725, 430. Barry reported that Volnay grapes (Pinot Noir) were so delicate that they were not allowed to ferment in the vat for more than 12 to 18 hours resulting in a color

reminiscent of "the eye of a partridge." Barry confirms that the wines could be drunk within one year of the vintage. This is the earliest major work in English on the wines of the ancients and the first book in English that discusses modern wines. Notes to the author from Danny Shuster, an Australian winemaker, September, 1990.

13. Shaw, Thomas George. *Wine, the Vine and the Cellar*, London: 1864, 342.
14. PTJ, XI: 417.
15. PTJ, XI: 417. Volnay became his favorite Burgundy red table wine but the particular vineyard was not identified.

Paris, October 12, 1787, The Hermitage, a monastery

1. TJ to Madame de Corny, June 30, 1787.
2. *Passions*, 133.
3. PTJ, XII: 199, 214. Two months after his visit to the Hermitage, he wrote a friend, "I sometimes think of building a little hermitage at the Natural Bridge, and of passing there a part of the year at least. TJ to William Carmichael, Sept 26, 1786.
4. *Passions*, 133. The vineyards gave way to military fortifications in 1840, and following World War I it became a cemetery for Americans killed in the war.
5. *Passions*, 133.
6. Dion, Roger. *Histoire de la Vigne et du Vin en France*, 1959, 215, 659, 673.
7. Fremyne de Fontenille to TJ, Oct 23, 1787; TJ to Fontenille, Oct 24, 1787.
8. *Diary of John Adams*, Vol. 3, 37.
9. *Passions*, 59-60.
10. TJ to Lafayette, April 11, 1787.

Paris, May 5, 1788, Hôtel de Langeac, Shippen, Rutledge

1. *Passions*, 158.

2. Jefferson mailed them letters of introduction and a detailed outline of his travel notes on June 19, 1788.
3. *Jefferson's Memorandum Books*; PTJ, XI: 423; TJ to Madame de Tessé, March 20, 1787.
4. *Passions*, 81.
5. Smollet, 710-11.
6. Redding, 121-2; Jullien, 129.
7. Admired through the ages, its architectural proportions and symmetry were later used by Jefferson in designing the State Capitol in Richmond, Virginia and during Napoleon's reign as the model for the Church de la Madeleine in Paris.
8. *Passions*, 83-4.
9. *Passions*, 84-5.
10. PTJ, XIII: 274; *Jefferson's Memorandum Books*.
11. *Passions*, 84.
12. TJ to Martha Jefferson, March 28, 1787.
13. TJ to William Short, April 7, 1787.
14. Short to TJ, March 13, 1787.
15. Jullien, 138-40.
16. TJ to Chastellux, April 4, 1787; TJ to Mazzei, April 4, 1787.
17. TJ to Short, April 9, 1787.
18. PTJ, XI: 427-9, XIII: 273-4; TJ to John Jay, May 4, 1787.
19. *Diary of John Quincy Adams*, 1981, Vol. 1, 263n. By the time Jefferson left Paris, the barriers had increased in number to fifty-two.
20. For a fuller discussion of the foods available throughout southern France see Appendix H. Tobias Smollet's account of foods available in southern France.
21. TJ to Francis Eppes, May 26, 1787.
22. To drink a First Growth Bordeaux of an outstanding vintage in less than seven years would be considered infanticide today—ten or more years of bottle age would be preferable. Jefferson's opinion is puzzling since present-day vinification methods are designed to bring more rapid maturation than earlier, primitive

systems. Was Jefferson drinking the great clarets too soon? In the opinions of Elie de Rothschild, former managing director of Chateau Lafite-Rothschild, Jean Delmas, former manager of Chateau Haut-Brion, and Jean-Paul Gardere, former manager of Chateau Latour, Jefferson was drinking the Bordeaux Grands Crus before they were "ready to give complete satisfaction." See *Passions: The Wines and Travels of Thomas Jefferson*, 118-19 for a fuller explanation.

23. John Locke's book is titled *Observations upon the Growth and Culture of Vines and Olives, the Production of Silk and Preservation of Fruits.* For a detailed account of Locke's time in France and interests in wine see *Wine into Words: A History and Bibliography of Wine Books in the English Language*, 230-32.

Paris, June, 1788, Hôtel de Langeac—Lafayette and Houdon

1. Passions, 31.
2. *Jefferson's Memorandum Books*; PTJ, XIII: 31-2.
3. TJ to Nicholas Lewis Sept 17, 1787; PTJ, XII: 135; TJ to Baron Geismar, July 13, 1788.
4. TJ to James Monroe, 1817.
5. PTJ, XI: 427-8. Jefferson's notes give the cellar temperature at 9 ½ degrees Reaumur, a scale developed in 1730 by French scientist René-Antoine Ferchault de Reaumur. Reaumur's temperature scale was fairly widely used in the 18th century but has now practically disappeared. See O.T. Zimmerman and Irvin Lavin, *Industrial Research Services Conversion Factors and Tables*, Dover, N.H., 1961, 539.
6. TJ to Mazzei, April 4, 1787.
7. Stephen Cathalan to TJ, June 5, 1816.
8. TJ to Lafayette, April 11, 1787.
9. Jefferson had a dramatic change of opinion about the wines of Bellet. On the spot Jefferson said the Bellet wines were good "though not of the first quality." Still, he ordered them. A little

later he called them "remarkably good." In a letter to President Monroe in April 1817 he said, "Vin de Nice. The crop called Bellet, of M. Sasserno, is the best. This is the most elegant every-day wine in the world and cost 31 cents the bottle." Jefferson continued to order the Bellet wines well into his retirement. Were Sasserno's wines red or white? Jefferson never says specifically but he esteemed the red wines. This is confirmed by André Jullien, a wholesale Paris wine merchant who wrote in 1816 a marvelous book about the wines of the world, *Topographic de tous les Vignobles Connus.* Jullien says that the only wine of repute from the vineyards of Bellet was a red wine that he described as "delicate and agreeable." Jullien, 188.

10. Stein, Susan R. *The Worlds of Thomas Jefferson at Monticello,* 1993, 337, 340.

11. TJ to Short, April 12, 178.

12. PTJ, XI: 442-3; Young, 191-2.

13. Young, 192.

14. *Passions,* 96. The description of ascending and descending the Col de Tende is from Smollet's account of his travels in Italy about 25 years before Jefferson's travels there.

15. *Jefferson's Memorandum Books*; PTJ XI: 435, XIII: 272; Young, 194, 254-5.

16. PTJ, XI: 436; TJ to John Jay, 4 May 1787; TJ to Edward Rutledge, 14 July 1787; Ralph Izard to TJ, 10 November 1787; Leon Drayton to TJ, 25 November 1787.

17. PTJ, XI: 435, XIII: 272.

18. PTJ, XI: 437–40; XIII: 272; TJ to J. Skinner, Feb 24, 1820. James Boswell visited Simonetta twenty-two years before Jefferson and fired a pistol "from the window of an upper story opposite to a wall" and counted the sound repeat fifty-eight times. Boswell, 43.

19. *Passions,* 100.

20. The wine descriptions are not Jefferson's but those of Alexander Henderson, an English physician, who wrote *The History of Ancient and Modern Wines.* Henderson devotes fourteen chapters to

modern wines and many of his observations are as valid now as
then.

21. *Jefferson's Memorandum Books*; Smollett, 203–04. James Boswell
    also left Genoa aboard a felucca and because of contrary winds
    had to put ashore. The description of the felucca and crew is
    Boswell's. See Boswell, 225. TJ to William Short, May 1, 1787.
22. PTJ, XI: 441-4.
23. PTJ, XI: 442; XIII: 271.
24. PTJ, XI: 442-3; XIII: 271.

Paris, April 8, 1789, Good Friday, Easter Parade

1. Morris entered into his diary under date of April 8, 1789, "Dine
   early with Jefferson to see the Procession to Longchamps."
2. Bill Of Rights Institute, "Gouverneur Morris 1752-1816," 7.
3. Monticello website, "Philip Mazzei," Research & Collections
   Museum.
4. *Diary of John Quincy Adams*, Vol. 1, 239.
5. *Diary of John Adams*, Vol. 4: 62-3.
6. *Passions*, 105 and citations at page 258. Lisbon wines were fortified, having had their fermentation stopped by the addition of
   brandy, and even the dry Lisbon wines were sweet to some degree. By 1825 Vin Blanc de Rochegude was not available at any
   price because production ceased following the Marquis's death.
   Letters from Robert Bailey to the author dated July 12 and 27,
   1974. Although the Marquis's records do not tell us what grape
   varietal made his Vin Blanc de Rochegude, Jefferson's description
   strongly suggests that it was a sweet fortified white wine. With
   only one exception, the wines produced today in these same vineyard areas are wines made primarily from red grapes such as
   Grenache, Syrah, Mourvedre, Cinsault and Carignan and sold as
   Côtes-du-Rhône-Villages. The exception is a sweet lightly fortified white wine made from the Muscat grape that is grown in the
   vicinity of the valley town of Beaumes-de-Venise lying between

Rochegude and Avignon and dating to Roman times. It is un-known when the Muscat grape was first planted here, but it is the only place in the southern Côtes du Rhône where it is plant-ed, evidence that the Marquis's Vin Blanc de Rochegude was the ancestor of today's Beaumes-de-Venise. Jullien, 138. Muscat de Beaumes-de-Venise is a first class wine with its own AOC desig-nation, and though called a vins doux naturel, it is a lightly fortified sweet wine having had its fermentation arrested by the addition of brandy. As an aperitif or dessert wine, it has been gaining in popularity. Many consider it France's best sweet Mus-cat wine and several excellent Beaumes-de-Venise wines are available in the United States. Livingstone–Learmonth, 77-85. One sou was equal to slightly less than 1 American cent but for conversion purposes, 1 sou equals 1 cent.

Paris, July 4, 1789, Hôtel de Langeac, Dinner Party

1. Stephen Cathalan to TJ, June 4, 1816.
2. *Passions*, 162-3
3. Young, 276-7.
4. See Appendix G.
5. Kierner Cynthia A. *Martha Jefferson Randolph, Daughter of Monticello: her life and times*, University of North Carolina Press, 2012.
6. Shepperson, Archibald Bolling. *John Paradise and Lucy Ludwell of London and Williamsburg*, 1942, 203.
7. See Kimball, Marie, *Thomas Jefferson's Cook Book*, for an account of "Thomas Jefferson's Paris Recipes," 29-38.
8. Shepperson, Archibald Bolling. *John Paradise and Lucy Ludwell of London and Williamsburg*, 1942, 207-11, 273-4, 293-5; PTJ, 10: 69, 255-6; 13: 457, 543-5.
9. TJ to James Madison, June 18, 1789.
10. TJ to John Jay, June 24, 1789.
11. Lafayette to TJ, July 9, 1789.

12. *Morris Diary*, July 4, 1789, 134.

Annapolis, Sept 10, 1790, Mann's Tavern, Jefferson, Madison

1. TJ to Elizabeth Eppes, March 7, 1790.
2. TJ to Thomas Mann Randolph, Jr., March 28, 1790.
3. TJ to Ferdinand Grand, April 4, 1790 and April 23, 1790.
4. TJ to Francis Eppes, July 1, 1790; TJ to Short, July 1, 1790; PTJ, XVI: 598. Ellis, Joseph J. *Founding Brothers - The Revolutionary Generation*, 2000, 49.
5. Jefferson may have met Hamilton in Philadelphia in early 1783 when Hamilton was a member of Congress. PTJ, VI: 217.
6. TJ to Short, August 20, 1790.
7. TJ to Fenwick, Sept 6, 1790.
8. Thomas Lee Shippen to Dr. William Shippen, Jr., Sept 15, 1790.
9. Thomas Lee Shippen to Dr. William Shippen, Jr., Sept 15, 1790.
10. *Maryland Gazette*, June 25, 1812; *Passions*, 12, note 42 at 231.
11. *Passions*, 12.
12. *Jefferson's Memorandum Books; Maryland Historical Magazine*, "Thomas Jefferson in Annapolis," 1946, Vol. 41, 115-23.
13. James McHenry to Margaret Caldwell, Dec 23, 1783; PTJ, VI: 402-14; *Passions*, 12-3.
14. Thomas Lee Shippen to Dr. William Shippen, Jr. Sept 15, 1790.

Philadelphia, April 11, Jefferson residence, Adams, Hamilton, Knox

1. Termo was a white wine, either sweet or dry, that came from vineyards in regions around Lisbon. Termo was a more specific wine designation than the more generic term "Lisbon" wine. In a note Jefferson calculated a pipe of Lisbon at 117 gallons.
2. TJ to Richard Peters, June 30, 1791.
3. TJ to Benjamin Rush, 16 January 1811. The actual date of the meeting and dinner at Jefferson's house was April 11, 1791. See

letter to Alexander Hamilton date April 9, 1791 from John Adams in which Adams says "we will meet next Monday at Mr. Jefferson's at two o'clock with the secretary of war ..." *Papers of Alexander Hamilton*. President Washington was on a trip through the southern states at the time.

4. McCullough, David. *John Adams*, 17-8.
5. Notes to Henry Sheaff: "Bordeaux red wines. There are four crops of them more famous than all the rest ..."
6. The wine descriptions are not Jefferson's but those of Alexander Henderson, an English physician, who wrote *The History of Ancient and Modern Wines*, London: 1824, 167. Henderson devotes fourteen chapters and 228 pages to modern wines, and many of his observations are as valid now as then.
7. TJ to Benjamin Rush, Jan 16, 1811.
8. TJ to Thomas Paine, June 19, 1792.
9. TJ to Benjamin Rush, Jan 16, 1811.
10. TJ to Thomas Paine, June 19, 1792.
11. Malone Vol II, 356.
12. TJ to Benjamin Rush, Jan 16, 1811.

Philadelphia, Feb. 20, 1792, President Washington's Residence

1. TJ to Short, August 20, 1790.
2. TJ to Short, Sept 6, 1790; TJ to Fenwick, Sept 6, 1790.
3. Fenwick to TJ, Feb 10, 1791; PTJ, XVIII: 630.
4. TJ to H. Remsen, Jr., May 16, 1791; PTJ, XVIII: 555.
5. TJ to Tobias Lear, June 24, 1791.
6. Hailman, John. *Thomas Jefferson on Wine*, 2009, 234.
7. Washington, a man of structured habits, followed a social schedule of regular Tuesday afternoon levees, Thursday afternoon state dinners for 10-22 guests, and frequent smaller dinners. Dinner began at three o'clock and was served by six or more servants in white or scarlet livery. If other ladies were not present Mrs.

Washington sat at one end of the table and the President's private secretary, Tobias Lear, at the other end. Washington sat in the center on one side of the table surrounded by guests. In mixed company Martha and George sat across from one another. The President's dinners did not wait for unpunctual guests. *History of George Washington: Bicentennial Celebration*, Vol. III Literature Series, 1932, 280; "Taverns: For the Entertainment of Friends and Strangers," Kym S. Rice, Fraunces Tavern Museum, 1893, 131-2.

8. *History of George Washington: Bicentennial Celebration*, Vol. III Literature Series, 1932, 280.

9. "Taverns: For the Entertainment of Friends and Strangers," Kym S. Rice for Fraunces Tavern Museum, 1893, 131-2; *History of George Washington: Bicentennial Celebration*, Vol. III Literature Series, 1932.

10. *Diary of William Maclay*, Kenneth Bowling and H. Veit, eds. Mount Vernon Ladies Association; Joshua Brooks, "Dinner at Mount Vernon, The New York Society Historical Society Quarterly XXXI 1947, 72-85. This was a typical meal served at President Washington's table according to Maclay. Thane, Elworth. *Washington's Lady*, 1960, 281-2; Freeman, Douglas Southall. *George Washington*, Vol. VI: Patriot and President, 1784-93, 1954, 199. Uninvited visitors to Mount Vernon could expect, Washington said, "A glass of wine and a bit of mutton are always welcome. Those who expect more will be disappointed." But those invited to dine with George and Martha a typical dinner often included game, boiled leg of mutton, roast beef, veal, turkey, duck, fowl, hams, fish, vegetables, fruits, puddings, cream trifle, jellies, oranges, nuts, figs, raisins, almonds. Cannon, Poppy and Patricia Brooks, *The President's Cookbook: Practical Recipes from George Washington to the Present*, 1968, 2, 8-9. For dessert a variety of cakes, macaroons, fruit pies and tarts were served. Martha Hess, Karen. *Martha Washington's Book of Cookery and Sweetmeats*, 1945. Joshua Brooks, a Mount Vernon dinner guest remembered

"leg of boiled pork at the head of the table, a goose at the foot, and in between roast beef, round cold boiled beef, mutton chops, hominy, cabbage, potatoes, pickles, fried tripe, and onions. Beverages offered during dinner, wine, porter and beer. The table cloth was wiped off before the second course of mince pies, tarts, cheese. The cloth was removed and port and madeira served along with nuts, raisins, apples." "A Dinner at Mount Vernon: From the Unpublished Journal of Joshua Brooks," R.W.G. Vail, ed. *The New York Historical Society Quarterly* 31, No. 2, April 1947, 75-6.

11. Benson, John Lossing. *Mary and Martha, the Mother and Wife of George Washington*, "Lear, Secretary and Companion," 1886, 243.

12. Lawler, Edward, Jr. "Hercules," The President's House in Philadelphia, www.UShistory.org. [Hereafter Lawler.] Hercules was described by Washington's step son George Washington Parke Custis as "a celebrated artiste ... as highly accomplished, as proficient in the culinary art as could be found in the United States."

13. *Diary of John Adams*, II: 292-94.

14. *Passions*, "Notes to Henry Sheaff," 184.

15. Prichard and his wife were condemned by the Revolutionary Tribunal and guillotined in 1794. Faith, Nicholas. *The Winemakers*, 1978, 47-50.

16. TJ to Bondfield, Dec 14, 1788.

Monticello, June 1800, Jefferson, Monroe, Randolph and Eppes.

1. Parton, James. *Life and Times of Benjamin Franklin*, Vol., II: 418.

2. TJ to Uriah McGregory, Aug 13, 1800.

3. *Thomas Paine: World Citizen.* "Presentation speech made by Joseph Lewis at the dedication of the Thomas Paine statue in Paris, January 29th, 1948.

4. James Monroe to Thomas Paine, Sept 18, 1794.

5. TJ to Elizabeth Trist, Aug 18, 1785.

6. TJ to Monroe, June 17, 1785.

7. TJ to Charles Bellini, Sept 30, 1785.

8. TJ to Pierre Guide, May 1 and May 16, 1791.

9. *Passions*, 36-7. 49-52.

10. John Trumbull to TJ, August 28, 1787; Papers, XII: 60. The French officers that Trumbull painted from life were Lafayette, Rochambeau, De Grasse, De Barras, Viomenil, Chastellux, St. Simon, young Viomenil, Choizy, Lauzun, de Custine, de Laval, Deuxponts, Pherson, and Damas. Trumbull, *Autobiography*, 152; *Passions*, 135.

11. Trumbull, *Autobiography*, 173-75. William Branch Giles (1762-1830) at the time was a member of the House of Representatives, later a Senator and Governor of Virginia. He was a Jeffersonian Democrat and an ardent opponent of Alexander Hamilton. William Maclay of Pennsylvania wrote in his journal on January 20, 1791 about Giles: "The frothy manners of Virginia were ever uppermost. Canvas-back ducks, ham and chickens, old Madeira, the glories of the Ancient Dominion, all fine, were his constant themes.

Monticello, Sept 21, 1802, Wm. & Anna Thornton, William Short

1. Monticello website, "Parlor," House and Gardens Menu. The Monticello parlor was not in the good condition as described here. Anna Thornton, her husband William, and her mother were guests at Monticello for five days, September 18 – 22, 1802, and she made diary entries describing the house in a dilapidated condition. I have set the parlor scene as Mrs. Thornton probably saw it when she returned four years later on a second visit and found the house "quite a handsome place." Peterson, Merrill D., Ed. *Visitors to Monticello*, "A Querulous Guest from Washington," 1989, 33-5.

2. Short to John Hartwell Cocke, July 8, 1828; Monticello website,

"William Short," Research and Collections Menu.

3. A sort of "dumbwaiter" food service idea Jefferson brought back from France. There were five of these "dumb waiters" in the President's private dining room. Kimball, Marie. *Thomas Jefferson's Cook Book*, University of Virginia Press, 1976, multiple printings, 17-8.

4. See *Thomas Jefferson's Cook Book*, 30-5. Jefferson used "macaroni" to describe pasta. The macaroni press that William Short bought for Jefferson in Italy came with a set of plates with holes of different sizes and shapes that could be changed to make different sorts of pasta such as spaghetti or linguini. Jefferson's "Notes on Macaroni," PTJ, XIV: 544.

5. TJ to Mrs. William Bingham, May 11, 1788.

6. TJ to Thomas Paine, July 13, 1789.

7. TJ to John Bondfield, 16 July 1789; TJ to John Mason, 16 July 1789; TJ to Thomas Paine, 17 July 1789; TJ to Richard Price, 17 July 1789; TJ to C.W.F. Dumas, 27 July 1789; TJ to Maria Cosway, 25 July 1789.

8. *Passions*, 202.

9. *Passions*, 187, 290, 293.

10. PTJ, 354-5.

11. TJ to Short, January 3, 1793.

12. Much of the narrative about Condorcet's last year has been taken from *Condorcet and Modernity* by David Williams, Cambridge University Press, 2007.

13. See *The Marquis: Lafayette Reconsidered* by Laura Auricchio, 2014.

14. ATJ.

15. TJ to Washington, May 2, 1788; TJ to James Madison, Dec 29, 1788.

16. TJ to John Langdon, March 5, 1810.

17. TJ to Walter Jones, Jan 2, 1814.

18. TJ to Tench Coxe, June 1, 1795.

White House, July 3, 1803, Meriwether Lewis

1. Jefferson recorded in his memorandum book on June 1, 1801 that he paid Dr. William Baker ten pounds to rent John Freeman on a monthly basis. Jefferson eventually purchased Freeman. Freeman worked in the dining room and traveled with Jefferson between Monticello and the President's House.

2. *Passions*, 195-8.

3. Horse races were held on an oval track west of the White House. *Jefferson's Memorandum Books.*

4. Roosevelt, Theodore. *Gouverneur Morris,* American Statesman Series, Vol. III, Boston: 1899, 287; *Passions*, 195. Morris was in Washington as a U.S. Senator.

5. Ellis, Richard J. *The Development of the American Presidency*, 2012, 154.

6. TJ to Short, Jan 23, 1804.

7. TJ to David R. Williams, Jan 31, 1806; "Jefferson's White House Dinner Guests," Charles T. Cullen, *White House History*, 2008, 313, 322.

8. Scofield, Merry Ellen. *The Fatigues of His Table: The Politics of Presidential Dining During the Jefferson Administration*, 2006, 457.

9. Scofield, 459.

10. Senator Plumer asked that question of Jefferson's friend and fellow Virginian, Senator William Branch Giles and that is the explanation Giles gave. Plumer, 211-2; Young, James Sterling. *The Washington Community 1800-1828*, 1966, 168.

11. Stanton, Lucia C. "Wine and Food at the White House, The Presidential Table," from *Jefferson and Wine*, 1976, 202-212, edited by Treville Lawrence, Sr.

12. William P. and Julia P. Cutler. *Life, Journals and Correspondence of Rev. Manasseh [Senator] Cutler*, Cincinnati, 1888.

13. Ambrose, Stephen. *Undaunted Courage*, 64.

14. Monticello website, "Preparing for the Expedition," Thomas Jef-

ferson Menu.

15. Ambrose, Stephen E. *Undaunted Courage: Meriwether Lewis, Thomas Jefferson, and he Opening of the American West*, New York: Simon & Schuster, 1996. [Hereafter cited as Ambrose.

16. Ziff Larzer. *Return Passages: Great American Travel Writing 1780–1910*, 39-42, New Haven: Yale University Press, 2000. [Hereafter cited as Ziff; BF & TJ, 154-6.

17. Ambrose, 70-1; BF&TJ, 156-7.

18. PTJ, XXV, 75-81.

19. Margaret Bayard Smith quoting Thomas Jefferson.

20. "Marine Corps Historical Perspective on The President's Own U.S. Marine Band, 200ᵗʰ Anniversary," by Master Gunnery Sergeant D. Michael Ressler, Chief Librarian of the U.S. Marine Band, National Archives, mcu.usmc.mil.,6. The U.S, Marine Band was created by act of Congress and signed by President John Adams on July 11, 1798. The band performed at festivities celebrating Jefferson's inauguration, March 4, 1801.

21. TJ to Thomas Mann Randolph, July 5, 1803.

22. TJ to Julian, Jan 27, 1825.

23. *Passions*, Appendix B, "The White House Wine Cellar with Annotations," 289, 292-3.

White House, Dec 2, 1803, British Ambassador Anthony Merry

1. Malone, Dumas. *Jefferson the President First Term 1801-1805*, 1970, 377, 382.

2. Merry to Hammond, Dec 7, 1803.

3. Parton, James. *Life of Thomas Jefferson, Third President of the United States*, 1883, 619; Brodi, Fawn McKay. *Thomas Jefferson: An Intimate History*, 413. An insight into how Jefferson dressed during his early years as President can be gleaned from a description recorded by Federalist Senator William Plumer of New Hampshire on first meeting Jefferson at the White House. "I

thought this man was a servant." Plumer described Jefferson as wearing "an old brown coat, red waistcoat, corduroy small clothes, much soiled, woolen hose, and slippers without heels." *Life of Plumer*, William Plumer to Jeremiah Smith, Dec 9, 1802; Stanton, 289. Sir August Foster, a British diplomat who served in Washington from 1805-07, and who knew the President well, said Jefferson "affected to despise dress." Davis, Richard Beale, Ed. *Jeffersonian America: Notes on the United States of America in the Years 1805-6-7 and 11-12* by Sir August Foster, 1954, 143-9.

4. Malone, Dumas. *Jefferson the President, First Term, 1801 – 1805*, 1970, 371-82.
5. Merry to Hawkesbury, Dec 6, 1803; Adams, Henry. *History of the United States During the Administrations of Thomas Jefferson*, II: 16; Malone, Dumas. *Jefferson the President, First Term, 1801 – 1805*, 1970, 371-82.
6. PTJ, VIII: 129; Van Doren, 723.
7. Brodie, 425.
8. "Isaac A. Coles Diary, 1806-1809." The foods listed and the second course that follows are the actual dinner menu served at the White House on April 7, 1807 as recorded in the diary of Isaac Coles, Jefferson's private secretary.
9. This exchange between Dolley Madison and Elizabeth Merry is reported to have taken place a few days later at a dinner given by the Madisons at their house on F Street on December 6, 1803.
10. TJ to Short, Jan 23, 1804.
11. TJ to Short, Jan 23, 1804; Jefferson's *pêle-mêle* (to mix) dining etiquette laid the foundation for a more egalitarian social society which allowed the host to choose the woman he wished to escort to the table putting representatives of the government on a preferential footing with foreign dignitaries. "The Politics of Dinner: Presidential Entertaining in the Early Republic," by Amanda Michelle Milian, Texas Christian University, 2006.
12. Merry to Hawkesbury, Dec 31, 1803.

White House, March 5, 1805, Commodore Preble and the Barbary Pirates

1. Monticello website. "Wigs," Research & Collections Menu.
2. Monticello website. "Jefferson's Clothing" Research & Collections Menu.
3. USSConstitutionMuseum.org website, "Gold Medals All Around," by Commander Tyrone G, Martin; Monticello website, "Edward Preble (Medals & Medallions)," and "The First Barbary War," Research & Collections Menu.
4. *Jefferson's Memorandum Books*, May 30, 1805; Monticello website, "Edward Preble (Medals & Medallions)," Research & Collections Menu; *Passions*, 291.
5. TJ to James Monroe, Nov. 11, 1784; PTJ, VII: 511-2. Tripoli is today Libya.
6. TJ and JA to John Jay, Mar. 28, 1786; PTJ IX: 358; TJ to Monroe, May 10, 1786.
7. TJ to John Adams, July 11, 1786; PTJ, X: 123-5.
8. Malone, Dumas. *Jefferson the President: Second Term 1805-1809*, 37-8.
9. Wheelan, Joseph. *Jefferson's war: First War on Terror*, 190-4, 214.
10. The actual menu of the first course served at the White House on Thursday, April 2, 1807 as reported by Isaac A. Coles in his diary.
11. Mackenzie, Alexander Slidell. *Life of Stephen Decatur: A Commodore in the Navy of the United States*, 1846, 66-7.
12. Mackenzie, 67-8.
13. Mackenzie, 70-9.
14. Malone, *Jefferson the President*, 37-8; Wheelan, 190-4, 203-7, 214; Whipple, 177-240. Jefferson was able to report in his sixth annual message to Congress, "The states on the coast of Barbary seem generally disposed at present to respect our peace and friendship."
15. Madame's Rozan's wine is known today as Rauzan-Ségla.

White House, Dec 9, 1805, Tunisian Ambassador Mellimelli asks for concubines

1. *Monticello* website. "Tunisian Envoy," Research and Collections Menu.
2. PTJ, VII: 511-12; PTJ, IX: 358; PTJ, X: 123-25.
3. Monticello website. "Tunisian Envoy," Research and Collections Menu.
4. George and Deborah Logan, Stenton House website.
5. Adams, Charles Francis, ed. *Memoirs of John Quincy Adams, 1874-77,* 330-31.
6. Adams *Memoirs,* 457-8.
7. Tinkcom, Margaret B. "Caviar Along the Potomac: Sir August John Foster's Notes on the United States, 1804-1812," *WMQ* January 1951, 80.
8. United States Presidential Election, 1800, Wikipedia.
9. *Samuel Latham Mitchill Papers 1802-1815,* William L Clements Library, University of Michigan; *Biographical Dictionary of the United States Congress*; *A Scientist in the Early Republic: Samuel Latham Mitchill 1764-1831,* Courtney Robert Smith, Russell & Russell, 1967. Senator Mitchill was not impressed by Mellimelli's dinner antics. He later complained that the American government has "given this half-savage the dignified title of ambassador."
10. Margaret Bayard Smith, *First Forty Years*; Monticello website, "Dining at The President's House," Research and Collections Menu.
11. "A Problem for President Jefferson in North African Diplomacy," Julia H. Mcleod, *The Virginia Quarterly Review,* 1944, Vol 20, #4; *Barbarians and Savages in the President's House,* Lucia S. Goodwin, 4; Monticello website, "Tunisian Envoy," Research and Collections Menu; *Encyclopedia of Muslin – American History,* "Early Dress Patterns," Edward E. Curtis, IV, 156.
12. Adams *Memoirs,* 378, under diary entry of Dec 9, 1805. Otto of

roses is a type of oil extracted from roses through a steam distillation process.

13. More than 65 years later, Thomas Jefferson Randolph, Jefferson's grandson, reported that Meriwether Lewis placed him between Mellimelli's secretaries "with a large silver goblet on each side, and a bottle of wine to be replenished. When exhausted I had orders to keep the goblets well filled. Altho Mahometans [Muslims], watching their master at the other end of a long table they emptied them repeatedly and seemed to enjoy and feel their wine." TJR recollections, ViU: 1397. President Jefferson's grandson probably heard about this unusual evening from his grandfather many times, but if he was present at the dinner, his recollection is inaccurate. First, Meriwether Lewis could not have given him the instructions he claims because on December 9, 1805 Meriwether Lewis was three thousand miles away at Fort Clatsop, Oregon. Second Thomas Jefferson Randolph was 13 years old at the time, and it is unlikely that his mother Martha, seated at the table, would allow her young son to sit between two unknown foreign men and ply them with wine. Third, Senator John Quincy Adams was in attendance and recorded in his diary the names of the dinner guests. Thomas Jefferson Randolph's name is not listed. Isaac Cole, Jefferson's secretary, was in attendance and usually took his place at the far end of the table and probably poured the wine for the two Muslim secretaries.

14. Monticello website. "Dining at the President's House," Research and Collections Menu.

15. This is the actual first course that was served at the White House on Tuesday, March 31, 1807 as recorded in the diary of Isaac Coles, Jefferson's personal secretary. It also the actual second course served that day. For a Jeffersonian recipe for beef bouilli, see *Dining at Monticello*, Damon Lee Fowler, ed., 2005, 114; recipes for braised leg of mutton and boiled leg of mutton, see *Thomas Jefferson's Cook Book* by Marie Kimball at pages 57 and 69, sixth printing 1993. These two cook books contain many au-

thentic recipes for breads, soups, meats, fowl, fish, vegetables, puddings, and desserts served at Thomas Jefferson's dining tables.

16. See *Passions*, 289-91 for the wines President Jefferson imported in 1801-1805.

17. TJ to Samuel I. Harrison, Sept 18, 1817; TJ to Monroe, April 8, 1817; TJ to Thomas Appleton, Jan 14, 1816.

18. *Passions*, 215-17, 222, 291.

19. Monticello website, "Tunisian Envoy," Research and Collections Menu.

20. Monticello website, "Tunisian Envoy," Research and Collections Menu. Senator William Plumer in his diary reported the payment for Mellimelli's concubines noting, "Our government has, on this application, provided him with one or more women, with whom he spends a portion of the night." Madison joked about the State Department's payment for Mellimelli's concubines in a letter to Jefferson and charged the expense to, "It is not amiss to avoid narrowing too much the scope of the *appropriations to foreign intercourse,* which are a term of great latitude, and may be drawn on by any urgent and unforeseen occurrence." The italicized words were underlined by Madison. Madison to TJ, Sept 27, 1806

21. Adams *Memoir*, Dec 9, 1805.

White House, April 3, 1807, Jefferson calls a Cabinet meeting

1. "The Aaron Burr Treason Trial," by Charles Hobson, Editor, *The Papers of John Marshall.*

2. This is the actual menu of the foods served that day at the White House as recorded in the diary of Isaac Coles, the President's secretary.

3. "Independence from Spain: Francisco de Miranda's 1806 Invasion of Venezuela," by Christopher Minster.

4. "Barbarians and Savages in the President's House," by Lucia S. Goodwin, 1983, 5-6.

5. "Barbarians and Savages in the President's House," by Lucia S. Goodwin, 1983, 10.

6. Bernard, 235, *Passions*, 199.

7. Coles did not report the wines served at this dinner but the four wines listed are the wines Cole's recorded as served at a presidential dinner two days earlier.

8. Bernard, 235; *Passions*, 199.

9. *Jefferson's Memorandum Books*; PTJ, XI: 435; PTJ, XIII: 272; Young 194 and 254-5. Jefferson's comments are out of character with the big, full-bodied, dry, tannic Barolo and Barbaresco wines made today in Piedmont from the Nebbiolo grape. Nebbiolo wines are not sweet nor do they effervesce, because the style of making these red wines has changed radically. Throughout the 18th century, and well into the 18th century, fermentation was never allowed to finish, leaving the wines sweet and often unstable. Redding talks of these red wines being "fermented but a short period and the best being Vin de Liqueur." It was not until the 1840s that the big, dry wines we know today as Barolos and Barbarescos emerged. The incomplete fermentation also left them frizzanti which probably explains the "brisk as Champagne" comment.

1. Redding, 246; Johnson, *Vintage*, 419; Jullien, 189; letter to author from Burton Anderson, October 1,9,1992. Mr. Anderson is the author of *The Wine Atlas of Italy and Traveller's Guide to the Vineyards*, 1990 and other books on Italian wines.

10. Madison to TJ, May 12, 1791; *Jefferson's Memorandum Books*.

11. N. Hazard to Alexander Hamilton, Nov 25, 1791.

12. TJ to Stephen Cathalan, Feb 1, 1816; TJ to Stephen Cathalan, Feb 13, 1816.

13. Rutland, Robert Allen. *James Madison: The Founding Father*, 1987, 178.

Monticello, May 6, 1816, Jean David, a young French vintner visits

1. TJ to DuPont de Nemours, March 2, 1809
2. TJ to [probably] William Short, Nov 24, 1821.
3. TJ to Monroe, April 8, 1817; TJ to Samuel I. Harrison, Sept 18, 1817.
4. TJ to John Dortie, Oct 1, 1811.
5. Jean David to TJ, Nov 26, 1815; TJ to Jean David Dec 25, 181; Jean David to TJ, Jan 1, 1816; PTJ Retirement Series, Vol., 9, 197-201, 311-2. TJ to John Adlum, Jan 13, 1816.Although Jefferson invited Jean David to Monticello on at least two occasions and David expressed an interest in coming to Monticello, there is no definitive evidence that they dined at Monticello. Jefferson's letters make it clear that he not only wanted to meet David, but he wanted to utilize David's viticulture talents in the growing of grapes and making wine in Virginia. Jefferson clearly planned on David planting vines at Monticello because in a letter to Monroe he says, "I have an opportunity of getting some vines planted next month . . . will you permit me to take the trimmings of your vines, it shall be done by John [sic Jean] David so as to insure no injury to them." TJ to Monroe, Jan 16, 1816.
6. Ibid.
7. TJ to Jean David, Jan 13, 1816.
8. TJ to Monroe, Jan 16, 1816. I have not been able to identify if the Monroe's cuttings were planted at Monticello, but if they were it did not result in the production of wine. In fact, there is no evidence that Jefferson ever successfully made wine from his Monticello vineyards. See Lawrence, R de Treville, Sr., *Jefferson and Wine*, "Quality No Matter the Wine," by James A. Bear, Jr., 13-4; and "Restoring the Vineyards," by Peter Hatch, 52-9.
9. TJ to S. Cathalan, May 26, 1819. Eighteenth century wine glasses were smaller than present wine glasses. The six wine glasses that remain at Monticello (all of which descend through Jeffer-

son's family) when filled to 3/8" from the top vary in capacity from about three ounces (85 ml.) to two ounces (55 ml.). Assuming Jefferson drank from the larger wine glass (a reasonable assumption given his love of wine) and that he drank three to four and a half glasses of wine a day, his daily wine consumption was in the range of a third to a half of a bottle of wine. The volume measurements were not taken with scientifically precise equipment and should be considered approximate.

10. TJ to Adlum, June 13, 1822; TJ to Judge William Johnson, May 10, 1817; TJ to Thomas Cox, June 3.1823, *Jefferson's Memorandum Books*, May1, 1817; TJ to Samuel Maverick, May 12, 1822.

11. TJ to Adlum, April 20, 1810.

12. TJ to Cathalan, May 26, 1819. See Henderson, 237-8.

13. This salad was identified as a Jefferson recipe in an article by Edythe Preet, June 27, 1991. It contains several French food items that were Jefferson favorites. Although the spelling is slightly different, the French word "salmagondis" means a hodge-podge or mix of disparate things.

14. Short to TJ, Feb 15, 1789.

15. PTJ, 14: 540; Thomas Jefferson Papers, Library of Congress.

Monticello, Nov 4, 1824, Lafayette visits Monticello

1. *Monticello* website, "Lafayette's Visit to Monticello (1824)," Research & Collections Menu.

2. TJ to John Adams, Oct 12, 1823.

3. Malone, Dumas, *The Sage of Monticello*, 1981, 402-08.

4. TJ to William H. Crawford, Nov 10, 1818.

5. TJ to Monsieur de Neuville, Dec 12, 1818

6. TJ to B. Peyton, Nov 21, 1784.

Franklin's Secretary, Edward Bancroft, Master Spy

1. Edward Bancroft to the Most Honorable Marquis of Carmarthen, September 17, 1784.

2. Brands, 609.

3. Lord North was convinced that all three American commissioners, Deane, Lee, and Franklin, were involved in stockjobbing through Bancroft, but probably only Deane was guilty. PBF, 25: 22–25, 417, note; Isaacson, 347; Van Doren, 582, 594.

4. BF to James Lind, October 25, 1769; PBF, 16: 224, note 4. This is Franklin's first mention of Bancroft.

5-9.Gabler, 164-75, and authorities cited therein.

10. Juliana Ritchie to BF, January 12, 1777; BF to Juliana Ritchie, January 9, 1777; Isaacson, 336; Van Doren, 569.

11. Edward Bancroft to Silas Deane, Arthur Lee and BF, October 3, 1777, PBF, 25: 22, 25.

12. PBF, 25: 22.

13. Izard, a friend of Arthur Lee's and a wealthy South Carolina planter, had come to Europe as envoy to Tuscany. When he was not received there, he ended up staying in Paris. Isaacson, 333.

14. Ralph Izard to BF, June 17, 1778, PBF, 26: 640–53.

15. Musco Livingston to American Commissioners, April 8, 1778; Ralph Izard to BF, June 17, 1778, PBF, 26: 256, note, 640–53; PBF, 27: 229.

16. Arthur Lee to BF and John Adams, February 7, 1779; PBF, 28: 479–80. John Adams in his diary makes mention of Bancroft living with a woman in France to whom he was not married. According to Adams, the French called her "la femme de Monsieur Bancroft." Apparently Bancroft did not take her out socially, because even though his friendship with Franklin brought him daily to his house where he often dined with Adams and Franklin, Adams said, "she never made her appearance." Butterfield, 4: 71–74.

17. Butterfield, 4: 72, note.

18. BF to Edward Bancroft, May 31, 1779, PBF, 29: 580; Idzerda, *Lafayette Papers*, Vol II: 268-9, 287n.

19. Van Doren, 597–99.

20. BF to Arthur Lee (unsent), April 3, 1778; Writings, 7: 132.

Made in the USA
Middletown, DE
05 November 2015